Joseph Masters

The Primer

Set Forth at Large with Many Godly and Devout Prayers

Joseph Masters

The Primer

Set Forth at Large with Many Godly and Devout Prayers

ISBN/EAN: 9783744747721

Printed in Europe, USA, Canada, Australia, Japan

Cover: Foto ©Lupo / pixelio.de

More available books at **www.hansebooks.com**

This Book will bind with The Book of Common Prayer, Oxford Nonpareil 16mo. edition, or with the Long Primer 24mo. edition, rubricated.

THE PRIMER.

The Primer

SET FORTH AT LARGE

WITH MANY GODLY AND DEVOUT PRAYERS.

"Seven times a day do I praise thee, because of thy righteous judgments."—Ps. cxix.

FOURTH THOUSAND.

LONDON:
JOSEPH MASTERS, 78, NEW BOND STREET.
MDCCCLX.

LONDON:
PRINTED BY J. MASTERS AND SON,
ALBION BUILDINGS, BARTHOLOMEW CLOSE.

PREFACE.

The Primer is the authorized Book of Family and Private Prayer, for the laity of the Church. Its sources are of antiquity equal with that of the Book of Common Prayer; and it was revised and published by the Bishops at the Reformation, at the same time with that Book. It is the only book of Private Devotion which has received the sanction of the English Church.

CONTENTS.

	PAGE
History of the Primer	ix
Plain directions for using the Hours	xxvi

Graces, &c.

Lord's Prayer	1
Creed	1
Ten Commandments	2
i. Grace before dinner	3
ii. Grace after dinner	3
iii. Grace before supper	4
iv. Grace before supper	5
v. Grace after supper	5
PRAYERS WHICH MAY BE SAID BEFORE ANY OF THE HOURS	6

HOURS OF PRAYER.

Matins	7
Lauds	18
Prime	31
Third Hour	37
Sixth Hour	40
Ninth Hour	43
Evensong	46
Compline	55

Seven Penitential Psalms.

	PAGE
Sunday	61
Monday	63
Tuesday	64
Wednesday	67
Thursday	69
Friday	72
Saturday	73
LITANY	76

Offices for Penitential Seasons.

Evensong	84
Matins	92
Lauds	102
FIFTEEN PSALMS OF PRAYER	113
PSALMS OF THE PASSION	186
THE PASSION OF OUR LORD FROM S. JOHN'S GOSPEL	197
CONTEMPLATION OF THE CROSS	206
PRAYERS OF THE PASSION	218

Prayers.

In the Morning (three Prayers)	223
At Night (three Prayers)	225
Before going to sleep	227
Prayer of Erasmus before receiving the Holy Communion	227
Prayer of the dying S. Jerome before Communicating	228
Thanksgiving after Communicating	230
On Sunday Morning	231
For trust in God	231
For patience in trouble	232
For concord of Christ's Church	233
Against the enemies of Christ's truth (Ps. cxl.)	234

CONTENTS.

	PAGE
To the Holy Ghost (two Prayers)	235
To keep the tongue and avoid the infection of the world	236
Prayer of any captive, according to the form of David	237
In great trouble of conscience (Ps. cxliii.)	238
Prayer of the Church against sin (Wisd. xv. 1)	240
In wars, the Prayer of King Asa (2 Chron. xiv. 11)	240
Prayer of Manasses, King of Judah (2 Chron. xxxvi.)	240
Prayer of Job, in his distress (Job i. 21)	242
Prayer of Jeremiah (Jer. xvii. 14)	242
Another (Jer. xxxi. 18)	242
Prayer of Solomon for a competent living (Prov. xxx. 7)	243
Prayer for obtaining of wisdom (Wisd. ix. 1)	243
Prayer of Jesus Son of Sirac, in necessity and for wisdom (Ecclus. li.)	244
Prayer to speak the Word of God boldly (Acts iv. 24)	246
Prayer of Erasmus, for the peace of the Church	247
For the keeping of a good name	254
Against worldly carefulness	255
Against pride and unchasteness	256
Against pride	256
Against envy	257
Against anger	257
In adversity	258
In prosperity	259
Prayer of S. Thomas Aquinas	260
Prayer of S. Bernardine	261
To be said at the hour of death	263
General confession of sins to God	264
For the desire of the life to come	268

Metrical Litanies.

Night Litany	269
Commendatory Litany	271
Litany of the Ascension	275

INDEX IN HORARIUM.

	PAGINA
Ante omnes Horas dicendæ Orationes	ii
Ad Matutinum	iii
Ad Laudes	xi
Ad Primam	xxii
Ad Tertiam	xxvi
Ad Sextam	xxviii
Ad Nonam	xxx
Ad Vesperas	xxxii
Ad Completorium	xxxix
SEPTEM PSALMI POENITENTIALES	xliv
Litania	lvi

HISTORY OF THE PRIMER.

THE Service of the Church of God has ever consisted of two distinct and separate parts : the one Divine, and instituted by Christ Himself on the eve of His Passion, the main substance of which is one and the same in every branch of the Catholic Church throughout the world, nor can be materially altered in its central parts without risk to the validity of the rite ; the other human, (so far as that can be called human which is in its essence probably of more than Apostolic antiquity,) and liable to any amount of adaptation and change in its details, according to the requirements of time or place.

The former of these, the Eucharist, is commonly called by us the *Holy Communion*, or the *Blessed Sacrament*, and by the Eastern Church the *Liturgy* (a term of Scriptural origin.) It consists of one nearly unvarying office, containing, in every branch of the Church both Eastern and Western, these main features in common, though not always in exactly the same order :—

    Prayer for the Church Militant.
    Prayer for the Departed.
    Sursum Corda (Lift up your hearts.)
    Preface.
    "Therefore with angels and archangels," &c.
    Invocation of the Holy Ghost (nearly lost in the Roman and Anglican Offices, but restored in the Scotch and American ritual of our Communion.)

CONSECRATION, with the words of Institution.
Oblation (restored to this place in the American book, but following the Communion in the Anglican.)
Communion.
Lord's Prayer.
Pax (The peace of God.)

No valid Communion Service in the world, orthodox or heretical, is to be found without these great features : some of the Eastern heretical bodies indeed have lost or dangerously paraphrased the words of Institution (probably from the ancient custom prescribed by the " Disciplina Arcani," of not writing them down, but leaving them for the priest to say from memory) and their rite is therefore considered by us to be invalid. But with this exception, if it be an exception—it is an all-important one certainly—these features are found in all Liturgies everywhere,—nor would the Church recognise any office of the Blessed Sacrament which should be devoid of them. They are believed to have been given by our Lord himself to the Apostles, after the Resurrection, when he " spoke to them of the things pertaining to the kingdom of God" during the forty days before his Ascension. Certainly their origin can be of no later date than the time when the Apostles were together in Jerusalem before their dispersion, to found the Churches in every part of the world, where these offices containing such features in common are to be found to this day; there being no period, after that time, in which representatives of those Churches could have composed such offices in common. Thus much then will suffice about the office for the "*Holy Communion*" or the "*Eucharist.*" The Primer has nothing in common with it (except in so far as all prayer in the Church is in a sense subsidiary to this great central act of devotion) nor is it in any way derived from it. It is with the second division of Public worship that the Primer is connected, and of this a more detailed description will be necessary.

The second great division of Public worship is that which, in our ritual, bears the names of MATINS and EVENSONG, consisting of Psalms, Lessons, Hymns, Creeds, and Prayers: the service, owing to later additions, being somewhat overweighted with the last of these elements. If the ancient offices from which ours are abridged be consulted, it will be seen that they consist almost entirely of Psalms, in beautiful arrangement, with the other elements in merely subordinary position, rather as supplements to the office than as necessary parts of it.

Matins and Evensong of the Common Prayer are not new offices, compiled from ancient ones, but simple abridgments of the ancient offices themselves. In preparing them for use at the Reformation, the pen was used for little else than erasure, not for doctrinal purposes, but to shorten and simplify the office for congregational use. These ancient offices were called the "*Canonical Hours of Prayer*," or simply "*The Hours*," and were seven in number.

I. MATINS. A night office of great length, with a subordinary office called LAUDS (or the Praises) to be sung at dawn. *Matins* begins with the *Lord's Prayer* and the *Versicles*, "O Lord, open thou my lips," "And my mouth," &c., then the *Gloria* and *Alleluia* (Praise ye the Lord:) after which the *Venite*; then the Hymn, after which come the Psalms, from ten to twenty in number, according to the day of the week; each day having its own Psalms. Next follow the *Lessons*, from three to nine in number (each Lesson consisting of about half-a-dozen verses, either from Holy Scripture or some Father of the Church,) with their Responsories. After the Lessons came the *Te Deum*, with which the office ended; and was followed immediately by LAUDS which, after the introductory *Versicles*, "O God, make speed to save me," &c., (with which all the Hours commence,) consists of seven Psalms with the *Benedicite* and the Canticle

Benedictus, followed by certain Versicles and Collects for different occasions called "*Memorials*."

II. PRIME said at the first hour (prima hora) of the day, or six o'clock a.m., contains three Psalms and the Athanasian Creed (on Sunday.)

III. IV. V. TIERCE, or Third Hour (nine o'clock a.m.;) SEXT, or Sixth Hour (Mid-day;) NONE, or Ninth Hour (three o'clock p.m.) are called the Lesser Hours, and divide Psalm CXIX. among them. These Hours do not vary with the days of the week.

VI. EVENSONG (or Vespers) said at six o'clock p.m. consists of five Psalms, according to the day of the week and the canticle *Magnificat*, followed by "*Memorials*," as in Lauds.

VII. COMPLINE (Completorium, i.e. the completion of the day) said at bedtime : a most beautiful office, consisting of four Psalms, the Canticle *Nunc Dimittis*, *Creed*, &c.

Such were the Seven Hours of Prayer in general outline. It will be seen from the above description that the Anglican MATINS is an abridgment of the ancient *Matins and Lauds*; and that the Anglican EVENSONG is an abridgment of the ancient *Evensong* (or *Vespers*) and *Compline*. As a fact when the Hours are said publicly abroad, it is usual to group them exactly in this way. If when doing so the officiants were to omit the repetitions, a good idea would be given of the rationale of the English Daily Office. Of the antiquity of these Seven Canonical Hours it is impossible to speak with the confidence with which we can speak of the antiquity of portions of the Eucharistic Office. It is difficult however to imagine, whence an office which is thoroughly Jewish in structure and build can have emanated, unless from the revising laboratory of the Apostolic age itself. This may be mentioned independently of the considerations arising from the strong internal evidence of their primitive antiquity, and from the allusion to them by very early Fathers in the Church. As regards their significance, the Seven Hours are coincident with the Acts of the Passion of our Blessed Lord, as is expressed in these lines of Durandus :

" At *Matins* bound, at *Prime* reviled, condemned to death at *Tierce*,
Nailed to the Cross at *Sext*; at *Nones* his Blessed Side they pierce;
They take him down at *Evensong*, in grave at *Compline* lay,
Who thenceforth bids his Church observe her Sevenfold Hours alway."

Over and above this commemoration of the Passion a special and independent significance has ever been attached to three of the Hours. (1.) To *Matins*, as being the service whose voice shall be rising to heaven when the Lord shall return to Judgment. (2.) To *Tierce*, or Third Hour, as sacred to the Holy Spirit, who descended at that hour on Whitsun Day. (3.) To *Vespers*, or *Evensong*, as sacred to the Incarnation, because at that hour the Body of Jesus, being taken from the Cross and borne to the tomb, destroyed for ever the gloom and terror of the grave. Hence it comes that *Matins* consists entirely of Praise, and the element of Prayer is almost wholly absent from it, that the Hymn at Tierce has special reference to the Holy Ghost, and that *Evensong* contains the *Magnificat*—the great canticle of the Incarnation. Such then in outline were the Seven Canonical Hours of the Church. They are still used in Religious Societies both among ourselves and abroad, and are enjoined for private recitation of the clergy abroad, but have long ceased (with the single exception of Sunday Vespers and Compline) to hold any place in the ordinary public worship of the sanctuary. It was a somewhat sanguine desire to revive their use which induced the Bishops of the Reformation to edit the Anglican edition of them which we now use in the Book of Common Prayer.

What the SEVEN CANONICAL HOURS OF PRAYER were for the public worship of the Church and for the clerical and Monastic orders, that the Primer is intended to be, for the use of the oratory, and of the lay members of the Church. Both underwent revision at the Reformation, Matins and Evensong being left for the public worship of the congregation and for the private recitation of all the clergy except the bishops and schoolmasters; the Primer being revised contemporaneously with Matins and Evensong of the Common Prayer for the use of the laity. There is much similarity between the two offices; indeed in outline the Canonical Hours and the Primer are identical, and in many parts (Hymns, Canticles, &c.) they are identical in substance also. The main difference is this: that in the Canonical Hours the Psalter is recited weekly with different sets of Psalms for each day, in the greater Hours, whereas in the Primer there are certain fixed Psalms to each Hour of Prayer, variety being gained by the substitution of Penitential services for particular days and occasions, and by the use of different Hours on different days, rather than by the introduction of perplexing variations in the body of the service itself. In origin, the Primer can be traced back as far as the seventh century, and it is generally supposed to be of an antiquity even remoter than this. It underwent revision at the hands of S. Peter Damian about the time of the Norman conquest. Its ancient name was "*Officium parvum*," or the "*Little Office*." When published in English it assumed the name of the Primer ("Prymer" or "Prymar.") Thus in the legend of Piers Plowman (A.D. 1365,)

> "The lomes that ich labour with, and lyflode deserve,
> Ys pater noster and my prymer."

It was also sometimes styled the "Sarum Hours," and it has also appeared under the designation of the "Enchiridion," or manual. In editing the Primer there was by no means the same careful uniformity observed as in the case of the Canonical Hours. On the contrary, though the Primer was in no sense a private publication, the editors for the time being allowed themselves considerable latitude in the details of their work, so that no two editions of the Primer are ever absolutely identical. This is the case even in the instance of the Primers published during the reign of Elizabeth—a fact which has made the editing of the present volume a matter demanding some judgment. The editions collated for the purpose have been those of the reign of Queen Elizabeth.

The only thing in the book which is taken from an edition not of the Elizabethan Recension is the version of the Litany. The Elizabethan Primers contain the Litany as it stands in the Common Prayer. It seems hardly necessary in these days to reprint this. The beautiful old Primer Litany therefore, which is in fact the ancient Anglo-Saxon Litany of the ninth century, is here reinstated from a Primer of 1543 in the Bodleian Library at Oxford. This is the latest edition of it, before the publication, in the King's Primer, only two years later, of the Litany with which modern Englishmen are familiar, in which for facility of recitation in public worship, the responses are thinned, and the petitions are massed together in verses. For private use unquestionably the original Litany is preferable, and is therefore here restored. It has been transcribed at Oxford expressly for this edition, as also the Latin version of it in the Horarium, p. lvi.

It is noteworthy that the revised Primer of the reign of Elizabeth was published in the same year with the finally established version of the Book of Common Prayer (1559), and also that in the year after (1560) a Latin version of the Primer (called the *Horarium*) appeared at the same time with the Latin version of the Common Prayer. This fact gives peculiar weight to this particular edition of the Primer. The Hours of the Horarium (collated with the Primer) are published at the end of the present edition, for the use of those who may prefer to recite them in the old ecclesiastical language. They will also be of much use for Church schools and colleges.

It will be observed that a few things are retained in the Reformed Primer from the old Offices, which are not retained in the Book of Common Prayer. Such as are,—

1. ANTHEMS, (or "*Antiphons*," the word is the same.) These are verses generally from Holy Scripture used before and after a Psalm, or a group of Psalms, and occasionally (as in the Laudal and Evensong Memorials) before a Collect. The Anthem is usually said entire after its Psalms, but only in the few first words before them, except in Festival and Penitential Offices, when the whole Anthem is said both before and after its Psalms. They are designed to give the key-note to that to which they are attached. For instance, in Compline, said immediately before bedtime, the Anthems are very beautiful in their application; the first Anthem, "Save us, O Lord, waking, and keep us sleeping; that we may wake in Christ and rest in peace," pointing to the verse in its first Psalm,

> "Consider and hear me, O Lord my God : lighten mine eyes, that I sleep not in death."

And to that in its second Psalm,

> "O send out thy light and thy truth, that they may lead me : and bring me unto thy holy hill, and to thy dwelling."

The second Anthem, "Grant us, O Lord, thy light, that we being delivered from the darkness of our hearts, may come to the true light which is Christ," pointing to the verse of the NUNC DIMITTIS which it accompanies.

> "To be a light to lighten the Gentiles, and to be the glory of thy people Israel."

2. HYMNS to each of the Hours. Except in the one instance of the Ordination Service, which retains the "*Veni, Creator Spiritus,*" there was no provision for rhymed Hymns in public worship made by the Reformers. It is curious that in the Third Hour, the Hymn is a mixture of two Hymns, the first verse being that of the Hymn "*Rector potens, verax Deus,*" and the two last being those verses of the old Hymn, proper to that Hour, "*Nunc sancte nobis Spiritus.*" The change is scarcely an improvement, as it to some extent obscures the connection of that Hour with the Pentecostal descent of the Holy Ghost.

3. RESPONSORIES after the Lessons. This most striking feature has been omitted in the ordinary Matin Lessons of the Reformed Primer, (as well as in the Lessons of the Book of Common Prayer,) but is retained in all its beauty in the Matins for the Penitential Seasons (Dirge) of the Primer. It consists of an alternate recitation of two short passages, the second having its application to the first indicated by the repetition after it of the last few words of the first. This will be easily understood by reference to the Responsories themselves. In the Responsory of the Third Lesson the Reclamation (or "Repetition") was doubled, with the *Gloria* interpolated. The following from the Matins of St. Agnes' Day, in the Canonical Hours, will give a good idea of the nature of these Responsories:

(AFTER LESSON I.)

℞. *Celebrate we the feast of the holy Virgin; how blessed Agnes suffered, let us recall to memory; in the thirteenth year of her age she lost death, and found life; because she loved the Author of life alone.*

℣. *Reckoned by years, hers was infancy: but the old age of her mind was venerable.*

Because she loved the Author of life alone.

(AFTER LESSON II.)

℟. (reciting the words of St. Agnes.) *He hath encircled my neck and mine arms with precious stones. He hath given to mine ears inestimable pearls: and he hath endued me with bright and sparkling gems.*

℣. *He hath set a sign upon my face, that I should own no lover but himself.*

And he hath endued me with bright and sparkling gems.

(AFTER LESSON III.)

℟. *Christ I love, into whose bridal-chamber I shall enter: whose Mother is a Virgin, whose Father knows not woman, the melody of whose notes already resounds in mine ear: whom when I shall have loved I am chaste; when I shall have touched, I am pure; when I shall have received, I am a virgin.*

℣. *With the ring of his faith he hath plighted me to himself: and hath adorned me with priceless jewels.*

Whom when I shall have loved, I am chaste; when I shall have touched, I am pure; when I shall have received, I am a virgin.

(AFTER LESSON IV.)

℟. *Come, Bride of Christ, receive the crown which the Lord hath prepared for thee for ever; for whose love thou hast poured forth thy blood: and thou hast entered with Angels into Paradise.*

℣. *Come, mine elect, and I will set thee upon my throne, because the King hath desired thy beauty.*

And thou hast entered with Angels into Paradise.
Glory be to the Father, &c.
And thou hast entered with Angels into Paradise.

4. THE LORD'S PRAYER, as said secretly, except the last two petitions, which are said aloud. This is probably a relic of the ancient "Disciplina Arcani," which enjoined the withholding of the treasures of

the faith from the derision of the heathen and unbaptized, a custom diametrically opposite to that which has found favour in modern days. As therefore the catechumens were admitted before baptism to be within hearing of portions of the Church Service, it was the custom, when solemn parts of the Service, such as the *Creed* or the *Lord's Prayer*, occurred, that those parts should be said in silence, with the exception only of the last two articles or petitions, which were said aloud alternately by the Priest and Choir. In the first editions of the Common Prayer itself, the Lord's Prayer was printed as it stands now in the Primer. In using the Primer it may perhaps be more convenient for the Reader to say it aloud by himself as far as, "But deliver us from evil," which is said in response by the worshippers.

5. The ALLELUIA after the introductory Versicles is retained instead of its translation, "Praise ye the Lord," as in the Common Prayer.

6. The CHAPTER (Capitulum.) A short text of Scripture, read after the Psalms, is retained in Lauds, Evensong, and Compline of the Reformed Primer, but omitted in the Minor Hours. In the Common Prayer it appears in the shape of the Lessons of Evensong. *Matins* never had a *Chapter*, and the Lessons there are in their right place in the Common Prayer. In Evensong they are peculiar to the Anglican ritual.

Such then are the only features in the Primer (besides the arrangement in VII. Hours of Prayer) with which those using the Common Prayer will not be familiar. The following table in parallel columns will give a general analysis of Matins and Lauds, Vespers (or Evensong) and Compline, of the Canonical Hours. In the left hand column will be seen by the italics what omissions have been made in arranging the Matins and Evensong of the English Church. In the right hand column will be seen, in the same manner, what alterations have been made in revising the Primer. It has been already stated that, in general outline, there was, before the Reformation, no difference between the Canonical Hours and the Primer. What the difference in substance was (as regards the Psalms), may be seen by a comparison of the two books.

MATINS AND LAUDS OF THE CANONICAL HOURS.

N.B. Those portions which are not retained in the English COMMON PRAYER *are printed in italics.*	*N.B. Those portions which are not retained in the English* PRIMER *are printed in italics.*
MATINS.	MATINS.
Our Father.	Our Father.
O Lord, open thou.	O Lord, open thou.
And my mouth.	And my mouth.
O God, make speed.	O God, make speed.
O Lord, make haste.	O Lord, make haste.
Glory be to the Father.	Glory be to the Father.
As it was in the beginning.	As it was in the beginning.
Alleluiah (Praise ye the Lord.)	Alleluiah.
Invitatory.	*Invitatory.*
Venite.	Venite.
Hymn.	*Hymn.*
Psalms, *with their Anthems.*	Psalms, with their Anthems.
V. R.	V. R.
Our Father (*not aloud*).	Our Father.
Absolution.	*Absolution.*

HISTORY OF THE PRIMER.

Benediction 1. ⎫ Lesson, Part 1. ⎬ *Responsory.* ⎭	Benediction 1. ⎫ Lesson, Part 1. ⎬ Responsory. ⎭
Benediction 2. ⎫ Lesson, Part 2. ⎬ *Responsory.* ⎭	Benediction 2. ⎫ Lesson, Part 2. ⎬ Responsory. ⎭
Benediction 3. ⎫ *Lesson, Part* 3. ⎬ *Responsory* or Te Deum. ⎭	Benediction 3. ⎫ Lesson, Part 3. ⎬ Responsory. Te Deum. ⎭

Lauds. / Lauds.

O God, make speed. *O Lord, make haste.* *Glory be.* *As it was.* *Alleluiah.*	O God, make speed. O Lord, make haste. Glory be. As it was. Alleluiah.
Psalms, with Anthems.	Psalms, with Anthems.
Benedicite.	Benedicite.
Chapter (Second Lesson.)	Chapter.
Hymn.	Hymn.
Benedictus, *with Antiphon.*	Benedictus, with Antiphon.
Versicles.	*Versicles.*
Collect for the Day.	Collect *for the Day.*
Memorials, several in number, consisting each of an Antiphon, Verse and Response, and Collect.	Memorials, several in number, consisting each of an Anthem, Verse and Response, and Collect.

VESPERS AND COMPLINE OF THE CANONICAL HOURS.

N.B. Those portions which are not retained in the English COMMON PRAYER *are printed in italics.*

N.B. Those portions which are not retained in the English PRIMER *are printed in italics.*

VESPERS.

Our Father.
O God, make speed.
O Lord, make haste.
Glory be.
As it was.
Alleluiah (Praise ye the Lord.)
Psalms, *with their Anthems.*
Chapter (First Lesson.)
Hymn.
Magnificat.
Collect.
Memorials.

VESPERS.

Our Father.
O God, make speed.
O Lord, make haste.
Glory be.
As it was.
Alleluiah.
Psalms, with their Anthems.
Chapter.
Hymn.
Magnificat.
Collect.
Memorials.

Compline.

Turn us, O God our Saviour.
And let thine anger cease from us.
O God, make speed.
O Lord, make haste.
Glory be.
As it was.

COMPLINE.

Turn us, O God our Saviour.
And let thine anger cease from us.
O God, make speed.
O Lord, make haste.
Glory be.
As it was.

Alleluiah.	Alleluiah.
Psalms.	Psalms.
Chapter (Second Lesson.)	Chapter.
Hymn.	Hymn.
Nunc Dimittis.	Nunc Dimittis.
Lord, have mercy.	*Lord, have mercy.*
Christ, have mercy.	*Christ, have mercy.*
Lord, have mercy.	*Lord, have mercy.*
Our Father.	*Our Father.*
Ave Maria.	*Ave Maria.*
I believe in God, the Father.	I believe in God, the Father.
Confession.	*Confession.*
Absolution.	*Absolution.*
Versicles.	*Versicles.*
Collect for Aid.	Collect for Aid.
Collect for Peace of the Church.	*Collect for Peace of the Church.*
Fidelium animæ.	*Fidelium animæ.*
Let us bless the Lord.	Let us bless the Lord.
Thanks be to God.	Thanks be to God.

Such then were the changes effected in the Older Offices with a view to their more general use in the Public and Private worship of the English Church. It will be noticed that the Primer retains the outline of the original Four Hours without much alteration. And this is the case also in the remaining Minor Hours,—*Prime, Tierce*, or Third Hour, *Sext* or Sixth Hour, *None* or Ninth Hour. Though in the Reformed Primer these Hours are greatly shortened, only one Psalm being used for each.

The *Penitential Offices* receive their name of "Dirge" from the first word of the Latin Anthem to the first Matin Psalm in the Office of the Canonical Hours,—" *Dirige*, Domine Deus meus, in conspectu tuo viam meam." In the same way Penitential Evensong of the Canonical Hours was sometimes called " PLACEBO" from the first word of the opening anthem, "*Placebo* Domino, in regione vivorum." (In the Primer this anthem is placed at the beginning of Matins.) And the term " REQUIEM" has still lingered in use, in the sense of a funeral chant, from the fact that, at the end of every Psalm of this office in the Canonical Hours, instead of the usual Gloria, the following chant was sung from 2 Esdras ii. 34, 35,

"Requiem æternam dona eis Domine : et lux perpetua luceat eis."

In the Primer the Gloria is retained after the Psalms, and the above is given as one of the Versicles and Responses after the Lord's Prayer in Lauds and Evensong, and before it in Matins.

Of the GRACES given at the beginning of the Primer No. II. is of very great interest, as being unquestionably the oldest Christian grace in existence. By writers in the time of Constantine, little more than 150 years after the death of those who had conversed with Apostles, it was spoken of with reverence as being of unknown age. Both S. Athanasius and S. Chrysostom quote it. The latter Father, speaking of the Monastic customs in the Egyptian desert, writes thus,—

"I praise and admire the Monks who have taken up their abode in the desert, for this Office among other things. For they, after having breakfasted, or rather after dinner,—for they know nothing of breakfast, being well assured that the present is a season of sorrow and fasting,—after dinner then, when saying grace to God, they offer also this memorial chant. And if you are desirous of hearing their hymn, in order that you yourselves also may constantly say it, I will repeat to you all that sacred Ode. The words of it then run thus :—'Blessed be God, who hath fed me from my tender age and giveth sustenance to all flesh. Replenish our hearts with joy and gladness, that we alway having sufficient may abound unto every good work in Christ Jesus our Lord; with whom to thee be glory, honour, and might, with the Holy Ghost, for ever and ever. Amen. Glory to thee, O Lord; Glory to thee, O Holy One; Glory to thee, O King; for thou hast given us meat for gladness. Fill us with the Holy Spirit, that we may be found well-pleasing in thy sight, and may not be ashamed when thou renderest to every man according to his works.' In every respect therefore this hymn is worthy of admiration, but especially this ending."—*Homily on S. Matth. xvi.* 24.

The PRAYER OF ERASMUS, p. 247, "For the Peace of the Church," is remarkable as owing its translation into English to the hand of Queen Mary, daughter of Henry VIII., when Princess. The prayer occurs in his "Precationes aliquot," published shortly before the death of Erasmus for the use of a young friend.

The Primer was in the hands of the notorious Thomas Cranmer, Earl of Essex, in the reign of Henry VIII., at the time of his execution. He recited aloud the Prayer (p. 263) "TO BE SAID AT THE HOUR OF DEATH," immediately before laying his head upon the block. It is quoted at full length by Mr. Anthony Froude, in a publication called by him "The History of England," as the "last words of Thomas Cranmer."

The XV. PSALMS OF PRAYER, p. 113, were composed by the good Bishop Fisher, of Rochester, in prison, during the year which preceded his execution by the State for defending the liberties of the Church. They are published in the Elizabethan Primer of 1566 and 1575, but in English so rugged that it was impossible in any way to use it: and they have therefore been translated anew from the original Latin for the present edition.

PLAIN DIRECTIONS FOR USING THE HOURS.

When one says his prayers alone, the circumstances are free to be governed by his own devotion. But if two or more say together, it is convenient that they agree on some rules: for which purpose the following are proposed, yet so as to be altered by their own discretion, as they please.

Those saying the Hours may stand and kneel as most convenient to themselves, avoiding however kneeling with their faces in an opposite direction to that in which they have been standing. Thus each will be able distinctly to read his book. In the following directions A. will indicate the Reader or Officiant; B. the one or more persons who respond in the Office.

Matins.

First, both stand awhile to put themselves in the presence of God, and implore his assistance either without set form of words, or with any Collect which they may choose for themselves, e.g., one of the Collects at the end of the Communion Service, such as that beginning, "PREVENT US, O LORD, IN ALL OUR DOINGS," &c.

Then A. says, "In the name of the Father, and of the Son, and of the Holy Ghost," (p. 6.)

B. responds, "Amen."

Then both kneel, and A. says the Collect, "O Lord my God and Father," &c.

B. "Amen."

Then both together, "Our Father which art in heaven," &c.

Then A. says with a loud voice, "O Lord, open thou my lips."

B. "And my mouth shall show forth thy praise."

A. "O God, make speed to save me."

B. "O Lord, make haste to help me."

Then, both standing up, A. says, "Glory be to the Father," &c.

B. "As it was in the beginning," &c.

Then A. says, "ALLELUIA," and the first verse of the VENITE. (In Lent however "ALLELUIA" is always omitted, both here and in the other Hours.)

B. then says the second verse of the VENITE, A. the third, and so on to the end, as in reciting the Services in the Book of Common Prayer.

Then A. recites the first line of the Hymn, and B. the second: A. the third, and so on to the end, as in the Hymn, *Veni Creator*, in the Ordination Service.

Then A. says the Anthem, "Christ is able to save," and the first verse of the Psalm; B. the second, and so on.

At the end of the Psalm or Psalms both recite the Anthem together, (p. 12,) and then A. says the Versicle, "He hath entered into heaven itself." B. responds, "Now to appear in the presence of God for us."

Then A. alone says the Lord's Prayer in a low and reverential tone, as far as the end of the petition, "And lead us not into temptation," which he says in a loud voice, and B. responds, "But deliver us from evil."

A. then says the Blessing, "The everlasting Father bless us with his blessing everlasting."

B. "Amen."

Then by any one is read the FIRST LESSON, ending with the ascription, in a loud voice, "Thus saith the Lord, Turn unto me and ye shall be saved."

A. says the Blessing, "God the Son of God," &c.
B. "Amen."

Then the Second and Third Lessons, as the First.

After which A. begins the *Te Deum*, which is recited alternately like the Psalms.

At the end of the *Te Deum* A. says the Versicle, "The earth, O Lord, is full of thy mercy."

B. "O teach me thy statutes."

Thus MATINS concludes. But in Advent and Lent it is usual to omit the *Te Deum*, and the Office may conclude, if so desired, with one of the *Penitential Psalms*, (p. 61,) said kneeling.

Lauds

begins, as in Matins, with the introductory Prayers, (p. 6,) after silent prayer, as directed above in Matins. Thus,—

A. "In the name," &c.
B. "Amen."
A. (both kneeling,) "O Lord my God and Father."
B. "Amen."

Both together, "Our Father."
A. "O God, make speed," (p. 18.)
B. "O Lord, make haste."
A. (both standing,) "Glory be."
B. "As it was."
A. "Alleluia." "Behold the eye of the Lord." And the first verse of the Psalm.
B. The second verse, and so on.

At the end of the Psalms both together recite the full Anthem, (p. 22,) "Behold the eye of the Lord," &c.

Then A. reads the CHAPTER, "Thus saith the Lord."

B. responds, "Thanks be to God."

Then A. recites the first line of the Hymn; B. the second, and so on, as in Matins.

A. says the Versicle, "Blessed be the name," &c.

B. "From this time forth," &c.

A. says the Anthem, "The kindness and love," and recites the first verse of the *Benedictus*.

After the *Benedictus*, both together say the Anthem, "The kindness and love," &c., (p. 24.)

Then A. says the Versicle, and B. responds.

A. says, "Let us pray," and reads the COLLECT FOR THE DAY from the Book of Common Prayer.

After that, the LAUDAL COLLECT, "Grant, we beseech thee, O Lord our God." Then he says, "Let us bless the Lord," and B. responds, "Thanks be to God."

Then two or more of the MEMORIALS are read, p. 25—29, thus: A. gives out the page and title of the Memorial to be used, and then recites the Anthem and the Versicle which follows it. B. responds with the Answer. A. says, "Let us pray," and says the Collect. (Each Memorial consisting of this combination of Anthem, Versicle and Answer, and Collect.)

After saying the MEMORIALS, A. says, (p. 30,) "Let us bless the Lord."

B. "Thanks be to God."

A. "The glorious Passion," &c.

B. "Amen."

Then the Lord's Prayer in silence, with which the Office concludes.

Prime

begins as in Lauds. Thus,—

A. "In the name," &c., (p. 6.)

B. "Amen."

A. (both kneeling,) "O Lord my God and Father," &c.

B. "Amen."

Both together, "Our Father."

A. "O God, make speed," &c., (p. 18.)

B. "O Lord, make haste."

A. (both standing up,) "Glory be to the Father," &c.

B. "As it was in the beginning," &c.
A. "Alleluia," and begins the Hymn, reading the first line; B. the second, and so on.

Then A. recites the Anthem, "Blessed are the poor," and says the first verse of the Psalm; B. the second, and so on.

At the end of the Psalm, both recite the full Anthem (p. 34) and the Creed.

Then A. says, "Lord, hear my prayer."
B. "And let my cry come unto thee."

Then (both kneeling) A. says the Collect for the Day from the Book of Common Prayer. Then the Prime Collect, "O Lord Jesu Christ." After which he says, "Let us bless the Lord."
B. "Thanks be to God."

The Office concluding with the Lord's Prayer in silence.

Third, *Sixth*, and *Ninth* Hours

are said in the same way as Prime in every respect.

Evensong

is said in the same way as Lauds.

Compline

is said in the same way as the other Hours. As however it will be from its nature more generally used than any of the other Hours, particular directions are here added for the sake of convenience. After silent prayer A. says, "In the name," &c., (p. 6.)
B. "Amen."
A. (both kneeling,) "O Lord my God and Father," &c.
B. "Amen."
Both together, "Our Father."
A. "Turn us, O God our Saviour," (p. 55.)

B. "And let thine anger cease from us."
A. "O God, make speed to save me."
B. "O Lord, make haste to help me."
A. (both standing up,) "Glory be to the Father," &c.
B. "As it was in the beginning," &c.
A. "Alleluia;" "Save us, O Lord;" and then says the first verse of the Psalm; B. the second, and so on.

After the Psalms both recite the full Anthem together (p. 57,) "Save us," &c.

Then A. slowly and reverentially reads *The Chapter*, "Thou, O Lord," &c.

B. "Thanks be to God."

A. reads the first line of the Hymn; B. the second; A. the third, and so on.

A. "Whoso dwelleth under the defence," &c.
B. "Shall abide under the shadow," &c.

A. says the Anthem, "Grant us, O Lord, thy light," and the first verse of the *Nunc Dimittis*; B. the second, and so on.

Then both recite the full Anthem together, "Grant us," &c., and the Creed. After which A. says, "Lord, hear our prayer."

B. "And let our cry come unto thee."

A. (both kneeling,) "Let us pray." Then he recites the COLLECT FOR THE DAY from the Book of Common Prayer: then the Compline Collects, "Lighten our darkness," &c. After which he says, "Let us bless the Lord."

B. "Thanks be to God."

A. "The grace of our Lord," &c.

And the office concludes with the Lord's Prayer in silence.

Offices for Penitential Seasons.

Each of these Offices begins with silent prayer (said standing.) Then both together (without further preface) recite the full ANTHEM at the beginning of the office, and then A. says the first verse of the Psalm, B. the second, and so on.

At the end of the Psalms both together repeat the Anthem again.

The rest of the office is said as in the other Hours. In Matins (p. 97) the following directions may be useful.

A. says, "Lord, grant thy people eternal rest."

B. "And let thine everlasting light shine upon them."

Then A. alone says the LORD'S PRAYER in a low and reverential tone as far as the end of the petition, "And lead us not into temptation," which he says in a loud voice, and B. responds, "But deliver us from evil."

Then any one reads the FIRST LESSON, after which B. says the first verse of the RESPONSORY, "I know that my Redeemer liveth," &c.

A. "Whom I shall see for myself," &c.

Both together, "And though after my skin," &c.

Then the SECOND and THIRD LESSONS with their RESPONSORIES, the last of which is here given in full length to obviate any chance of difficulty.

B. "Deliver me, O Lord, from eternal death in that dreadful day when the heaven and the earth shall be moved, and thou shalt judge the world by fire: this day is the day of wrath, of trouble and distress, the great day and very bitter."

A. "Deliver not to the lion, O Lord, the souls of them that confess thee, and forget not at length the souls of thy poor people."

FOR USING THE HOURS. xxxiii

B. "This day is the day of wrath, of trouble and distress, the great day and very bitter."
A. "Glory be to the Father, and to the Son, and to the Holy Ghost."
Both together, "Deliver me, O Lord, from eternal death, in that dreadful day, when the heaven and the earth shall be moved, and thou shalt judge the world by fire: this day is the day of wrath, of trouble and distress, the great day and very bitter."

Then both kneel and say the *Miserere Psalm*, with which and the Lord's Prayer (in silence) the office concludes.

WHAT HOURS TO USE, AND WHEN.

Speaking generally, any of the Morning Hours (i.e *Matins, Lauds, Prime, Third,* or *Sixth Hours*) may be used at any time before mid-day, and any of the Evening Hours (sc. *Ninth Hour, Evensong,* or *Compline*) at any time in the afternoon or evening. Thus every day in the week may have a different office, which the head of a household may arrange according to his own taste. He may for instance note down at the end of his Primer some such arrangement as this:

Sunday morning. *Sixth Hour, and one of the Passion Psalms.*
Sunday evening. *Ninth Hour, and one of the Passion Psalms.*
Monday morning. *Matins for Penitential Seasons.*
Monday evening. *Evensong for Penitential Seasons.*
Tuesday morning. *Matins, or Prime.*
Tuesday evening. *Compline.*
Wednesday morning. *Litany.*

Wednesday evening. *Evensong, or Compline and Litany.*
Thursday morning. *Lauds.*
Thursday evening. *Ninth Hour, or Compline.*
Friday morning. *Lauds for Penitential Seasons.*
Friday evening. *Litany;* or one of the *Penitential Psalms;* or both, with the Litany last.
Saturday morning. *Third Hour.*
Saturday evening. *Compline.*

On any days in Advent and Lent, when the offices for Penitential Seasons are not recited, one of the *Penitential Psalms* may be used either in addition to the Hours or as a separate office, with the *Preface* (p. 6) and any Collect to conclude. The *Psalms of the Passion* may be used in the same way in *Holy Week*. Indeed the use of the different offices in the book may be varied to almost any amount, according to the taste and discretion of those who use it. It will generally be found however that for evening prayers before bed-time *Compline* will be the most suitable Hour, and one which, from its rare beauty, never palls upon the taste. It is remarkably well adapted for choral rendering; as, owing to its unvarying structure, it is soon known by heart, and can be sung without book at any place or at any evening hour.

It may be added that the very large circulation of the Primer in England and America during the last few years is a sign that the style of Family worship as set forth in its pages is rapidly regaining the position which it once exclusively held. Much pains has been taken in re-editing the present issue in a manner worthy of its popularity.

G. M.

SOUTH LEIGH VICARAGE.
S. Luke's Day, 1870.

THE PRIMER.

Graces,
ETC., ETC.

LORD'S PRAYER.

OUR Father, which art in heaven, hallowed be thy name. Thy kingdom come. Thy will be done in earth, as it is in heaven. Give us this day our daily bread. And forgive us our trespasses, as we forgive them that trespass against us. And lead us not into temptation, but deliver us from evil. Amen.

THE CREED.

I BELIEVE in God the Father Almighty, Maker of heaven and earth:

And in Jesus Christ his only Son our Lord, Who was conceived by the Holy Ghost, Born of the Virgin Mary, Suffered under Pontius Pilate, Was crucified, dead, and buried, He descended into hell; The third day he rose again from the dead, He ascended into heaven, And sitteth on the right hand of God the Father Almighty; From thence he shall come to judge the quick and the dead.

I believe in the Holy Ghost; The holy Catholic Church; The Communion of Saints; The Forgiveness of sins; The Resurrection of the body, And the life everlasting. Amen.

TEN COMMANDMENTS.

THOU shalt have none other gods but me.

II. Thou shalt not make to thyself any graven image, nor the likeness of any thing that is in heaven above, or in the earth beneath, or in the waters under the earth. Thou shalt not bow down to them, nor worship them: for I the Lord thy God am a jealous God, and visit the sins of the fathers upon the children unto the third and fourth generation of them that hate me, and show mercy unto thousands in them that love me, and keep my commandments.

III. Thou shalt not take the name of the Lord thy God in vain: for the Lord will not hold him guiltless that taketh his name in vain.

IV. Remember that thou keep holy the Sabbath-day. Six days shalt thou labour, and do all that thou hast to do; but the seventh day is the Sabbath of the Lord thy God. In it thou shalt do no manner of work, thou, and thy son, and thy daughter, thy man-servant and thy maid-servant, thy cattle, and the stranger that is within thy gates. For in six days the Lord made heaven and earth, the sea, and all that in them is, and rested the seventh day; wherefore the Lord blessed the seventh day, and hallowed it.

V. Honour thy father and thy mother, that thy days may be long in the land which the Lord thy God giveth thee.

VI. Thou shalt do no murder.

VII. Thou shalt not commit adultery.

VIII. Thou shalt not steal.

IX. Thou shalt not bear false witness against thy neighbour.

X. Thou shalt not covet thy neighbour's

house, thou shalt not covet thy neighbour's wife, nor his servant, nor his maid, nor his ox, nor his ass, nor any thing that is his.

Vers. Lord, into thy hands I commend my spirit.

Ans. Thou hast redeemed me, O Lord, thou God of truth.

I.
GRACE BEFORE DINNER.

THE eyes of all wait upon thee, O Lord: and thou givest them their meat in due season.

Ans. Thou openest thine hand: and fillest all things living with plenteousness.

Glory be to the Father, and to the Son: and to the Holy Ghost.

As it was in the beginning, is now, and ever shall be: world without end. Amen.

𝔅lessing. The King of eternal glory make us partners of the heavenly table. *Amen.*

Ans. God is love, and he that dwelleth in love, dwelleth in God, and God in him.

God grant us all to dwell in him. *Amen.*

II.
GRACE AFTER DINNER.

THE God of peace and love vouchsafe alway to dwell with us; and thou, Lord, have mercy upon us.

Glory, honour, and praise be unto thee, O Lord: who hast fed us from our infancy, and givest sustenance to every living thing.

Replenish our hearts with joy and gladness:

that we, alway having sufficient, may be rich and plentiful in all good works, through Jesus Christ our Lord. Amen.

Glory be to thee, O Lord; glory be to thee, O Holy One; glory be to thee, O King : for thou hast given us meat for gladness.

O fill us with thine Holy Spirit : that we may be found well-pleasing in thy sight, and may not be ashamed when thou renderest to every man according to his works.

Lord, have mercy upon us.

Christ, have mercy upon us.

Lord, have mercy upon us.

Our Father, &c.
And lead us not into temptation.

But deliver us from evil.

Lord, hear my prayer.

And let my cry come unto thee.

From the fiery darts of the devil, both in weal and woe : our Saviour Christ be our defender, shield, and buckler. *Amen.*

God save the Church, our Queen, and realm : and send us peace in Christ. *Amen.*

III.

GRACE BEFORE SUPPER.

O LORD Jesu Christ, without whom is no sweetness nor savour, we beseech thee to bless us and our supper, and with thy blessed presence to cheer our hearts; that in all our meats and drinks our savour may be of thee, to thy honour and glory. *Amen.*

IV.
GRACE BEFORE SUPPER.

CHRIST, who at his last Supper gave himself unto us, promising his body to be crucified, and his blood to be shed for our sins, bless us and our supper. *Amen.*

V.
GRACE AFTER SUPPER.

BLESSED be God in all his gifts : and holy in all his works.

Our help standeth in the name of the Lord : who hath made heaven and earth.

Blessed be the name of the Lord : from this time forth for evermore.

Collect.

MOST mighty Lord and merciful Father, we yield thee hearty thanks for our bodily sustenance; and we beseech thee, of thy goodness, so to feed us with the food of thy heavenly grace, that we may ever truly glorify thy holy name in this life, and hereafter be partakers of the life everlasting, through Jesus Christ our Lord. Amen.

God save the Church, our Queen, and realm : and send us peace in Christ. Amen.

PRAYERS WHICH MAY BE SAID BEFORE ANY OF THE HOURS.

IN the name of the Father, and of the Son, and of the Holy Ghost.

Ans. Amen.

O LORD, my God and Father, blessed be thy name for ever: dispose my heart, open my lips, and guide me by thy Holy Spirit to a true confession of all my sins, that my prayers may be heard of thee in the name of thine only Son our Saviour Jesus Christ.

Ans. Amen.

OUR Father, which art in heaven, hallowed be thy name. Thy kingdom come. Thy will be done in earth, as it is in heaven. Give us this day our daily bread. And forgive us our trespasses, as we forgive them that trespass against us. And lead us not into temptation, but deliver us from evil. Amen.

HOURS OF PRAYER.

THE ORDER FOR
Matins.

EARLY MORNING.

O Lord, open thou my lips.

And my mouth shall show forth thy praise.

O God, make speed to save me.

O Lord, make haste to help me.

Glory be to the Father, and to the Son : and to the Holy Ghost;

As it was in the beginning, is now, and ever shall be : world without end. Amen.

ALLELUIA.

VENITE EXULTEMUS DOMINO.
Psalm xcv.
A Song inviting to the praise of God.

O COME, let us sing unto the Lord : let us heartily rejoice in the strength of our salvation.

Let us come before his presence with thanksgiving : and show ourselves glad in him with Psalms.

For the Lord is a great God : and a great King above all gods.

In his hand are all the corners of the earth : and the strength of the hills is his also.

The sea is his, and he made it : and his hands prepared the dry land.

O come, let us worship, and fall down : and kneel before the Lord our Maker.

For he is the Lord our God : and we are the people of his pasture, and the sheep of his hand.

To day if ye will hear his voice, harden not your hearts : as in the provocation, and as in the day of temptation in the wilderness ;

When your fathers tempted me : proved me, and saw my works.

Forty years long was I grieved with this generation, and said : It is a people that do err in their hearts, for they have not known my ways.

Unto whom I sware in my wrath : that they should not enter into my rest.

Glory be to the Father, &c.

As it was in the beginning, &c.

HYMN. *Jam lucis orto sidere.*

Now that the sun is gleaming bright,
  Implore we, bending low,
That he, the uncreated light,
  May guide us as we go :

No sinful word, nor deed of wrong,
  Nor thoughts that idly rove,
But simple truth be on our tongue,
  And in our hearts be love.

And while the hours in order flow,
  O Christ, securely fence
Our gates beleaguered by the foe,
  The gate of every sense:

And grant that to thine honour, Lord,
  Our daily toil may tend;
That we begin it at thy word,
  And in thy favour end. Amen.

¶ *Then one or more of the following Psalms, preceded and followed by their* ANTHEM, *as here placed.*

Ant. Christ is able to save.

PSALM VIII. *Domine, Dominus noster.*

Of the praise, honour, and glory of Christ.

O LORD our Governor, how excellent is thy name in all the world : thou that hast set thy glory above the heavens!

Out of the mouth of very babes and sucklings hast thou ordained strength, because of thine enemies : that thou mightest still the enemy, and the avenger.

For I will consider thy heavens, even the works of thy fingers : the moon and the stars, which thou hast ordained.

What is man, that thou art mindful of him : and the son of man, that thou visitest him?

Thou madest him lower than the angels : to crown him with glory and worship.

Thou makest him to have dominion of the

works of thy hands : and thou hast put all things in subjection under his feet :

All sheep and oxen : yea, and the beasts of the field;

The fowls of the air, and the fishes of the sea : and whatsoever walketh through the paths of the seas.

O Lord our Governor : how excellent is thy name in all the world!

Glory be to the Father, &c.

As it was in the beginning, &c.

PSALM XIX. *Cœli enarrant.*

Of the glory of God which shineth forth in his creation, and of his holy law.

THE heavens declare the glory of God : and the firmament showeth his handy work.

One day telleth another : and one night certifieth another.

There is neither speech nor language : but their voices are heard among them.

Their sound is gone out into all lands : and their words into the ends of the world.

In them hath he set a tabernacle for the sun : which cometh forth as a bridegroom out of his chamber, and rejoiceth as a giant to run his course.

It goeth forth from the uttermost part of the heaven, and runneth about unto the end of it again : and there is nothing hid from the heat thereof.

The law of the Lord is an undefiled law,

converting the soul : the testimony of the Lord is sure, and giveth wisdom unto the simple.

The statutes of the Lord are right, and rejoice the heart : the commandment of the Lord is pure, and giveth light unto the eyes.

The fear of the Lord is clean, and endureth for ever : the judgments of the Lord are true, and righteous altogether.

More to be desired are they than gold, yea, than much fine gold : sweeter also than honey, and the honey-comb.

Moreover, by them is thy servant taught : and in keeping of them there is great reward.

Who can tell how oft he offendeth : O cleanse thou me from my secret faults.

Keep thy servant also from presumptuous sins, lest they get the dominion over me : so shall I be undefiled, and innocent from the great offence.

Let the words of my mouth, and the meditation of my heart : be alway acceptable in thy sight,

O Lord : my strength and my redeemer.

Glory be to the Father, &c.

As it was in the beginning, &c.

PSALM XXIV. *Domini est terra.*

Of the innocence of those who shall go to heaven, and of the resurrection of Christ.

THE earth is the Lord's, and all that therein is : the compass of the world, and they that dwell therein.

For he hath founded it upon the seas : and prepared it upon the floods.

Who shall ascend into the hill of the Lord : or who shall rise up in his holy place?

Even he that hath clean hands, and a pure heart : and that hath not lift up his mind unto vanity, nor sworn to deceive his neighbour.

He shall receive the blessing from the Lord : and righteousness from the God of his salvation.

This is the generation of them that seek him : even of them that seek thy face, O Jacob.

Lift up your heads, O ye gates, and be ye lift up, ye everlasting doors : and the King of glory shall come in.

Who is the King of glory : it is the Lord strong and mighty, even the Lord mighty in battle.

Lift up your heads, O ye gates, and be ye lift up, ye everlasting doors : and the King of glory shall come in.

Who is the King of glory : even the Lord of hosts, he is the King of glory.

Glory be to the Father, &c.

As it was in the beginning, &c.

Ant. Christ is able to save them to the uttermost that come unto God by him : seeing he ever liveth to make intercession for them. _{Heb. vii. 25.}

Vers. He hath entered into heaven itself:

Ans. Now to appear in the presence of God for us.

¶ *Then by the Reader alone,*

OUR Father, which art in heaven, hallowed be thy name. Thy kingdom come. Thy will be done in earth, as it is in heaven. Give us this day our daily bread. And forgive us our trespasses, as we forgive them that trespass against us.

And lead us not into temptation,

But deliver us from evil.

𝕭𝖑𝖊𝖘𝖘𝖎𝖓𝖌. The everlasting Father bless us with his blessing everlasting.

Ans. Amen.

THE FIRST LESSON. Isa. xi. 1.

THERE shall come forth a rod out of the stem of Jesse, and a branch shall grow out of his roots: and the Spirit of the Lord shall rest upon him, the spirit of wisdom and understanding, the spirit of counsel and might, the spirit of knowledge and of the fear of the Lord; and shall make him of quick understanding in the fear of the Lord: and he shall not judge after the sight of his eyes, neither reprove after the hearing of his ears: but with righteousness shall he judge the poor, and reprove with equity for the meek of the earth: and he shall smite the earth with the rod of his mouth, and with the breath of his lips shall he slay the wicked. And righteousness shall be the girdle of his loins, and faithfulness the girdle of his reins. THUS SAITH THE LORD; TURN UNTO ME, AND YE SHALL BE SAVED.

Blessing. God, the Son of God, vouchsafe to bless and succour us.

Ans. Amen.

THE SECOND LESSON. S. Luke i. 26.

THE Angel Gabriel was sent from God unto a city of Galilee, named Nazareth, to a virgin espoused to a man whose name was Joseph, of the house of David; and the virgin's name was Mary. And the Angel came in unto her, and said, Hail, thou that art highly favoured, the Lord is with thee: blessed art thou among women. And when she saw him she was troubled at his saying, and cast in her mind what manner of salutation this should be. And the Angel said unto her, Fear not, Mary; for thou hast found favour with God. And behold thou shalt conceive in thy womb, and shalt bring forth a Son, and shalt call his name JESUS. He shall be great, and shall be called the Son of the Highest: and the Lord God shall give unto him the throne of his Father David: and he shall reign over the house of Jacob for ever; and of his kingdom there shall be no end. THUS SAITH THE LORD; TURN UNTO ME, AND YE SHALL BE SAVED.

Blessing. The grace of the Holy Ghost illumine us in heart and body.

Ans. Amen.

THE THIRD LESSON.

THEN said Mary unto the Angel, How shall this be, seeing I know not a man? And the Angel answered and said unto her, The Holy Ghost shall come upon thee, and the power of the Highest shall overshadow thee; therefore also that holy thing which shall be born of thee shall be called the Son of God. And behold thy cousin Elizabeth, she hath also conceived a son in her old age; and this is the sixth month with her who was called barren. For with God nothing shall be impossible. And Mary said, Behold the handmaid of the Lord; be it unto me according to thy word. THUS SAITH THE LORD; TURN UNTO ME, AND YE SHALL BE SAVED.

TE DEUM LAUDAMUS.

The praise of God the Father, the Son, and the Holy Ghost.

WE praise thee, O God: we acknowledge thee to be the Lord.

All the earth doth worship thee: the Father everlasting.

To thee all Angels cry aloud: the Heavens, and all the Powers therein.

To thee Cherubin, and Seraphin: continually do cry,

Holy, holy, holy : Lord God of Sabaoth ;

Heaven and earth are full of the Majesty : of thy Glory.

The glorious company of the Apostles : praise thee.

The goodly fellowship of the Prophets : praise thee.

The noble army of Martyrs : praise thee.

The holy church throughout all the world : doth acknowledge thee ;

The Father : of an infinite majesty ;

Thine honourable, true : and only Son ;

Also the Holy Ghost : the Comforter.

Thou art the King of Glory : O Christ.

Thou art the everlasting Son : of the Father.

When thou tookest upon thee to deliver man : thou didst not abhor the Virgin's womb.

When thou hadst overcome the sharpness of death : thou didst open the kingdom of heaven to all believers.

Thou sittest at the right hand of God : in the glory of the Father.

We believe that thou shalt come : to be our Judge.

We therefore pray thee, help thy servants : whom thou hast redeemed with thy precious blood.

Make them to be numbered with thy Saints : in glory everlasting.

O Lord, save thy people : and bless thine heritage.

Govern them : and lift them up for ever.

Day by day : we magnify thee ;

And we worship thy name : ever world without end.

Vouchsafe, O Lord : to keep us this day without sin.

O Lord, have mercy upon us : have mercy upon us.

O Lord, let thy mercy lighten upon us : as our trust is in thee.

O Lord, in thee have I trusted : let me never be confounded.

Vers. The earth, O Lord, is full of thy mercy.

Ans. O teach me thy statutes.

THE ORDER FOR
Lauds.

Early Morning.

¶ *Introductory Prayers, p. 6.*

O God, make speed to save me.

O Lord, make haste to help me.

Glory be to the Father, and to the Son : and to the Holy Ghost ;

As it was in the beginning, is now, and ever shall be : world without end. Amen.

ALLELUIA.

¶ *Then shall be said or sung one or more of the following Psalms with their* Anthem.

Ant. Behold the eye of the Lord.

PSALM LXVII. *Deus misereatur.*

A prayer for the favour and knowledge of God, and that his praise may be spread throughout all the world.

GOD be merciful unto us, and bless us : and show us the light of his countenance, and be merciful unto us :

That thy way may be known upon earth : thy saving health among all nations.

Let the people praise thee, O God : yea, let all the people praise thee.

O let the nations rejoice and be glad : for thou shalt judge the folk righteously, and govern the nations upon earth.

Let the people praise thee, O God : yea, let all the people praise thee.

Then shall the earth bring forth her increase : and God, even our own God, shall give us his blessing.

God shall bless us : and all the ends of the world shall fear him.

Glory be to the Father, &c.

As it was in the beginning, &c.

BENEDICITE.

Dan. iii. 57.

The song of the three children, praising God as they walked in the fire.

O ALL ye works of the Lord, bless ye the Lord : praise him, and magnify him for ever.

O ye Angels of the Lord, bless ye the Lord : ye Heavens, bless ye the Lord.

O ye waters that be above the Firmament, bless ye the Lord : all ye powers of the Lord, bless ye the Lord.

O ye Sun and Moon, bless ye the Lord : ye stars of heaven, bless ye the Lord.

O ye Showers and Dew, bless ye the Lord : ye Winds of God, bless ye the Lord.

O ye Fire and Heat, bless ye the Lord : ye Winter and Summer, bless ye the Lord.

O ye Dews and Frosts, bless ye the Lord : ye Frost and Cold, bless ye the Lord.

O ye Ice and Snow, bless ye the Lord : ye Nights and Days, bless ye the Lord.

O ye Light and Darkness, bless ye the Lord : ye Lightnings and Clouds, bless ye the Lord.

O let the Earth bless the Lord : yea let it praise him, and magnify him for ever.

O ye Mountains and Hills, bless ye the Lord : all ye green things upon the Earth, bless ye the Lord.

O ye Wells, bless ye the Lord : ye Seas and Floods, bless ye the Lord.

O ye Whales, and all that move in the waters, bless ye the Lord : all ye fowls of the air, bless ye the Lord.

O all ye Beasts and Cattle, bless ye the Lord : ye Children of Men, bless ye the Lord.

O let Israel bless the Lord : praise him, and magnify him for ever.

O ye Priests of the Lord, bless ye the Lord : ye servants of the Lord, bless ye the Lord.

O ye spirits and souls of the Righteous, bless ye the Lord : ye holy and humble men of heart, bless ye the Lord.

O Ananias, Azarias, and Misael, bless ye the Lord : praise him, and magnify him for ever.

Let us bless the Father, the Son, and the

Holy Ghost : let us praise him, and magnify him for ever.

Blessed art thou, Lord, in the firmament of heaven : and above all to be praised and glorified for ever.

PSALM CXLVIII. *Laudate Dominum.*

All creation is invited to the praise of God.

O PRAISE the Lord of Heaven : praise him in the height.

Praise him, all ye angels of his : praise him, all his host.

Praise him, sun and moon : praise him, all ye stars and light.

Praise him, all ye heavens : and ye waters that are above the heavens.

Let them praise the name of the Lord : for he spake the word, and they were made; he commanded, and they were created.

He hath made them fast for ever and ever : he hath given them a law which shall not be broken.

Praise the Lord upon earth : ye dragons and all deeps;

Fire and hail, snow and vapours : wind and storm, fulfilling his word;

Mountains, and all hills : fruitful trees and all cedars;

Beasts and all cattle : worms and feathered fowls.

Kings of the earth and all people : princes and all judges of the world;

Young men and maidens, old men and

children, praise the name of the Lord : for his name only is excellent, and his praise above heaven and earth.

He shall exalt the horn of his people; all his saints shall praise him : even the children of Israel, even the people that serveth him.

Glory be to the Father, &c.

As it was in the beginning, &c.

Ant. Behold the eye of the Lord is upon them that fear him, and upon them that put their trust in his mercy : to deliver their soul from death, and to feed them in the time of dearth. *Ps. xxxiii. 17.*

THE CHAPTER. Jer. ix. 23.

THUS saith the Lord, Let not the wise man glory in his wisdom, neither let the mighty man glory in his might, let not the rich man glory in his riches : but let him that glorieth glory in this, that he understandeth and knoweth me, that I am the Lord, which exercise lovingkindness, judgment, and righteousness, in the earth.

Ans. Thanks be to God.

HYMN. *Ales diei nuncius.*

The winged herald of the day
Proclaims the morn's approaching ray;
And Christ the Lord our souls excites,
And so to endless life invites.

With earnest cry, with tearful care,
Call we the Lord to hear our prayer,
While supplication, pure and deep,
Forbids each chastened heart to sleep.

Do thou, O Christ, our slumbers wake;
Do thou the chains of darkness break;
Purge thou our former sins away,
And in our souls new light display.

Vers. Blessed be the name of the Lord.

Ans. From this time forth for evermore.

𝔄nt. The kindness and love.

BENEDICTUS.

The Song of Zacharias.

S. Luke i. 68.

Thanksgiving for the performance of God's promise.

BLESSED be the Lord God of Israel : for he hath visited and redeemed his people.

And hath raised up a mighty salvation for us : in the house of his servant David;

As he spake by the mouth of his holy Prophets : which have been since the world began;

That we should be saved from our enemies : and from the hands of all that hate us;

To perform the mercy promised to our forefathers : and to remember his holy Covenant;

To perform the oath which he sware to

our forefather Abraham : that he would give us;

That we being delivered out of the hand of our enemies : might serve him without fear;

In holiness and righteousness before him : all the days of our life.

And thou, Child, shalt be called the Prophet of the Highest : for thou shalt go before the face of the Lord to prepare his ways :

To give knowledge of salvation unto his people : for the remission of their sins,

Through the tender mercy of our God : whereby the dayspring from on high hath visited us;

To give light to them that sit in darkness, and in the shadow of death : and to guide our feet into the way of peace.

Glory be to the Father, &c.

As it was in the beginning, &c.

Ant. The kindness and love of God our Saviour toward man appeared, not by works of righteousness which we have done, but according to his mercy he saved us, by the washing of regeneration and renewing of the Holy Ghost; which he shed on us abundantly through Jesus Christ our Saviour; that being justified by his grace we should be made heirs according to the hope of eternal life. _{Tit. iii. 4.}

Vers. O Lord, show thy mercy upon us.

Ans. And grant us thy salvation.

LAUDS.

Let us pray.

¶ *Here may be said the* COLLECT *for the day, all kneeling: then as follows.*

GRANT, we beseech thee, O Lord our God, that thy servants may enjoy continual health of body and soul, that we may be delivered from the present sorrow and have the fruition of eternal joy; through Christ our Lord.

Let us bless the Lord.

Ans. Thanks be to God.

¶ *Then may be said one or more of the following* MEMORIALS, *ending with the blessing and Lord's Prayer at the conclusion, p. 30.*

Memorials.

OF THE HOLY GHOST.

Ant. Come, Holy Spirit of God, inspire the hearts of thy faithful people; and kindle in them the fire of thy love.

Vers. When thou sendest forth thy Spirit, they are created.

Ans. And thou renewest the face of the earth.

Let us pray.

GOD, who didst teach the hearts of thy faithful people, by sending to them the light of thy

Holy Spirit; Grant us, by the same Spirit, to have a right judgment in all things, and evermore to rejoice in his holy comfort: through the merits of Christ Jesus our Saviour, who liveth and reigneth with thee in the unity of the same Spirit, one God, world without end. *Amen.*

II.

OF THE HOLY TRINITY.

Ant. Deliver us, save us, justify us, O Blessed Trinity.

Vers. Blessed be the Father, and the Son, and the Holy Ghost.

Ans. Let us praise him and magnify him above all for ever.

Let us pray.

ALMIGHTY and everlasting God, who hast given unto us, thy servants, grace by the confession of a true faith, to acknowledge the glory of the eternal Trinity, and in the power of the divine majesty to worship the unity; we beseech thee that thou wouldest keep us stedfast in this faith, and evermore defend us from all adversities, who livest and reignest, one God, world without end. *Amen.*

III.

FOR HOLINESS.

Ant. Hereby we know that we know God, if we keep his commandments: he that saith, I know him, and keepeth not his commandments, is a liar, and the truth is not in him: but whoso keepeth his word, in him verily is the love of God perfected.

1 S. John iii. 2.

Vers. Teach us, O Lord, to do the thing that pleaseth thee.

Ans. For thou art our God.

Let us pray.

GRANT to us, Lord, we beseech thee, the spirit to think and do always such things as be rightful; that we, who cannot do anything that is good without thee, may by thee be enabled to live according to thy will: through Jesus Christ our Lord. *Amen.*

IV.

FOR GRACE.

Ant. The Lord is full of compassion and mercy, long-suffering, and of great goodness. For look how high the heaven is in comparison of the earth, so great is his mercy also toward them that fear him. Look how wide also the east is from the west, so far hath he set our sins from us. Yea, like as a father pitieth his own children, even so is the Lord merciful to them that fear him. Ps. ciii. 11.

Vers. My heart, O Lord, is joyful in thy salvation.

Ans. I will sing of the Lord because he hath dealt so lovingly with me; yea, I will praise the name of the Lord most highest.

Let us pray.

LORD, we pray thee that thy grace may always prevent and follow us, and make us continually to be given to all good works; through Jesus Christ our Lord. *Amen.*

V.

FOR THE QUEEN.

Ant. Because thou hast been my helper, O Lord, therefore under the shadow of thy wings will I rejoice. My soul hangeth upon thee, thy right hand hath upholden me. Those also that seek the hurt of my soul, they shall go under the earth, but the King shall rejoice in God. Ps. lxiii. 8.

Vers. O Lord, save the Queen.

Ans. And mercifully hear us when we call upon thee.

Let us pray.

O LORD God, most merciful Father, who, of thy favour towards us, hast sent Victoria thy servant, our Queen, to reign over us: Keep her, we beseech thee, under thine almighty protection; save and defend her from all her enemies, both ghostly and bodily; give her grace to rule thy people according to thy law, that she may here govern to thy honour and glory, and after this life may receive and enjoy the inheritance of thy heavenly kingdom, in life and bliss everlasting; through Jesus Christ our Lord. *Amen.*

VI.

FOR PEACE.

Ant. Give peace in our time, O Lord, because there is none other that fighteth for us, but only thou, O God.

Vers. Peace be within thy walls.

Ans. And plenteousness within thy palaces.

Let us pray.

O GOD, from whom all holy desires, all good counsels, and all just works do proceed; give unto thy servants that peace which the world cannot give; that both our hearts may be set to obey thy commandments, and also that by thee we being defended from the fear of our enemies may pass our time in rest and quietness; through the merits of Jesus Christ our Saviour. *Amen.*

VII.

OF THE PASSION.

Ant. Christ suffered for us, leaving us an example that we should follow his steps; who did no sin, neither was guile found in his mouth. 1 S. Pet. ii. 21.

Vers. We worship thee, O Christ, with praise and benediction.

Ans. For thou hast redeemed the world from endless affliction.

Let us pray.

O LORD Jesu Christ, Son of the living God, set thine holy passion, cross, and death, between thy judgment and our souls, both now and in the hour of death. And vouchsafe, we beseech thee, to grant unto the living mercy and grace, to the dead pardon and rest, to thy holy Church peace and concord, and to us miserable sinners life and joy everlasting; who livest and reignest with the Father and the Holy Ghost, one God, world without end. *Amen.*

Let us bless the Lord.

Ans. Thanks be to God.

THE glorious Death and Passion of our Lord Jesus Christ deliver us from sorrow and trouble, and bring us to the joys of Paradise.

Ans. Amen.

¶ *Then the Lord's Prayer, as follows, which may be said in silence.*

OUR Father, which art in heaven, hallowed be thy Name. Thy kingdom come. Thy will be done in earth, as it is in heaven. Give us this day our daily bread. And forgive us our trespasses, as we forgive them that trespass against us. And lead us not into temptation, but deliver us from evil. Amen.

THE ORDER FOR Prime.

EARLY MORNING.

¶ *Introductory Prayers, p. 6.*

O God, make speed to save me.

O Lord, make haste to help me.

Glory be to the Father, and to the Son: and to the Holy Ghost;

As it was in the beginning, is now, and ever shall be : world without end. Amen.

ALLELUIA.

HYMN. *Consors paterni luminis.*

Fellow of thy Father's light,
  Light of light, eternal day,
Victor o'er the shades of night,
  Aid us, Jesu, when we pray.

Night, and gloom, and mists of hell,
  All the powers of evil chase :
Darkness of the soul dispel
  With the glory of thy face.

When our chant on wings of love,
  Riseth in the morning air,
Shed thy bright beams from above,
  Touch with life the lips of prayer. Amen.

Ant. Blessed are the poor.

PSALM CXVIII. *Confitemini Domino.*

All men are exhorted to praise and magnify the Lord God.

O GIVE thanks unto the Lord, for he is gracious : because his mercy endureth for ever.

Let Israel now confess, that he is gracious : and that his mercy endureth for ever.

Let the house of Aaron now confess : that his mercy endureth for ever.

Yea, let them now that fear the Lord confess : that his mercy endureth for ever.

I called upon the Lord in trouble : and the Lord heard me at large.

The Lord is on my side : I will not fear what man doeth unto me.

The Lord taketh my part with them that help me : therefore shall I see my desire upon mine enemies.

It is better to trust in the Lord : than to put any confidence in man.

It is better to trust in the Lord : than to put any confidence in princes.

All nations compassed me round about : but in the name of the Lord will I destroy them.

They kept me in on every side, they kept

me in, I say, on every side: but in the name of the Lord will I destroy them.

They came about me like bees, and are extinct even as the fire among the thorns: for in the name of the Lord I will destroy them.

Thou hast thrust sore at me, that I might fall: but the Lord was my help.

The Lord is my strength, and my song: and is become my salvation.

The voice of joy and health is in the dwellings of the righteous: the right hand of the Lord bringeth mighty things to pass.

The right hand of the Lord hath the pre-eminence: the right hand of the Lord bringeth mighty things to pass.

I shall not die, but live: and declare the works of the Lord.

The Lord hath chastened and corrected me: but he hath not given me over unto death.

Open me the gates of righteousness: that I may go into them, and give thanks unto the Lord.

This is the gate of the Lord: the righteous shall enter into it.

I will thank thee, for thou hast heard me: and art become my salvation.

The same stone which the builders refused: is become the head-stone in the corner.

This is the Lord's doing: and it is marvellous in our eyes.

This is the day which the Lord hath made : we will rejoice and be glad in it.

Help me now, O Lord : O Lord, send us now prosperity.

Blessed be he that cometh in the name of the Lord : we have wished you good luck, ye that are of the house of the Lord.

God is the Lord who hath showed us light : bind the sacrifice with cords, yea, even unto the horns of the altar.

Thou art my God, and I will thank thee : thou art my God, and I will praise thee.

O give thanks unto the Lord, for he is gracious : and his mercy endureth for ever.

Glory be to the Father, &c.

As it was in the beginning, &c.

Ant. Blessed are the poor in spirit, for theirs is the kingdom of heaven : blessed are they that mourn, for they shall be comforted.

S. Matth. v. 3.

¶ *Then the* APOSTLES' CREED, *all standing and turning reverently to the East.*

I BELIEVE in God the Father Almighty, Maker of heaven and earth :

And in Jesus Christ his only Son our Lord, Who was conceived by the Holy Ghost, Born of the Virgin Mary, Suffered under Pontius Pilate, Was crucified, dead, and buried, He descended into hell; The third day he rose again from the dead, He ascended into heaven, And sitteth on the right hand of God the Father Almighty;

From thence he shall come to judge the quick and the dead.

I believe in the Holy Ghost; The holy Catholic Church; The Communion of Saints; The Forgiveness of sins; The Resurrection of the body, And the life everlasting. Amen.

¶ *And after that these Prayers following, all devoutly kneeling; the Reader first pronouncing with a loud voice,*

Lord, hear my prayer.

Ans. And let my cry come unto thee.

Let us pray.

¶ *Here may be said the* COLLECT FOR THE DAY, *after which shall be said as follows.*

O LORD Jesu Christ, most poor and mild of spirit, who didst mourn and lament for our sins and infidelity; grant us to be like thee, even of a meek and lowly spirit, and so to mourn for our sins that we may have our part in thy heavenly kingdom, who livest and reignest with the Father and the Holy Ghost, one God, world without end. Amen.

Let us bless the Lord.

Ans. Thanks be to God.

¶ *Then the* LORD'S PRAYER *as follows, which may be said in silence.*

OUR Father, which art in heaven, hallowed be thy name. Thy kingdom come. Thy will be done in earth, as it is in heaven. Give us this day our daily bread. And forgive us our trespasses, as we forgive them that trespass against us. And lead us not into temptation, but deliver us from evil. Amen.

¶ *Here may follow (when so desired) the* LITANY, *p.* 76, *or one of the* SEVEN PENITENTIAL PSALMS, *p.* 61, *or one of the* PSALMS OF THE PASSION.

THE ORDER FOR
The Third Hour.
(9 A.M., OR EARLIER.)

¶ *Introductory Prayers, p.* 6.

O God, make speed to save me.

O Lord, make haste to help me.

Glory be to the Father, and to the Son : and to the Holy Ghost;

As it was in the beginning, is now, and ever shall be : world without end.   Amen.

ALLELUIA.

HYMN.   *Rector potens, verax Deus.*

O God of truth, O Lord of might,
Who orderest time and change aright,
Brightening the morn with golden gleams,
Kindling the noon-day's fiery beams :

Quench thou in us the flames of strife,
From passion's heat preserve our life,
Our bodies keep from perils free,
And give our souls true peace in thee.

By every power, by heart and tongue,
By act and deed, thy praise be sung ;

Inflame with perfect love each sense,
That others' souls may kindle thence. Amen.

Ant. Blessed are the meek.

PSALM CXX. *Ad Dominum.*

A prayer to be delivered from the vanity of the world.

WHEN I was in trouble I called upon the Lord : and he heard me.

Deliver my soul, O Lord, from lying lips : and from a deceitful tongue.

What reward shall be given or done unto thee, thou false tongue : even mighty and sharp arrows, with hot burning coals.

Woe is me, that I am constrained to dwell with Mesech : and to have my habitation among the tents of Kedar.

My soul hath long dwelt among them : that are enemies unto peace.

I labour for peace, but when I speak unto them thereof : they make them ready to battle.

Glory be to the Father, &c.

As it was in the beginning, &c.

Ant. Blessed are the meek, for they shall inherit the earth : blessed are they which do hunger and thirst after righteousness, for they shall be filled. S. Matth. v. 5.

Lord, hear my prayer.

Ans. And let my cry come unto thee.

Let us pray.

¶ *Here may be said the* COLLECT FOR THE DAY, *all kneeling; after which, as follows.*

O LORD Jesu Christ, whose whole life was given to humility and meekness, who alone art our very Righteousness; Grant us to serve and honour thee with humble and meek heart, and in all our life and conversation to be occupied in the works of righteousness; who livest and reignest with the Father and the Holy Ghost, one God, world without end. *Amen.*

Let us bless the Lord.

Ans. Thanks be to God.

¶ *Then the* LORD'S PRAYER *as follows, which may be said in silence.*

OUR Father, which art in heaven, hallowed be thy name. Thy kingdom come. Thy will be done in earth, as it is in heaven. Give us this day our daily bread. And forgive us our trespasses, as we forgive them that trespass against us. And lead us not into temptation, but deliver us from evil. Amen.

¶ *Here may follow (when so desired) the* LITANY, *p.* 76, *or one of the* SEVEN PENITENTIAL PSALMS, *p.* 61, *or one of the* PSALMS OF THE PASSION.

THE ORDER FOR
The Sixth Hour.

(MID-DAY, OR EARLIER.)

¶ *Introductory Prayers, p. 6.*

O God, make speed to save me.

O Lord, make haste to help me.

Glory be to the Father, and to the Son : and to the Holy Ghost ;

As it was in the beginning, is now, and ever shall be : world without end.   Amen.

ALLELUIA.

HYMN.   *Rerum Creator omnium.*

Maker of all things, heavenly King,
Who light and life to all dost bring ;
In glory shines the mid-day sun,
Aid thou our work for thee begun.

Thee, Christ, with chant and hymn we bless,
Eternal Sun of Righteousness ;
Shed down thy bright beams from above,
And light the clear flame of thy love.

O let it burn so clear, so bright,
That all shall pass beneath the light,

All secret sins be burnt away
Before that searching heavenly ray. Amen.

Ant. Blessed are the merciful.

PSALM CXXIII. *Ad te levavi oculos meos.*

A prayer to be delivered from the scorn of the wicked.

UNTO thee lift I up mine eyes : O thou that dwellest in the heavens.

Behold, even as the eyes of servants look unto the hand of their masters, and as the eyes of a maiden unto the hand of her mistress : even so our eyes wait upon the Lord our God, until he have mercy upon us.

Have mercy upon us, O Lord, have mercy upon us : for we are utterly despised.

Our soul is filled with the scornful reproof of the wealthy : and with the despitefulness of the proud.

Glory be to the Father, &c.

As it was in the beginning, &c.

Ant. Blessed are the merciful, for they shall obtain mercy : blessed are the pure in heart, for they shall see God.   S. Matth. v. 7.

Lord, hear my prayer.

Ans. And let my cry come unto thee.

Let us pray.

¶ *Here may be said the* COLLECT FOR THE DAY, *all kneeling; after which, as follows.*

O LORD Jesu Christ, whose property is ever to be merciful, who art ever pure and clean, without spot of sin: Grant us grace to follow thee in showing loving-kindness towards our neighbours, and always to bear a pure heart and a clear conscience towards thee; that we may, after this life, see thee in thine everlasting glory; who livest and reignest with the Father and the Holy Ghost, one God, world without end. *Amen.*

Let us bless the Lord.

Ans. Thanks be to God.

¶ *Then the* Lord's Prayer *as follows, which may be said in silence.*

OUR Father, which art in heaven, hallowed be thy name. Thy kingdom come. Thy will be done in earth, as it is in heaven. Give us this day our daily bread. And forgive us our trespasses, as we forgive them that trespass against us. And lead us not into temptation, but deliver us from evil. Amen.

¶ *Here may follow (when so desired) the* Litany, *p.* 76, *or one of the* Seven Penitential Psalms, *p.* 61, *or one of the* Psalms of the Passion.

THE ORDER FOR
The Ninth Hour.
(AFTERNOON.)

¶ *Introductory Prayers, p.* 6.

O God, make speed to save me.

O Lord, make haste to help me.

Glory be to the Father, and to the Son : and to the Holy Ghost;

As it was in the beginning, is now, and ever shall be : world without end. Amen.

ALLELUIA.

HYMN. *Æterni cœli gloria.*

Eternal glory of the sky,
Blest hope of frail mortality,
Thou well-belov'd, thou radiant Child
Of God and Mary undefiled,

To thee the lost creation cries,
Raise thou thine hand and bid it rise ;
O sinful soul, cast off thy fear,
Thy Saviour and thy Lord is here.

To thee, O Christ our God, we call,
Light thou the light of faith in all :

That as the beams of day decline,
Thy heavenly ray may clearer shine.   Amen.

Ant. Blessed are the peacemakers.

PSALM XV.   *Domine, quis habitabit.*

The innocent shall enter into everlasting life.

LORD, who shall dwell in thy tabernacle : or who shall rest upon thy holy hill ?

Even he that leadeth an uncorrupt life : and doeth the thing that is right, and speaketh the truth from his heart.

He that hath used no deceit in his tongue, nor done evil to his neighbour : and hath not slandered his neighbour.

He that setteth not by himself, but is lowly in his own eyes : and maketh much of them that fear the Lord.

He that sweareth unto his neighbour, and disappointeth him not : though it were to his own hindrance.

He that hath not given his money upon usury : nor taken reward against the innocent.

Whoso doeth these things : shall never fall.

Glory be to the Father, &c.
As it was in the beginning, &c.

Ant. Blessed are the peacemakers, for they shall be called the children of God : blessed are they which are persecuted for righteousness' sake, for theirs is the kingdom of heaven.

S. Matth. v. 9.

NINTH HOUR.

Lord, hear my prayer.

Ans. And let my cry come unto thee.

Let us pray.

¶ *Here may be said the* COLLECT FOR THE DAY, *all kneeling; after which, as follows.*

O LORD Jesu Christ, who madest peace between God the Father and us miserable sinners, and notwithstanding didst suffer unjustly many injuries and persecutions: Grant us grace to seek the peace which thou hast made, and patiently to bear all injuries and persecutions; that we may be called thy children, and may inherit thy heavenly kingdom; who livest and reignest, with the Father and the Holy Ghost, one God, world without end. *Amen.*

Let us bless the Lord.

Ans. Thanks be to God.

¶ *Then the* LORD'S PRAYER *as follows, which may be said in silence.*

OUR Father, which art in heaven, hallowed be thy name. Thy kingdom come. Thy will be done in earth, as it is in heaven. Give us this day our daily bread. And forgive us our trespasses, as we forgive them that trespass against us. And lead us not into temptation, but deliver us from evil. Amen.

¶ *Here may follow (when so desired) the* LITANY, *p.* 76, *or one of the* SEVEN PENITENTIAL PSALMS, *p.* 61, *or one of the* PSALMS OF THE PASSION.

THE ORDER FOR
Evensong.

¶ *Introductory Prayers, p. 6.*

O God, make speed to save me.

O Lord, make haste to help me.

Glory be to the Father, and to the Son: and to the Holy Ghost;

As it was in the beginning, is now, and ever shall be: world without end.   Amen.

ALLELUIA.

¶ *Then shall be said or sung one or more of the following Psalms, with their* ANTHEM.

Ant. A new commandment.

PSALM CXIII.   *Laudate pueri.*

We are exhorted to praise and magnify the Lord.

PRAISE the Lord, ye servants : O praise the name of the Lord.

Blessed be the name of the Lord : from this time forth for evermore.

The Lord's name is praised : from the rising up of the sun unto the going down of the same.

The Lord is high above all heathen : and his glory above the heavens.

Who is like unto the Lord our God, that hath his dwelling so high : and yet humbleth himself to behold the things that are in heaven and earth?

He taketh up the simple out of the dust : and lifteth the poor out of the mire;

That he may set him with the princes : even with the princes of his people.

He maketh the barren woman to keep house: and to be a joyful mother of children.

Glory be to the Father, &c.

As it was in the beginning, &c.

PSALM CXXXV. *Laudate nomen.*

God is to be praised for his wonderful works and benefits.

O PRAISE the Lord, laud ye the name of the Lord : praise it, O ye servants of the Lord :

Ye that stand in the house of the Lord : in the courts of the house of our God.

O praise the Lord, for the Lord is gracious : O sing praises unto his name, for it is lovely.

For why? the Lord hath chosen Jacob unto himself: and Israel for his own possession.

For I know that the Lord is great : and that our Lord is above all gods.

Whatsoever the Lord pleased, that did he in heaven, and in earth : and in the sea, and in all deep places.

He bringeth forth the clouds from the

ends of the world : and sendeth forth lightnings with the rain, bringing the winds out of his treasures.

He smote the first-born of Egypt : both of man and beast.

He hath sent tokens and wonders into the midst of thee, O thou land of Egypt : upon Pharaoh and all his servants.

He smote divers nations : and slew mighty kings ;

Sehon king of the Amorites, and Og the king of Basan : and all the kingdoms of Canaan ;

And gave their land to be an heritage : even an heritage unto Israel his people.

Thy name, O Lord, endureth for ever : so doth thy memorial, O Lord, from one generation to another.

For the Lord will avenge his people : and be gracious unto his servants.

As for the images of the heathen, they are but silver and gold : the work of men's hands.

They have mouths and speak not : eyes have they, but they see not.

They have ears, and yet they hear not : neither is there any breath in their mouths.

They that make them are like unto them : and so are all they that put their trust in them.

Praise the Lord, ye house of Israel : praise the Lord, ye house of Aaron.

Praise the Lord, ye house of Levi : ye that fear the Lord, praise the Lord.

Praised be the Lord out of Sion : who dwelleth at Jerusalem.

Glory be to the Father, &c.

As it was in the beginning, &c.

PSALM CXXXVIII. *Confitebor tibi.*

A praise and thanksgiving to God.

I WILL give thanks unto thee, O Lord, with my whole heart : even before the gods will I sing praise unto thee.

I will worship toward thy holy temple, and praise thy name because of thy lovingkindness and truth : for thou hast magnified thy name, and thy word above all things.

When I called upon thee thou heardest me : and enduedst my soul with much strength.

All the kings of the earth shall praise thee, O Lord : for they have heard the words of thy mouth.

Yea, they shall sing in the ways of the Lord : that great is the glory of the Lord.

For though the Lord be high, yet hath he respect unto the lowly : as for the proud, he beholdeth them afar off.

Though I walk in the midst of trouble, yet shalt thou refresh me : thou shalt stretch forth thy hand upon the furiousness of mine enemies, and thy right hand shall save me.

The Lord shall make good his lovingkindness toward me : yea, thy mercy, O Lord, endureth for ever; despise not then the works of thine own hands.

Glory be to the Father, &c.
As it was in the beginning, &c.

Ant. A new commandment I give unto you, That ye love one another, as I have loved you: by this shall all men know that ye are my disciples, if ye have love one to another.
S. John xiii. 34.

THE CHAPTER. Isaiah lxv., lv.

REJOICE ye with Jerusalem, and be glad with her, all ye that love her: rejoice for joy with her, all ye that mourn for her: that ye may drink and be satisfied with her consolations. Ho, every one that thirsteth, come ye to the waters, and he that hath no money, come, buy wine and milk without money and without price.

Ans. Thanks be to God.

HYMN. *Salvator mundi, Domine.*

O Saviour of the world forlorn,
Who, man to save, as man wast born:
Protect us through this coming night,
And ever save us through thy might.

Be with us, Lord, in mercy nigh,
And spare thy servants, when they cry;
Our sins blot out, our prayers receive,
Our darkness lighten, and forgive.

O let not sleep o'ercome the soul,
Nor Satan with his spirits foul;
Our flesh keep chaste, that it may be
An holy temple unto thee.

To thee, who makest souls anew,
With heartfelt vows we humbly sue;
That pure in heart, and free from stain,
We from our beds may rise again. Amen.

Vers. Make me a clean heart, O God.

Ans. And renew a right spirit within me.

Ant. If God be for us.

MAGNIFICAT.

S. Luke i.

The song of Mary, rejoicing and praising the goodness of God.

MY soul doth magnify the Lord : and my spirit hath rejoiced in God my Saviour.

For he hath regarded : the lowliness of his handmaiden.

For behold, from henceforth : all generations shall call me blessed.

For he that is mighty hath magnified me : and holy is his Name.

And his mercy is on them that fear him : throughout all generations.

He hath showed strength with his arm : he hath scattered the proud in the imagination of their hearts.

He hath put down the mighty from their seat : and hath exalted the humble and meek.

He hath filled the hungry with good things : and the rich he hath sent empty away.

He remembering his mercy hath holpen

his servant Israel : as he promised to our forefathers, Abraham and his seed, for ever.

Glory be to the Father, &c.

As it was in the beginning, &c.

Ant. If God be for us, who can be against us? He that spared not his own Son, but delivered him up for us all, how shall he not with him also freely give us all things?
_{Rom. viii. 31.}

Lord, hear my prayer.

Ans. And let my cry come unto thee.

Let us pray.

¶ *Here may be said the* COLLECT FOR THE DAY, *all kneeling: then as follows.*

ALMIGHTY God, by whose order and will night and darkness are drawing on, we beseech thee, of thy loving-kindness, mercifully to receive us under thy protection, that the spirits of darkness may have no power over us; and when we take our sleep for the body's need, yet may our hearts and minds keep watch unto thee; that in thy sight we be not found children of night and of darkness, but of the day and the light, for ever; who livest and reignest, one God, world without end. Amen.

Let us bless the Lord.

Ans. Thanks be to God.

¶ *Here may be said (if so desired) any of the* LAUDAL MEMORIALS, *p.* 25, *concluding with the following* MEMORIAL OF THE PASSION, *as there placed.*

MEMORIAL OF THE PASSION.

Ant. Christ suffered for us, leaving us an example that we should follow his steps; who did no sin, neither was guile found in his mouth.   1 S. Pet. ii. 21.

Vers. We worship thee, O Christ, with praise and benediction.

Ans. For thou hast redeemed the world from endless affliction.

Let us pray.

O LORD Jesu Christ, Son of the living God, set thine holy passion, cross, and death, between thy judgment and our souls, both now and in the hour of death. And vouchsafe, we beseech thee, to grant unto the living mercy and grace, to the dead pardon and rest, to thine holy Church peace and concord, and to us miserable sinners life and joy everlasting; who livest and reignest with the Father and the Holy Ghost, one God, world without end. Amen.

Let us bless the Lord.

Ans. Thanks be to God.

THE glorious death and passion of our Lord Jesus Christ deliver us from sorrow and trouble, and bring us to the joys of Paradise.

Ans. Amen.

¶ *Then the* LORD'S PRAYER, *which may be said in silence.*

OUR Father, which art in heaven, hallowed be thy name. Thy kingdom come. Thy will be done in earth, as it is in heaven. Give us this day our daily bread. And forgive us our trespasses, as we forgive them that trespass against us. And lead us not into temptation, but deliver us from evil. Amen.

THE ORDER FOR
Compline.
(BEDTIME.)

¶ *Introductory Prayers, p. 6.*

Turn us, O God our Saviour.

And let thine anger cease from us.

O God, make speed to save me.

O Lord, make haste to help me.

Glory be to the Father, and to the Son : and to the Holy Ghost ;

As it was in the beginning, is now, and ever shall be : world without end.   Amen.

ALLELUIA.

Ant. Save us, O Lord.

PSALM XIII.   *Usquequo, Domine.*

A prayer against temptation.

HOW long wilt thou forget me, O Lord, for ever : how long wilt thou hide thy face from me?

How long shall I seek counsel in my soul,

and be so vexed in my heart : how long shall mine enemies triumph over me?

Consider, and hear me, O Lord my God : lighten mine eyes, that I sleep not in death.

Lest mine enemy say, I have prevailed against him : for if I be cast down, they that trouble me will rejoice at it.

But my trust is in thy mercy : and my heart is joyful in thy salvation.

I will sing of the Lord, because he hath dealt so lovingly with me : yea, I will praise the name of the Lord most Highest.

Glory be to the Father, &c.

As it was in the beginning, &c.

PSALM XLIII. *Judica me, Deus.*

A prayer to be delivered from our adversaries, that we may sing the praise of God.

GIVE sentence with me, O God, and defend my cause against the ungodly people : O deliver me from the deceitful and wicked man.

For thou art the God of my strength, why hast thou put me from thee : and why go I so heavily, while the enemy oppresseth me?

O send out thy light and thy truth, that they may lead me : and bring me unto thy holy hill, and to thy dwelling.

And that I may go unto the altar of God, even unto the God of my joy and gladness : and upon the harp will I give thanks unto thee, O God, my God.

Why art thou so heavy, O my soul : and why art thou so disquieted within me?

O put thy trust in God: for I will yet give him thanks, which is the help of my countenance, and my God.

Glory be to the Father, &c.

As it was in the beginning, &c.

Ant. Save us, O Lord, waking, and guard us, sleeping; that we may wake in Christ, and rest in peace.

THE CHAPTER. Jer. xiv. 9.

THOU, O Lord, art in the midst of us, and we are called by thy name; leave us not, O Lord our God.

Ans. Thanks be to God.

HYMN. *Rerum creator omnium.*

Maker of all, to thee we pray,
As fades the light of dying day,
Defend us, by thy grace, this night,
From Satan's malice infinite.

From dream or fancy, born of sin,
Keep us, O Lord, all pure within;
And let our spirits wake with thee,
Nor slumber in impurity.

Almighty Father, heavenly Son,
Eternal Spirit, three in one,
Send down the fulness of thy grace
And hear from heaven thy dwelling-place.
Amen.

Vers. Whoso dwelleth under the defence of the most High.

Ans. Shall abide under the shadow of the Almighty.

Ant. Grant us, O Lord, thy light.

NUNC DIMITTIS.
S. Luke ii. 29.
The song of Simeon the Just.

LORD, now lettest thou thy servant depart in peace : according to thy word.

For mine eyes have seen : thy salvation.

Which thou hast prepared : before the face of all people ;

To be a light to lighten the Gentiles : and to be the glory of thy people Israel.

Glory be to the Father, &c.

As it was in the beginning, &c.

Ant. Grant us, O Lord, thy light; that we, being delivered from the darkness of our hearts, may come to the true light which is Christ.

¶ *Then the* APOSTLES' CREED, *all standing and turning reverently to the east.*

I BELIEVE in God the Father Almighty, Maker of heaven and earth :

And in Jesus Christ his only Son our Lord, Who was conceived by the Holy Ghost, Born of the Virgin Mary, Suffered under Pontius Pilate, Was crucified, dead, and buried, He descended into hell; The third day he rose again from the dead, He ascended into heaven, And sitteth on the right hand of God the Father Almighty; From thence he shall come to judge the quick and the dead.

I believe in the Holy Ghost; The holy Catholic Church; The Communion of Saints; The Forgiveness of sins; The Resurrection of the body, And the life everlasting. Amen.

¶ *And after that, these Prayers following, all devoutly kneeling; the Reader first pronouncing with a loud voice,*

Lord, hear my prayer.

Ans. And let my cry come unto thee.

Let us pray.

¶ *Here may be said the* COLLECT FOR THE DAY, *after which as follows.*

LIGHTEN our darkness, we beseech thee, O Lord; and by thy great mercy defend us from all perils and dangers of this night, for the love of thine only Son our Saviour Jesus Christ. *Amen.*

Or this.

O LORD Jesu Christ, Redeemer of the world, eternal Word of the Father, by whom all things were created and are preserved, we beseech thee to receive us this night beneath the shadow of thy mercy, nor to suffer us to fall, nor to be visited by the terrors of Satan. Cause us to see light in the darkness, O thou who art the everlasting light; who with the Father and the Holy Ghost livest and reignest, one God, world without end. *Amen.*

Let us bless the Lord.

Ans. Thanks be to God.

2 Cor. xiii.

THE grace of our Lord Jesus Christ, and the love of God and the fellowship of the Holy Ghost, be with us all evermore. *Amen.*

¶ *Then the* LORD'S PRAYER, *which may be said in silence.*

OUR Father, which art in heaven, hallowed be thy name. Thy kingdom come. Thy will be done in earth, as it is in heaven. Give us this day our daily bread. And forgive us our trespasses, as we forgive them that trespass against us. And lead us not into temptation, but deliver us from evil. Amen.

¶ *Here may follow (when so desired) the* LITANY, *p.* 76, *or one of the* SEVEN PENITENTIAL PSALMS, *p.* 61, *or one of the* PSALMS OF THE PASSION.

THE SEVEN PENITENTIAL PSALMS.

WITH SHORT COLLECTS CONTAINING THE SUBSTANCE OF EACH PSALM.

***

Ant. Remember not.

I. SUNDAY.

PSALM VI. *Domine, ne in furore.*

A fervent prayer of the sinner that he may be healed and his enemies vanquished.

O LORD, rebuke me not in thine indignation : neither chasten me in thy displeasure.

Have mercy upon me, O Lord, for I am weak : O Lord, heal me, for my bones are vexed.

My soul also is sore troubled : but, Lord, how long wilt thou punish me?

Turn thee, O Lord, and deliver my soul : O save me for thy mercy's sake.

For in death no man remembereth thee : and who will give thee thanks in the pit?

I am weary of my groaning; every night wash I my bed: and water my couch with my tears.

My beauty is gone for very trouble: and worn away because of all mine enemies.

Away from me, all ye that work vanity: for the Lord hath heard the voice of my weeping.

The Lord hath heard my petition: the Lord will receive my prayer.

All mine enemies shall be confounded, and sore vexed: they shall be turned back, and put to shame suddenly.

Glory be to the Father, &c.

As it was in the beginning, &c.

Let us pray.

O LORD, who in thy terrible and dreadful majesty shalt come to judge mankind, have mercy upon us miserable sinners in this life, that in the day of anger, wrath, and vengeance, we be not condemned to eternal punishment. Vouchsafe also to turn thyself from the sternness of justice to the lovingkindness of mercy, that thou mayest both deliver our souls from the powers of darkness, and in all our troubles and infirmities we may ever be defended by thy grace: through Jesus Christ our Lord. *Amen.*

II. MONDAY.

PSALM XXXII. *Beati, quorum.*

How the penitent person should bewail his sins, pray unto God, and rejoice in him.

BLESSED is he whose unrighteousness is forgiven : and whose sin is covered.

Blessed is the man unto whom the Lord imputeth no sin : and in whose spirit there is no guile.

For while I held my tongue : my bones consumed away through my daily complaining.

For thy hand is heavy upon me day and night : and my moisture is like the drought in summer.

I will acknowledge my sin unto thee : and mine unrighteousness have I not hid.

I said, I will confess my sins unto the Lord : and so thou forgavest the wickedness of my sin.

For this shall every one that is godly make his prayer unto thee in a time when thou mayest be found : but in the great waterfloods they shall not come nigh him.

Thou art a place to hide me in, thou shalt preserve me from trouble : thou shalt compass me about with songs of deliverance.

I will inform thee, and teach thee in the way wherein thou shalt go : and I will guide thee with mine eye.

Be ye not like to horse and mule, which have no understanding : whose mouths must be held with bit and bridle, lest they fall upon thee.

Great plagues remain for the ungodly: but whoso putteth his trust in the Lord, mercy embraceth him on every side.

Be glad, O ye righteous, and rejoice in the Lord : and be joyful, all ye that are true of heart.

Glory be to the Father, &c.

As it was in the beginning, &c.

Let us pray.

WE beseech thee, O Lord, vouchsafe to grant unto us the knowledge of thy heavenly wisdom, and of thy loving-kindness so furnish us in this path of our pilgrimage with the armour of righteousness, by bending on us who confess our unrighteousness the eyes of thy grace and mercy; that our sins being covered by thy pardon and love, and our former offences being no more imputed unto us, we may rejoice together with thy saints and elect, for ever and ever. *Amen.*

III. TUESDAY.

PSALM XXXVIII. *Domine, ne in furore.*

The sinner, oppressed by the burden of sin, imploreth God's assistance, to whose mercy he committeth himself.

PUT me not to rebuke, O Lord, in thine anger : neither chasten me in thy heavy displeasure.

For thine arrows stick fast in me : and thy hand presseth me sore.

There is no health in my flesh, because of thy displeasure : neither is there any rest in my bones, by reason of my sin.

For my wickednesses are gone over my head : and are like a sore burden, too heavy for me to bear.

My wounds stink, and are corrupt: through my foolishness.

I am brought into so great trouble and misery : that I go mourning all the day long.

For my loins are filled with a sore disease : and there is no whole part in my body.

I am feeble, and sore smitten : I have roared for the very disquietness of my heart.

Lord, thou knowest all my desire : and my groaning is not hid from thee.

My heart panteth, my strength hath failed me : and the sight of mine eyes is gone from me.

My lovers and my neighbours did stand looking upon my trouble : and my kinsmen stood afar off.

They also that sought after my life laid snares for me : and they that went about to do me evil talked of wickedness, and imagined deceit all the day long.

As for me, I was like a deaf man, and heard not : and as one that is dumb, who doth not open his mouth.

I became even as a man that heareth not : and in whose mouth are no reproofs.

For in thee, O Lord, have I put my trust : thou shalt answer for me, O Lord my God.

I have required that they, even mine enemies, should not triumph over me : for when my foot slipped, they rejoiced greatly against me.

And I, truly, am set in the plague : and my heaviness is ever in my sight.

For I will confess my wickedness : and be sorry for my sin.

But mine enemies live, and are mighty : and they that hate me wrongfully are many in number.

They also that reward evil for good are against me : because I follow the thing that good is.

Forsake me not, O Lord my God : be not thou far from me.

Haste thee to help me : O Lord God of my salvation.

Glory be to the Father, &c.

As it was in the beginning, &c.

Let us pray.

O LORD, rebuke us not in thy fiery anger, neither condemn us for ever with the lost. We acknowledge our faults, and pray for pardon. The remembrance of our sins is heavy upon us; our soul is distressed; there is no health in our flesh. Forsake us not, O Lord our God; withdraw not thy grace from us; but haste thee to help us, O Author of our salvation, Jesu Christ, who art blessed for evermore. *Amen.*

IV. WEDNESDAY.

PSALM LI. *Miserere mei, Deus.*

The sinner acknowledgeth and bewaileth his evil life; seeketh to be cleansed; imploreth the Spirit of God; that he may be renewed and strengthened.

HAVE mercy upon me, O God, after thy great goodness : according to the multitude of thy mercies do away mine offences.

Wash me throughly from my wickedness : and cleanse me from my sin.

For I acknowledge my faults : and my sin is ever before me.

Against thee only have I sinned, and done this evil in thy sight : that thou mightest be justified in thy saying, and clear when thou art judged.

Behold, I was shapen in wickedness : and in sin hath my mother conceived me.

But lo, thou requirest truth in the inward parts : and shalt make me to understand wisdom secretly.

Thou shalt purge me with hyssop, and I shall be clean : thou shalt wash me, and I shall be whiter than snow.

Thou shalt make me hear of joy and gladness : that the bones which thou hast broken may rejoice.

Turn thy face from my sins : and put out all my misdeeds.

Make me a clean heart, O God : and renew a right spirit within me.

Cast me not away from thy presence : and take not thy Holy Spirit from me.

O give me the comfort of thy help again : and stablish me with thy free Spirit.

Then shall I teach thy ways unto the wicked : and sinners shall be converted unto thee.

Deliver me from blood-guiltiness, O God, thou that art the God of my health : and my tongue shall sing of thy righteousness.

Thou shalt open my lips, O Lord : and my mouth shall show thy praise.

For thou desirest no sacrifice, else would I give it thee : but thou delightest not in burnt-offerings.

The sacrifice of God is a troubled spirit : a broken and contrite heart, O God, shalt thou not despise.

O be favourable and gracious unto Sion : build thou the walls of Jerusalem.

Then shalt thou be pleased with the sacrifice of righteousness, with the burnt-offerings and oblations : then shall they offer young bullocks upon thine altar.

Glory be to the Father, &c.

As it was in the beginning, &c.

Let us pray.

DO away our offences, we beseech thee, O Lord, according to thy great mercy. Cleanse us and wash us whiter than snow from our sins, wherein we have done evil in thy sight. Our humble and contrite hearts despise not thou, O Lord, but renew within us thine Holy Spirit; that we may be enabled to tell of thy praise, and being strengthened and confirmed by thy free Spirit the Comforter we may at length attain to the heavenly Jerusalem; through Jesus Christ our Lord. Amen.

V. THURSDAY.

PSALM CII. *Domine, exaudi.*

The complaint of the righteous, vexed by the wicked, and imploring the assistance of Almighty God.

HEAR my prayer, O Lord : and let my crying come unto thee.

Hide not thy face from me in the time of my trouble : incline thine ear unto me when I call; O hear me, and that right soon.

For my days are consumed away like smoke : and my bones are burnt up as it were a fire-brand.

My heart is smitten down, and withered like grass : so that I forget to eat my bread.

For the voice of my groaning : my bones will scarce cleave to my flesh.

I am become like a pelican in the wilderness : and like an owl that is in the desert.

I have watched, and am even as it were a sparrow : that sitteth alone upon the house-top.

Mine enemies revile me all the day long :

and they that are mad upon me are sworn together against me.

For I have eaten ashes as it were bread : and mingled my drink with weeping;

And that because of thine indignation and wrath : for thou hast taken me up, and cast me down.

My days are gone like a shadow : and I am withered like grass.

But thou, O Lord, shalt endure for ever : and thy remembrance throughout all generations.

Thou shalt arise, and have mercy upon Sion : for it is time that thou have mercy upon her, yea, the time is come.

And why? thy servants think upon her stones : and it pitieth them to see her in the dust.

The heathen shall fear thy name, O Lord : and all the kings of the earth thy Majesty;

When the Lord shall build up Sion : and when his glory shall appear;

When he turneth him unto the prayer of the poor destitute : and despiseth not their desire.

This shall be written for those that come after : and the people which shall be born shall praise the Lord.

For he hath looked down from his sanctuary : out of the heaven did the Lord behold the earth;

That he might hear the mournings of such as are in captivity : and deliver the children appointed unto death;

That they may declare the name of the Lord in Sion : and his worship at Jerusalem ;

When the people are gathered together : and the kingdoms also, to serve the Lord.

He brought down my strength in my journey : and shortened my days.

But I said, O my God, take me not away in the midst of mine age : as for thy years, they endure throughout all generations.

Thou, Lord, in the beginning hast laid the foundation of the earth : and the heavens are the work of thy hands.

They shall perish, but thou shalt endure : they all shall wax old, as doth a garment;

And as a vesture shalt thou change them, and they shall be changed : but thou art the same, and thy years shall not fail.

The children of thy servants shall continue : and their seed shall stand fast in thy sight.

Glory be to the Father, &c.

As it was in the beginning, &c.

Let us pray.

O KIND Saviour, open to us the bosom of thine infinite love, that the heavenly inheritance, which we lost through sin, we may recover through penitence. And grant us grace to offer worthy fruits of repentance, that we may obtain remission of all the sins which we have committed; and so to reverence thy name, that thou too, in the rich abundance of thy mercy, mayest receive our prayers, and we and our seed may attain to everlasting life; through thy grace and pity, O Lord Jesu Christ, who with the Father and the Holy Ghost livest and reignest, one God, world without end. *Amen.*

VI. FRIDAY.

PSALM CXXX. *De profundis.*

The sinner being punished for his sins, desireth to be delivered both from sin and from punishment.

OUT of the deep have I called unto thee, O Lord : Lord, hear my voice.

O let thine ears consider well : the voice of my complaint.

If thou, Lord, wilt be extreme to mark what is done amiss : O Lord, who may abide it?

For there is mercy with thee : therefore shalt thou be feared.

I look for the Lord; my soul doth wait for him : in his word is my trust.

My soul fleeth unto the Lord : before the morning watch, I say, before the morning watch.

O Israel, trust in the Lord, for with the Lord there is mercy : and with him is plenteous redemption.

And he shall redeem Israel : from all his sins.

Glory be to the Father, &c.

As it was in the beginning, &c.

Let us pray.

OUT of the deep of the heart we call unto thee, O Lord, to deliver us from the deep of our sins. For with thee, the only true God, is propitiation and our atonement. Mark not, then, our iniquities, who hope in thy mercy, and who have been redeemed by thy precious blood, O Lord our God. *Amen.*

VII. SATURDAY.

PSALM CXLIII. *Domine, exaudi.*

The just man, being in adversity, prayeth to be delivered from all evil.

HEAR my prayer, O Lord, and consider my desire: hearken unto me for thy truth and righteousness' sake.

And enter not into judgment with thy servant: for in thy sight shall no man living be justified.

For the enemy hath persecuted my soul, he hath smitten my life down to the ground: he hath laid me in the darkness, as the men that have been long dead.

Therefore is my spirit vexed within me: and my heart within me is desolate.

Yet do I remember the time past, I muse upon all thy works: yea, I exercise myself in the works of thy hands.

I stretch forth my hands unto thee: my soul gaspeth unto thee as a thirsty land.

Hear me, O Lord, and that soon, for my spirit waxeth faint: hide not thy face from me, lest I be like unto them that go down into the pit.

O let me hear thy lovingkindness betimes in the morning, for in thee is my trust: show thou me the way that I should walk in, for I lift up my soul unto thee.

Deliver me, O Lord, from mine enemies: for I flee unto thee to hide me.

Teach me to do the thing that pleaseth thee, for thou art my God: let thy loving Spirit lead me forth into the land of righteousness.

Quicken me, O Lord, for thy name's sake: and for thy righteousness' sake bring my soul out of trouble.

And of thy goodness slay mine enemies: and destroy all them that vex my soul; for I am thy servant.

Glory be to the Father, &c.

As it was in the beginning, &c.

Let us pray.

HIDE not, O Lord, as in anger, the face of thy mercy from us who repent; nor enter thou into judgment with us, O Lord, in whose sight no man living shall be justified: but quickly hear and help us, who hope in thee alone, and lift up our souls to the fountain of thy grace. Bring, we pray thee, our souls out of trouble: let us hear thy lovingkindness betimes in the morning: and show thou us thy way, that, walking rightly in it, we may finally attain to our heavenly home; for thy name's sake, which is JESUS. *Amen.*

Ant. Remember not, O Lord God, our old sins, but have mercy upon us, and that soon: for we are come to great misery. Help us, O God of our salvation, for the glory of thy name: O deliver us and be merciful unto our sins, for thy name's sake. Let not the wicked say: Where is now their God? So we, that are thy people, and the sheep of thy pasture, shall give thee thanks for ever: and will always be showing forth thy praise from generation to generation: to whom be honour and glory, world without end. *Amen.*

¶ *One or more of the Penitential Psalms may be used either as a short office by itself, ending with the Lord's Prayer; or after any of the Hours, as there directed.*

THE LITANY.

¶ *To be said by all, devoutly kneeling; either by itself, or after any of the Hours of prayer.*

Lord, have mercy upon us.

Lord, have mercy upon us.

Christ, have mercy upon us.

Christ, have mercy upon us.

Lord, have mercy upon us.

Lord, have mercy upon us.

O Christ, hear us.

Graciously hear us, O Christ.

O God the Father, of heaven, *Have mercy upon us.*

O God the Son, Redeemer of the world, *Have mercy upon us.*

O God the Holy Ghost, *Have mercy upon us.*

Holy Trinity, one God, *Have mercy upon us.*

Be merciful: *Spare us, O Lord.*

From all evil, *Deliver us, O Lord.*

From the crafts of the devil, *Deliver us, O Lord.*

From everlasting damnation, *Deliver us, O Lord.*

From imminent danger of our sins, *Deliver us, O Lord.*

From the assaults of evil spirits, *Deliver us, O Lord.*

From the spirit of fornication, *Deliver us, O Lord.*

From the desire of vainglory, *Deliver us, O Lord.*

From all uncleanness of body and of soul, *Deliver us, O Lord.*

From wrath and hatred, *Deliver us, O Lord.*

From unclean thoughts, *Deliver us, O Lord.*

From blindness of heart, *Deliver us, O Lord.*

From lightning and tempest, *Deliver us, O Lord.*

From sudden and unprovided death, *Deliver us, O Lord.*

By the mystery of thy holy Incarnation, *Deliver us, O Lord.*

By thy Nativity, *Deliver us, O Lord.*

By thy Circumcision, *Deliver us, O Lord.*

By thy Baptism, *Deliver us, O Lord.*

By thy Fasting, *Deliver us, O Lord.*

By thy Cross and Passion, *Deliver us, O Lord.*

By thy precious Death, *Deliver us, O Lord.*

By thy glorious Resurrection, *Deliver us, O Lord.*

By thy marvellous Ascension, *Deliver us, O Lord.*

By the grace of the Holy Ghost, *Deliver us, O Lord.*

In the hour of death, *Succour us, O Lord.*

In the day of judgment, *Deliver us, O Lord.*

We sinners, *Beseech thee to hear us.*

That it may please thee to give us peace, *We beseech thee to hear us.*

That thy mercy and thy pity may keep us, *We beseech thee to hear us.*

That it may please thee to govern and protect thy Church, *We beseech thee to hear us.*

That the Apostolic gift and all degrees of holy religion may be kept and preserved, *We beseech thee to hear us.*

That it may please thee to give peace and concord to our Queen and Generals, and also victory, *We beseech thee to hear us.*

That it may please thee to keep all our

Bishops in holy religion, *We beseech thee to hear us.*

That it may please thee to keep all the congregation of saints in thine holy service, *We beseech thee to hear us.*

That it may please thee to preserve all Christian people whom thou hast redeemed with thy precious blood, *We beseech thee to hear us.*

That it may please thee to give unto all our benefactors everlasting happiness, *We beseech thee to hear us.*

That it may please thee to deliver our souls and the souls of our parents from everlasting damnation, *We beseech thee to hear us.*

That it may please thee to give and preserve the fruits of the earth, *We beseech thee to hear us.*

That it may please thee to cast upon us thy merciful eyes, *We beseech thee to hear us.*

That it may please thee to cause the performance of our service to be reasonable, *We beseech thee to hear us.*

That it may please thee to raise our minds to heavenly desires, *We beseech thee to hear us.*

That it may please thee to give everlasting rest to all thy faithful people, both the living and the departed, *We beseech thee to hear us.*

That it may please thee to hear us, *We beseech thee to hear us.*

Son of God, *We beseech thee to hear us.*

Son of God, *We beseech thee to hear us.*

Son of God, *We beseech thee to hear us.*

O Lamb of God : that takest away the sins of the world, *Hear us, O Lord.*

O Lamb of God : that takest away the sins of the world, *Spare us, O Lord.*

O Lamb of God : that takest away the sins of the world, *Have mercy upon us.*

Lord, have mercy upon us.

Christ, have mercy upon us.

Lord, have mercy upon us.

¶ *Then by the Reader alone.*

OUR Father, which art in heaven, hallowed be thy name. Thy kingdom come. Thy will be done in earth, as it is in heaven. Give us this day our daily bread. And forgive us our trespasses, as we forgive them that trespass against us.

And lead us not into temptation.

But deliver us from evil.

O Lord, show thy mercy upon us.

And grant us thy salvation.

Let thy loving mercy come unto us, O Lord.

Even thy salvation, according to thy word.

We have sinned with our fathers.

We have done amiss, and dealt wickedly.

O Lord, deal not with us according to our sins.

Neither reward us according to our iniquities.

Let us pray for every degree in the Church.

Let thy priests be clothed with righteousness, and let thy saints rejoice.

For our brethren and sisters.

Save, O Lord, thy servants and handmaidens who put their trust in thee.

Let us pray for all Christian people.

Save thy people, O Lord, and bless thine heritage; govern them, and lift them up for ever.

Send peace within our walls, O God.

And plenteousness in every country.

For the souls of all thy servants and handmaidens.

May they rest in peace. Amen.

Lord, hear my prayer.

And let my cry come unto thee.

COLLECTS.

¶ *To be said, one or more.*

O GOD, whose nature and property is ever to have mercy and to forgive, receive our humble petitions; and though we be tied and bound with the chain of our sins, yet let the pitifulness of thy great mercy loose us; for the honour of Jesus Christ, our Mediator and Advocate. *Amen.*

ALMIGHTY and everlasting God, who alone workest great marvels; Send down upon our Bishops, and Curates, and all congregations committed to their charge, the healthful Spirit of thy grace; and that they may truly please thee, pour upon them the continual dew of thy blessing. Grant this, O Lord, for the honour of our Advocate and Mediator, Jesus Christ. *Amen.*

O GOD, who pourest the gifts of charity into the hearts of the faithful, through the grace of the Holy Ghost, grant unto thy servants and handmaidens, for whom we pray unto thy mercy, health of body and of soul; that they may love thee with all their heart, and cheerfully perform those things which thou wouldest have done, through Christ our Lord. *Amen.*

O GOD, from whom all holy desires, all good counsels, and all just works do proceed; Give unto thy servants that peace which the world cannot give; that both our hearts may be set to obey thy commandments, and also that by thee we being defended from the fear of our enemies may pass our time in rest and quietness; through the merits of Jesus Christ our Saviour. *Amen.*

THE grace of our Lord Jesus Christ, and the love of God, and the fellowship of the Holy Ghost, be with us all evermore. *Amen.*

OFFICES FOR PENITENTIAL SEASONS,

COMMONLY CALLED

THE DIRGE.

Evensong.

¶ *The Office to begin with one or more of the following Psalms, without further Preface.*

Ant. I will walk before the Lord in the land of the living. _{Ps. cxvi. 9.}

PSALM CXVI. *Dilexi, quoniam.*

For laud and praise of God, through whose benefits we are preserved in adversity.

I AM well pleased : that the Lord hath heard the voice of my prayer;

That he hath inclined his ear unto me : therefore will I call upon him as long as I live.

The snares of death compassed me round about : and the pains of hell gat hold upon me.

I found trouble and heaviness, and I called

upon the name of the Lord : O Lord, I beseech thee, deliver my soul.

Gracious is the Lord, and righteous : yea, our God is merciful.

The Lord preserveth the simple : I was in misery, and he helped me.

Turn again then unto thy rest, O my soul : for the Lord hath rewarded thee.

And why? thou hast delivered my soul from death : mine eyes from tears, and my feet from falling.

I will walk before the Lord : in the land of the living.

Glory be to the Father, &c.

As it was in the beginning, &c.

PSALM XLI. *Beatus qui intelligit.*

Happy is he that hath compassion upon the poor; whom God delivereth from his enemies and preserveth accordingly.

BLESSED is he that considereth the poor and needy : the Lord shall deliver him in the time of trouble.

The Lord preserve him, and keep him alive, that he may be blessed upon earth : and deliver not thou him into the will of his enemies.

The Lord comfort him when he lieth sick upon his bed : make thou all his bed in his sickness.

I said, Lord, be merciful unto me : heal my soul, for I have sinned against thee.

Mine enemies speak evil of me : When shall he die, and his name perish?

And if he come to see me, he speaketh vanity, and his heart conceiveth falsehood within himself, and when he cometh forth he telleth it.

All mine enemies whisper together against me : even against me do they imagine this evil.

Let the sentence of guiltiness proceed against him : and now that he lieth, let him rise up no more.

Yea, even mine own familiar friend, whom I trusted : who did also eat of my bread, hath laid great wait for me.

But be thou merciful unto me, O Lord : raise thou me up again, and I shall reward them.

By this I know thou favourest me : that mine enemy doth not triumph against me.

And when I am in my health, thou upholdest me : and shalt set me before thy face for ever.

Blessed be the Lord God of Israel : world without end. Amen.

Glory be to the Father, &c.

As it was in the beginning, &c.

PSALM CXLVI. *Lauda, anima mea.*

An exhortation to praise God, and to put our trust in him and not in man.

PRAISE the Lord, O my soul, while I live will I praise the Lord : yea, as long as I have any being, I will sing praises unto my God.

PENITENTIAL SEASONS.

O put not your trust in princes, nor in any child of man: for there is no help in them.

For when the breath of man goeth forth he shall turn again to his earth : and then all his thoughts perish.

Blessed is he that hath the God of Jacob for his help : and whose hope is in the Lord his God;

Who made heaven and earth, the sea, and all that therein is : who keepeth his promise for ever;

Who helpeth them to right that suffer wrong : who feedeth the hungry.

The Lord looseth men out of prison : the Lord giveth sight to the blind.

The Lord helpeth them that are fallen : the Lord careth for the righteous.

The Lord careth for the strangers, he defendeth the fatherless and widow : as for the way of the ungodly, he turneth it upside down.

The Lord thy God, O Sion, shall be King for evermore : and throughout all generations.

Glory be to the Father, &c.

As it was in the beginning, &c.

Ant. I will walk before the Lord in the land of the living. <small>Ps. cxvi. 9.</small>

¶ *Any appropriate Anthem or Hymn may be sung here.*

MAGNIFICAT.

S. Luke i.

MY soul doth magnify the Lord : and my spirit hath rejoiced in God my Saviour.

For he hath regarded : the lowliness of his handmaiden.

For behold, from henceforth : all generations shall call me blessed.

For he that is mighty hath magnified me : and holy is his name.

And his mercy is on them that fear him : throughout all generations.

He hath showed strength with his arm : he hath scattered the proud in the imagination of their hearts.

He hath put down the mighty from their seat : and hath exalted the humble and meek.

He hath filled the hungry with good things : and the rich he hath sent empty away.

He remembering his mercy hath holpen his servant Israel : as he promised to our forefathers, Abraham and his seed, for ever.

Glory be to the Father, &c.

As it was in the beginning, &c.

¶ *Then shall be said as follows, all devoutly kneeling.*

Let us pray.

Lord, have mercy upon us.

Christ, have mercy upon us.

Lord, have mercy upon us.

PENITENTIAL SEASONS.

¶ *Then by the Reader alone.*

OUR Father, which art in heaven, hallowed be thy name. Thy kingdom come. Thy will be done in earth, as it is in heaven. Give us this day our daily bread. And forgive us our trespasses, as we forgive them that trespass against us.

And lead us not into temptation.

But deliver us from evil.

Lord, grant thy people eternal rest,

And let thine everlasting light shine on them.

From the gates of hell

Deliver their souls, O Lord.

I believe verily to see the goodness of the Lord,

In the land of the living.

Lord, hear my prayer.

And let my cry come unto thee.

Let us pray.

¶ *Then shall be said one or more of the following Collects.*

O GOD, whose nature and property is ever to have mercy and to forgive, receive our humble petitions; and though we be tied and bound with the chain of our sins, yet let the pitifulness of thy great mercy loose us; for the honour of Jesus Christ our Mediator and Advocate. *Amen.*

WE beseech thee, O Lord, to show upon us thine exceeding great mercy, which no tongue can worthily express; and that it may please thee to deliver us from all our sins, and also from the punishment that we deserve for the same. Grant this, O Lord, through our Mediator and Advocate, Jesus Christ. *Amen.*

O GOD, who by the mouth of S. Paul thine apostle hast taught us not to weep for them that sleep in Christ; Grant, we beseech thee, that in the coming of thy Son our Lord Jesus Christ, both we, and all other faithful people being departed, may be brought by thy grace unto joys everlasting; who shalt come to judge the quick and the dead, and the world by fire. *Amen.*

ALMIGHTY, and eternal God, to whom there never is any prayer made without hope of mercy, be merciful to the souls of thy servants being departed from this world in the confession of thy name, that they may be associate to the company of thy saints; through Christ our Lord. *Amen.*

O LORD, bow thine ears unto our prayers, wherein we devoutly call upon thy mercy; that thou wilt bestow the souls of thy servants, which thou hast commanded to depart from this world, in the country of peace and rest, and cause them to be made partners with thy holy servants; through Christ our Lord. *Amen.*

Let us bless the Lord.

Ans. Thanks be to God.

¶ *Here may be said or sung the Psalm* DE PROFUNDIS *with its* COLLECT, *p.* 72.

Matins for Penitential Seasons.

¶ *To begin with one or more of the following Psalms, without further preface.*

Ant. I believe verily to see the goodness of the Lord in the land of the living. Ps. xxvii. 13.

PSALM V. *Verba mea auribus.*

The godly man desireth to be defended by God, that the intents of his adversaries may be stopped, and that the goodness of God may be showed among the righteous.

PONDER my words, O Lord : consider my meditation.

O hearken thou unto the voice of my calling, my King, and my God : for unto thee will I make my prayer.

My voice shalt thou hear betimes, O Lord : early in the morning will I direct my prayer unto thee, and will look up.

For thou art the God that hast no pleasure in wickedness : neither shall any evil dwell with thee.

Such as be foolish shall not stand in thy sight : for thou hatest all them that work vanity.

Thou shalt destroy them that speak leasing : the Lord will abhor both the bloodthirsty and deceitful man.

But as for me, I will come into thine house, even upon the multitude of thy mercy : and in thy fear will I worship toward thy holy temple.

Lead me, O Lord, in thy righteousness, because of mine enemies : make thy way plain before my face.

For there is no faithfulness in his mouth : their inward parts are very wickedness.

Their throat is an open sepulchre : they flatter with their tongue.

Destroy thou them, O God, let them perish through their own imaginations : cast them out in the multitude of their ungodliness, for they have rebelled against thee.

And let all them that put their trust in thee rejoice : they shall ever be giving of thanks, because thou defendest them, they that love thy name shall be joyful in thee;

For thou, Lord, wilt give thy blessing unto the righteous : and with thy favourable kindness wilt thou defend him as with a shield.

Glory be to the Father, &c.

As it was in the beginning, &c.

PSALM XXVII. *Dominus illuminatio.*

The goodness of God towards his people, whereby they are encouraged to trust in God, notwithstanding their adversaries; to rejoice in his aid, and to magnify him.

THE Lord is my light, and my salvation, whom then shall I fear : the Lord is the strength of my life, of whom then shall I be afraid?

When the wicked, even mine enemies, and my foes, came upon me to eat up my flesh : they stumbled and fell.

Though an host of men were laid against me, yet shall not my heart be afraid : and though there rose up war against me, yet will I put my trust in him.

One thing have I desired of the Lord, which I will require : even that I may dwell in the house of the Lord all the days of my life, to behold the fair beauty of the Lord, and to visit his temple.

For in the time of trouble he shall hide me in his tabernacle : yea, in the secret place of his dwelling shall he hide me, and set me up upon a rock of stone.

And now shall he lift up mine head : above mine enemies round about me.

Therefore will I offer in his dwelling an oblation with great gladness : I will sing, and speak praises unto the Lord.

Hearken unto my voice, O Lord, when I call unto thee : have mercy upon me, and hear me.

My heart hath talked of thee, Seek ye my face : Thy face, Lord, will I seek.

O hide not thou thy face from me : nor cast thy servant away in displeasure.

Thou hast been my succour : leave me not, neither forsake me, O God of my salvation.

When my father and my mother forsake me : the Lord taketh me up.

Teach me thy way, O Lord : and lead me in the right way, because of mine enemies.

Deliver me not over into the will of mine adversaries : for there are false witnesses risen up against me, and such as speak wrong.

I should utterly have fainted : but that I believe verily to see the goodness of the Lord in the land of the living.

O tarry thou the Lord's leisure : be strong, and he shall comfort thine heart, and put thou thy trust in the Lord.

Glory be to the Father, &c.

As it was in the beginning, &c.

PSALM XLII. *Quemadmodum.*

The righteous man is vexed with them that blaspheme God's religion, and with fervent complaint openeth his heart to God.

LIKE as the hart desireth the water-brooks : so longeth my soul after thee, O God.

My soul is athirst for God, yea, even for the living God : when shall I come to appear before the presence of God?

My tears have been my meat day and night : while they daily say unto me, Where is now thy God?

Now when I think thereupon, I pour out my heart by myself : for I went with the multitude, and brought them forth into the house of God;

In the voice of praise and thanksgiving : among such as keep holy-day.

Why art thou so full of heaviness, O my soul : and why art thou so disquieted within me?

Put thy trust in God : for I will yet give him thanks for the help of his countenance.

My God, my soul is vexed within me : therefore will I remember thee concerning the land of Jordan, and the little hill of Hermon.

One deep calleth another, because of the noise of the water-pipes : all thy waves and storms are gone over me.

The Lord hath granted his loving-kindness in the day-time : and in the night-season did I sing of him, and made my prayer unto the God of my life.

I will say unto the God of my strength, Why hast thou forgotten me : why go I thus heavily, while the enemy oppresseth me?

My bones are smitten asunder as with a sword : while mine enemies that trouble me cast me in the teeth ;

Namely, while they say daily unto me : Where is now thy God?

Why art thou so vexed, O my soul : and why art thou so disquieted within me?

O put thy trust in God : for I will yet thank him, which is the help of my countenance, and my God.

Glory be to the Father, &c.
As it was in the beginning, &c.

Ant. I believe verily to see the goodness of the Lord, in the land of the living. *Ps. xxvii. 13.*

Lord, grant thy people eternal rest.

Ans. And let thine everlasting light shine upon them.

¶ *Then by the Reader alone.*

OUR Father, which art in heaven, hallowed be thy name. Thy kingdom come. Thy will be done in earth, as it is in heaven. Give us this day our daily bread. And forgive us our trespasses, as we forgive them that trespass against us.

And lead us not into temptation:

But deliver us from evil.

THE FIRST LESSON. Job x. 8.

THINE hands have made me, and fashioned me together round about; yet thou dost destroy me. Remember, I beseech thee, that thou hast made me as clay; and wilt thou bring me into dust again? Thou hast clothed me with skin and flesh, and hast fenced me with bones and sinews. Thou hast granted me life and favour, and thy visitation hath preserved my spirit.

R. *I know that my Redeemer liveth, and that he shall stand at the latter day upon the earth: And though after my skin worms destroy this body, yet in my flesh shall I see God.*

℣. Whom I shall see for myself, and mine eyes shall behold, and not another.

℟. *And though after my skin worms destroy this body, yet in my flesh shall I see God.*

THE SECOND LESSON. S. John v. 24.

VERILY, verily, I say unto you, He that heareth my word and believeth on him that sent me, hath everlasting life, and shall not come into condemnation; but is passed from death unto life. Verily, verily, I say unto you, The hour is coming, and now is, when the dead shall hear the voice of the Son of God: and they that hear shall live. For as the Father hath life in himself, so hath he given to the Son to have life in himself; and hath given him authority to execute judgment also, because he is the Son of Man. Marvel not at this: for the hour is coming, in the which all that are in the graves shall hear his voice, and shall come forth; they that have done good unto the resurrection of life, and they that have done evil unto the resurrection of damnation.

℟. *Brethren, I would not have you to be ignorant concerning them which are asleep; That ye sorrow not even as others which have no hope.*

℣. For if we believe that Jesus died and rose again, even so them also which sleep in Jesus will God bring with him.

℟. *That ye sorrow not even as others which have no hope.*

THE THIRD LESSON. 1 Cor. xv. 51.

BEHOLD, I show you a mystery: we shall not all sleep, but we shall all be changed, in a moment, in the twinkling of an eye, at the last trump; for the trumpet shall sound, and the dead shall be raised incorruptible, and we shall be changed. For this corruptible must put on incorruption, and this mortal must put on immortality. So when this corruptible shall have put on incorruption, and this mortal shall have put on immortality; then shall be brought to pass the saying that is written, Death is swallowed up in victory. O death, where is thy sting? O grave, where is thy victory? The sting of death is sin, and the strength of sin is the law. But thanks be to God which giveth us the victory, through our Lord Jesus Christ.

℟. *Deliver me, O Lord, from eternal death, in that dreadful day when the heaven and the earth shall be moved, and thou shalt judge the world by fire: This day is the day of wrath, of trouble and distress, the great day and very bitter.*

℣. Deliver not to the lion, O Lord, the souls of them that confess thee, and forget not at length the souls of thy poor people.

℟. *This day is the day of wrath, of trouble and distress, the great day and very bitter.*

Glory be to the Father, and to the Son : and to the Holy Ghost.

℞. *Deliver me, O Lord, from eternal death, in that dreadful day, when the heaven and the earth shall be moved, and thou shalt judge the world by fire : this day is the day of wrath, of trouble and distress, the great day and very bitter.*

¶ *Then may be said or sung the Psalm* MISERERE, *as follows, all devoutly kneeling.*

PSALM LI. *Miserere mei, Deus.*

HAVE mercy upon me, O God, after thy great goodness : according to the multitude of thy mercies do away mine offences.

Wash me throughly from my wickedness : and cleanse me from my sin.

For I acknowledge my faults : and my sin is ever before me.

Against thee only have I sinned, and done this evil in thy sight : that thou mightest be justified in thy saying, and clear when thou art judged.

Behold, I was shapen in wickedness : and in sin hath my mother conceived me.

But lo, thou requirest truth in the inward parts : and shalt make me to understand wisdom secretly.

Thou shalt purge me with hyssop, and I shall be clean : thou shalt wash me, and I shall be whiter than snow.

Thou shalt make me hear of joy and gladness : that the bones which thou hast broken may rejoice.

Turn thy face from my sins : and put out all my misdeeds.

Make me a clean heart, O God : and renew a right spirit within me.

Cast me not away from thy presence : and take not thy Holy Spirit from me.

O give me the comfort of thy help again : and stablish me with thy free Spirit.

Then shall I teach thy ways unto the wicked : and sinners shall be converted unto thee.

Deliver me from blood-guiltiness, O God, thou that art the God of my health : and my tongue shall sing of thy righteousness.

Thou shalt open my lips, O Lord : and my mouth shall show thy praise.

For thou desirest no sacrifice, else would I give it thee : but thou delightest not in burnt-offerings.

The sacrifice of God is a troubled spirit : a broken and contrite heart, O God, shalt thou not despise.

O be favourable and gracious unto Sion : build thou the walls of Jerusalem.

Then shalt thou be pleased with the sacrifice of righteousness, with the burnt-offerings and oblations : then shall they offer young bullocks upon thine altar.

Glory be to the Father, &c.

As it was in the beginning, &c.

Our Father, &c.

Lauds for Penitential Seasons.

¶ *The Office to begin with one or more of the following Psalms, without further preface.*

Ant. I am the Resurrection and the Life; he that believeth in me, though he were dead, yet shall he live: and whosoever liveth and believeth in me shall never die.

S. John xi. 25.

PSALM XXX. *Exaltabo te, Domine.*

The goodness of God is praised, who for a little adversity sendeth much comfort.

I WILL magnify thee, O Lord, for thou hast set me up : and not made my foes to triumph over me.

O Lord my God, I cried unto thee : and thou hast healed me.

Thou, Lord, hast brought my soul out of hell : thou hast kept my life from them that go down to the pit.

Sing praises unto the Lord, O ye saints of his : and give thanks unto him for a remembrance of his holiness.

For his wrath endureth but the twinkling

of an eye, and in his pleasure is life : heaviness may endure for a night, but joy cometh in the morning.

And in my prosperity I said, I shall never be removed : thou, Lord, of thy goodness hast made my hill so strong.

Thou didst turn thy face from me : and I was troubled.

Then cried I unto thee, O Lord : and gat me to my Lord right humbly.

What profit is there in my blood : when I go down to the pit?

Shall the dust give thanks unto thee : or shall it declare thy truth?

Hear, O Lord, and have mercy upon me : Lord, be thou my helper.

Thou hast turned my heaviness into joy : thou hast put off my sackcloth, and girded me with gladness.

Therefore shall every good man sing of thy praise without ceasing : O my God, I will give thanks unto thee for ever.

Glory be to the Father, &c.

As it was in the beginning, &c.

SONG OF HEZEKIAH.

Isa. xxxviii. 10.

Thanksgiving to God for recovery.

I SAID in the cutting off of my days, I shall go to the gates of the grave : I am deprived of the residue of my years.

I said, I shall not see the Lord, even the

Lord, in the land of the living : I shall behold man no more with the inhabitants of the world.

Mine age is departed, and is removed from me as a shepherd's tent, I have cut off like a weaver my life : he will cut me off with pining sickness, from day even to night wilt thou make an end of me.

I reckoned till morning, that, as a lion, so will he break all my bones : from day even to night wilt thou make an end of me.

Like a crane or a swallow, so did I lament, I did mourn as a dove: mine eyes fail with looking upward, O Lord, I am oppressed, undertake for me.

What shall I say? he hath both spoken unto me, and himself hath done it : I shall go softly all my years in the bitterness of my soul.

O Lord, by these things men live, and in all these things is the life of my spirit : so wilt thou recover me, and make me to live.

Behold, for peace I had great bitterness, but thou hast in love to my soul delivered it from the pit of corruption : for thou hast cast all my sins behind thy back.

For the grave cannot praise thee, death cannot celebrate thee: they that go down into the pit cannot hope for thy truth.

The living, the living, he shall praise thee, as I do this day : the father to the children shall make known thy truth.

The Lord was ready to save me : therefore we will sing my songs to the stringed instruments all the days of our life in the house of the Lord.

Glory be to the Father, &c.

As it was in the beginning, &c.

PSALM LXXI. *In te, Domine, speravi.*

God is our only refuge: we must pray to him, and in him put all our trust.

IN thee, O Lord, have I put my trust, let me never be put to confusion : but rid me, and deliver me, in thy righteousness, incline thine ear unto me, and save me.

Be thou my strong hold, whereunto I may alway resort : thou hast promised to help me, for thou art my house of defence, and my castle.

Deliver me, O my God, out of the hand of the ungodly : out of the hand of the unrighteous and cruel man.

For thou, O Lord God, art the thing that I long for : thou art my hope, even from my youth.

Through thee have I been holden up ever since I was born : thou art he that took me out of my mother's womb, my praise shall be always of thee.

I am become as it were a monster unto many : but my sure trust is in thee.

O let my mouth be filled with thy praise : that I may sing of thy glory and honour all the day long.

Cast me not away in the time of age : forsake me not when my strength faileth me.

For mine enemies speak against me, and they that lay wait for my soul take their counsel together, saying : God hath forsaken him, persecute him, and take him, for there is none to deliver him.

Go not far from me, O God : my God, haste thee to help me.

Let them be confounded and perish that are against my soul : let them be covered with shame and dishonour that seek to do me evil.

As for me, I will patiently abide alway : and will praise thee more and more.

My mouth shall daily speak of thy righteousness and salvation : for I know no end thereof.

I will go forth in the strength of the Lord God : and will make mention of thy righteousness only.

Thou, O God, hast taught me from my youth up until now : therefore will I tell of thy wondrous works.

Forsake me not, O God, in mine old age, when I am gray-headed : until I have showed thy strength unto this generation, and thy power to all them that are yet for to come.

Thy righteousness, O God, is very high : and great things are they that thou hast done, O God, who is like unto thee?

O what great troubles and adversities hast thou showed me ! and yet didst thou turn and refresh me : yea, and broughtest me from the deep of the earth again.

Thou hast brought me to great honour: and comforted me on every side.

Therefore will I praise thee and thy faithfulness, O God, playing upon an instrument of music : unto thee will I sing upon the harp, O thou Holy One of Israel.

My lips will be fain when I sing unto thee : and so will my soul whom thou hast delivered.

My tongue also shall talk of thy righteousness all the day long : for they are confounded and brought unto shame that seek to do me evil.

Glory be to the Father, &c.

As it was in the beginning, &c.

Ant. I am the Resurrection and the Life: he that believeth in me, though he were dead, yet shall he live: and whosoever liveth and believeth in me shall never die.

S. John xi. 25.

¶ *Any appropriate Anthem or Hymn may be sung here.*

BENEDICTUS.

S. Luke i. 68.

BLESSED be the Lord God of Israel : for he hath visited and redeemed his people.

And hath raised up a mighty salvation for us : in the house of his servant David;

As he spake by the mouth of his holy Prophets : which have been since the world began;

That we should be saved from our enemies: and from the hands of all that hate us;

To perform the mercy promised to our forefathers : and to remember his holy Covenant;

To perform the oath which he sware to our forefather Abraham : that he would give us;

That we being delivered out of the hand of our enemies : might serve him without fear;

In holiness and righteousness before him : all the days of our life.

And thou, Child, shalt be called the Prophet of the Highest : for thou shalt go before the face of the Lord to prepare his ways.

To give knowledge of salvation unto his people : for the remission of their sins,

Through the tender mercy of our God : whereby the dayspring from on high hath visited us;

To give light to them that sit in darkness, and in the shadow of death : and to guide our feet into the way of peace.

Glory be to the Father, &c.

As it was in the beginning, &c.

¶ *Then shall be said as follows, all devoutly kneeling.*

Let us pray.

Lord, have mercy upon us.

Christ, have mercy upon us.

Lord, have mercy upon us.

PENITENTIAL SEASONS.

¶ *Then by the Reader alone,*

OUR Father, which art in heaven, hallowed be thy name. Thy kingdom come. Thy will be done in earth, as it is in heaven. Give us this day our daily bread. And forgive us our trespasses, as we forgive them that trespass against us.

And lead us not into temptation,

But deliver us from evil.

Lord, grant thy people eternal rest.

And let thine everlasting light shine upon them.

From the gates of hell

Deliver their souls, O Lord.

I believe verily to see the goodness of the Lord

In the land of the living.

Lord, hear my prayer.

And let my cry come unto thee.

Let us pray.

¶ *Then shall be said one or more of the following Collects.*

O GOD, whose nature and property is ever to have mercy and to forgive, receive our humble petitions; and though we be tied and bound with the chain of our sins, yet let the pitifulness of thy great mercy loose us; for the honour of Jesus Christ, our Mediator and Advocate. *Amen.*

WE beseech thee, O Lord, to show upon us thine exceeding great mercy, which no tongue can worthily express; and that it may please thee to deliver us from all our sins, and also from the pains that we deserve for the same. Grant this, O Lord, through our Mediator and Advocate, Jesus Christ. *Amen.*

O GOD, who by the mouth of S. Paul thine apostle hast taught us not to weep for them that sleep in Christ; Grant, we beseech thee, that in the coming of thy Son our Lord Jesus Christ, both we, and all other faithful people being departed, may be brought by thy grace unto joys everlasting; who shalt come to judge the quick and the dead, and the world by fire. *Amen.*

ALMIGHTY and eternal God, to whom there never is any prayer made without hope of mercy, be merciful to the souls of thy servants being departed from this world in the confession of thy Name, that they may be associate to the company of thy saints; through Christ our Lord. *Amen.*

O LORD, bow thine ears unto our prayers, wherein we devoutly call upon thy mercy; that thou wilt bestow the souls of thy servants, which thou hast commanded to depart from this world, in the country of peace and rest, and cause them to be made partners with thy holy servants; through Christ our Lord. *Amen.*

Let us bless the Lord.

Ans. Thanks be to God.

¶ *Here may be said or sung the Psalm* DE PROFUNDIS *with its* COLLECT, *p.* 72.

THE FIFTEEN PSALMS OF PRAYER,

TAKEN OUT OF HOLY SCRIPTURE,

VERY NECESSARY TO BE USED.

Psalm I.

For obtaining remission of sins.

O LORD of Lords, God Almighty, great and dreadful : who, by thy word, hast made the heaven, the earth, the sea, and all things that are therein;

Nothing is able to resist thy power : thy mercy is over all thy works.

All things are under thy dominion and rule : both man and beast, and all things living.

Thou art merciful to them on whom thou wilt have mercy : and hast compassion on whom it pleaseth thee.

Thy counsel shall stand for ever : and whatsoever thou wilt shall be done.

Power, dominion, and glory is thine : thou art above all things, and in all things, and in us all.

Thou art the Father of mercies, and God

of all grace, peace, and consolation : who wouldest not the death of a sinner, nor delightest in the damnation of souls.

O Lord God, who art rich in mercy, and of thine especial love towards us, even when we were thine enemies by sin, didst send into the world thine only begotten Son Jesus Christ : that whosoever believeth in him should not perish, but have everlasting life;

Have mercy upon me, have mercy upon me : according to thy great mercy.

And according to the multitude of thy mercies : put away mine offences.

O God most holy, wash me from my wickedness : cleanse me from my sin.

For I acknowledge, O Lord, my heinous sins : I accuse myself of mine unrighteous deeds.

I confess against myself the wickedness of my heart : which hath been ever unfaithful, rebelling against thy precepts.

I have been an untrue and froward child to thee : and have provoked thee with my vanities.

O Holy Father, I have offended thy divine majesty : and am not worthy to be called thy son.

Because I provoked thee to anger through the multitude of my sins ; and have not exercised myself in thy righteous laws.

I have turned back from thy ways : and done evil in thy sight.

I have dealt wickedly and behaved myself

unjustly : leaving thy commandments and murmuring against thy correction.

I have turned myself away, and not kept my promise made unto thee : I have walked in an evil way, after mine own thoughts and fancies, choosing the things that thou wouldst not.

O Lord God Almighty, I have not feared thee, nor showed due reverence unto thee : but I have been disobedient and stubborn unto thee.

As a common harlot is without shame, even so am I without shame of my sins : for behold I speak unto thee, and yet I sin more and more.

I have left that which is good, and gone back from thee; and I have not put my trust and hope in thee, my Father : but have sought for help and safeguard otherwise.

I have sown wickedness and reaped iniquity, and eaten the fruit of lies : because I have trusted in mine own way.

I have cast thy laws behind my back, not regarding thy commandments : nor leaving mine own evil ways.

I have not given my heart to return to thy paths : for I would not know thee, but have fallen through mine iniquity.

I never, unto this day, have turned truly unto thee with all my heart : but as a woman who breaketh her fidelity and promise unto her husband, even so, O Lord God, I have broken my promise unto thee.

For I have lived abominably, and have

had no remorse nor repentance for my evil deeds : but have run from sin to sin, following the fleshy desire of my heart.

Thou knowest all things, O Lord, how I have provoked thee to displeasure by my evil inventions : and none of all my sins are hid from thee.

I have hated thy teaching and thy correction : and have not regarded thy words and sayings.

I have not repented of my malice : but have increased in much vanity.

My heart hath been void of truth : and my hands have wrought unrighteousness.

My tongue hath spoken sinfully; and I have laboured with the imaginations of my heart to find out lies and deceits : and no truth hath been in my ways.

I have accustomed my tongue to speak trifles and vanities, fulfilling my fleshy desires and thoughts : my purposes and intentions have been contrary to thy will, whereby I have offended the eyes of thy majesty.

Thou hast seen all these things, O Lord, and hast holden thy peace : and yet they were evil in thy sight, and displeased thee.

In thine anger thou hast cast me away : and art divided from me now many days.

Thou hast given me up to the desires of my heart : to do the things which be unseemly.

Woe is me, that I have gone from thee : great is my misery that I have transgressed thy law.

Woe is me, that I have forsaken thee, to

follow after devices, not after thy mind : to accomplish my thoughts which have not proceeded of thy spirit, but have heaped up sin upon sin.

My shame and my reproach are daily before mine eyes : and for sorrow I dare hardly look up.

And now, O Lord God, why hast thou forgotten me : why withholdest thou so long thy mercy from me?

Hear now my cause graciously, although thou hast been so long displeased against me : for thou art merciful; be not angry for ever, I beseech thee.

Cast not away a contrite and penitent sinner : who humbly calleth upon thy name.

Turn thee again unto me, O Lord my God : and forgive me my transgressions.

Deal not with me according to my sins : nor punish me according to mine iniquities.

Show not forth thy power against a miserable sinner : nor be thou so severe on him in whom is no righteousness.

O let my prayers come before thy presence : and according to thy promises receive me into thy favour.

For I am thine, O righteous Father : whom thine only Son hath redeemed with his precious blood.

And now my soul doth abhor my life : and of thee, the judge of all, do I seek pardon.

I humble myself beneath thy mighty hand : since in anger thou rememberest mercy, and in time of trouble thou forgivest our sin.

And I confess that I am a sinner : beseeching thee, O Lord God Almighty, of thy goodness to deal with me according to thy great mercy.

I am confounded, and am ashamed to lift up my face unto thee : for my sins have gone up before thy countenance.

Against thee, against thee, O Father, have I sinned, and have done what is evil in thy sight : for my sin is great before thee.

Truly against thee have I been deceitful, from my cradle even unto this day : doing that which is evil, from my mother's breast.

Behold, I was born in iniquity : and in sin hath my mother conceived me.

The grain of evil seed is sown in my heart : great is the harvest of wickedness which hath sprung therefrom, even unto this day.

My transgressions are ever before me : and I bear the reproach of my youth even until now.

Behold, O Lord, I am sold under sin : and I find no good thing in my flesh.

The good which I desire, I do not : and that evil which I hate, that I do.

Every thought of my heart is inclined to evil : from the time of my youth.

Yet wherefore do I die in my sins, O Lord God Almighty : since thou wouldest not the death of a sinner, but rather that he be converted and live.

For thou art good and easy to be entreated : seeing thou savest even the unworthy, according to thy great mercy.

For though the vengeance of thy wrath against sinners is unendurable : yet infinite and unsearchable is the loving-kindness of thy promise.

Thou hast showed mercy in a thousand generations of old : that thou mightest make thy name great, as it is even unto this day.

Our fathers cried unto thee in their distress, and thou didst hear them : they hoped in thee and were not confounded.

When they had nothing more which they could do, this alone remained unto them : that they should lift up their eyes unto thee.

Thou savedst them according to thy name : that thou mightest show thy mightiness among them.

Many a time they provoked thee with their iniquities : and turned thy goodness to anger.

But when thou hast seen their trouble : and how they made supplication unto thee,

Thou didst think upon thy covenant : and it repented thee according to the multitude of thy mercies.

Have mercy upon me, have mercy upon me, O Lord God Almighty, for I am miserable and cast down : heal me, I beseech thee, whom thou hast stricken for mine iniquity.

My soul is sore troubled : how long, O Lord, wilt thou not regard me?

How long wilt thou refuse the prayer of

him that crieth unto thee? for ever: how long wilt thou hide thy face from me?

Where are thy loving-kindnesses of old, O Lord: which thou hast confirmed in thy truth?

Wilt thou cease to pity, O Lord: wilt thou refrain thy goodness in anger?

Hast thou rejected me for ever: and wilt thou not show thy loving-kindness again from henceforth?

Thine hand is not weak, that it cannot help: neither are thine ears heavy that they cannot hear.

How long shall I have bitter thoughts in my mind: how long shall sorrow vex my heart?

How long shall mine enemy have the mastery over me: look upon me and hear me, O Lord my God.

Lighten mine eyes, for I have slept too long in death: and mine iniquities have prevailed against me.

Return, O Lord, return and deliver my soul: and save me for thy great mercy's sake.

Behold, now is the acceptable time: behold, now is the day of salvation and grace.

In death who will remember thee: or who will give thee thanks in the pit?

The living, the living, he shall praise thee: and shall make known thy mercy.

O Lord, rebuke me not in thine anger: neither chasten me in thine heavy displeasure.

Cast not at me with thy darts : nor lay thy heavy hand upon me.

Thine anger have I borne too long : and I have drunk overmuch of the cup of thy wrath.

There is no health in my flesh in the presence of thine anger : there is no peace for me in the presence of my sins.

Mine iniquities have gone over my head : and like a sore burden oppress me daily.

My wounds are corrupt : by reason of my foolishness.

I am miserable, and cast away from thy presence : I go mourning all the day long.

My soul is full of impurity : and there is no whole part within me.

Hence it is that mine enemies persecute me : I mourn in the greatness of my sorrow.

My heart melteth within me : and my strength is gone from me.

O Lord, my desire is known unto thee : and my wants are not hid from thee.

Be merciful to my sins for thine own sake, O Lord God Almighty : let my wickedness be blotted out in thy sight; for according to thy goodness thou hast promised forgiveness of sins to all them that truly repent.

For the glory of thy name, have mercy upon me, O Lord; and forget thine indignation against me : then shalt thou be justified in thy sayings, and clear when thou art judged.

Wherein shall the greatness of thy grace be known : when thou shalt have pitied them who have not wherewith they may boast in thy sight.

And all the dwellers in the earth shall learn thy goodness, when thou hast helped us according to thy great name : and not according to our evil ways, nor according to our perversities.

Verily, O Lord God, unless thy mercy be multiplied upon us, life will not come into the world and upon them that dwell therein : unless thou givest of thy bounty, how shall they be raised from their sins who have wrought iniquity ?

Have mercy upon me, have mercy upon me, O good Father : and be no more angry with me for thy great name.

And for the name of thy holy Son Jesus, whom thou hast sent as an atonement for our sins, through faith in his blood : be thou merciful to me a sinner.

Behold, O holy Father, behold thy Son whom thou hast chosen : behold thy beloved Son, in whom thy soul is well-pleased.

Thou didst pour out thy spirit upon him, and didst send him to preach the gospel to the poor, to heal the broken-hearted : to comfort the mourners, to proclaim forgiveness to the captives, and to give sight to the blind.

Behold thy Child who is born unto us; behold thy Son, who was given for us : whom thou didst not spare, but didst deliver him up to death for us all, as a sacrifice for a sweet-smelling savour.

Truly he himself bare our sins in his own body : and himself carried our sorrows.

He was wounded for our transgressions : he was bruised for our iniquities.

The chastisement of our peace was upon him : and with his stripes we are healed.

All we, like sheep, have gone astray; we have turned every one to his own way; and thou, O Lord, hast laid on him the iniquity of us all : striking him for the transgression of thy people.

He gave his back to the smiters, and his cheeks to them that plucked off the hair : he hid not his face from shame and spitting.

In his love and in his pity he redeemed the lost, making peace through the blood of his cross : reconciling all things to God, whether they be things in earth or things in heaven.

He poured out his soul unto death : and he made intercession for the transgressors.

Behold, O most merciful Father, who is he who suffered : and remember, I beseech thee, for whom he suffered.

This is that innocent one, whom, when we were sinners, thou gavest up to death for us : shall we not much more, being now justified by his blood, be saved from wrath through him?

If, when we were yet sinners, we were reconciled to thee, by the death of thy Son :

shall we not much more, being reconciled, be saved by his life?

Behold the spotless Lamb, who taketh away the sins of the world : by whose precious blood we are redeemed from our iniquities.

Behold the most gentle Innocent, who was led as a sheep to the slaughter : and when he was oppressed and afflicted yet he opened not his mouth.

Behold thine only Son, whom thou didst beget of thine Almighty virtue : yet thou wouldest that he should be partaker of mine infirmity.

Who, being in the form of God, and thinking it not robbery to be equal to God, humbled himself and took upon him the form of a servant : and coming in the likeness of human flesh he condemned sin in the flesh.

He humbled himself unto thee, O Father, even to the death of the cross : and there he blotted out the handwriting of ordinances, which was against us.

He took it out of the way; he nailed it to his cross : wherein having spoiled principalities and powers he made a show of them openly, triumphing over them in himself.

Turn again, O Lord God, the eyes of thy majesty : upon the work of ineffable love.

Look upon thy dear Son : extended with his whole body upon the tree.

Consider all his limbs, from the crown of his head to the sole of his foot : and no sorrow shall be found like unto his sorrow.

Regard, O loving Father, the holy head of thy beloved child : circled with rude thorns, sprinkling his divine countenance with living blood.

Behold his fair body is scourged, his naked breast is smitten, his bleeding side is pierced : his panting heart doth beat, his extended nerves are strained.

His beautiful eyes do faint, his royal brow is pale, his eloquent tongue doth keep still silence : his heart within him is desolate, his arms are stiff and pallid.

His bones are parted asunder, his comely knees are weakened : a stream of purple blood washeth his innocent feet.

Behold, O most merciful Creator, the manhood of thy dear Son : and pity the weakness of us thy handiwork.

Regard, O Holy Father, the torn limbs of thy well-beloved child : and remember, I beseech thee, how frail is my substance.

Look upon the punishment of the God-Man : and lighten the misery of man whom thou hast created.

Cast thine eyes upon the suffering of the Redeemer : and forgive the sin of the redeemed.

Put far away from me the way of wickedness : and teach me, by thy Holy Spirit, to choose the holy way of truth.

I beseech thee, O King of Saints, by this Saint of Saints, by this my Redeemer, that thou wilt bring me back into the right way : that I may be made one with him in spirit, who did not abhor to be clothed in my flesh.

Direct my paths in thy ways : and make me to hate all the paths of iniquity.

Wash my heart from malice : and cleanse me from secret sins.

Make atonement for me, O Holy Father, by the blood of the eternal covenant of thy beloved Son : who loved us, and washed us from our sins in his own blood, and redeemed us from all iniquity.

Purify my heart, by the sanctification of thy Spirit, and the sprinkling of the blood of thy Son : from all impurity of sin, and from an evil conscience.

O Almighty God, be merciful to me a sinner, for thy great name : and have not thou my sins in remembrance any more.

For thou art God, loving, merciful, and patient towards us : nor wouldest that any should perish, but that all should return to repentance.

Make me to return, O Lord my God, from mine evil ways : and from my wrongful imaginations.

O remember not mine old sins, nor the offences of my youth : according to thy mercy be mindful of me, for thy goodness, O Lord.

Set not thy countenance against me for evil : for there is none who dareth to give testimony for me.

Enter not into judgment with thy servant :

for if thou accuse me, I shall never be absolved.

If thou makest inquisition for sin, O Lord, who shall stand in thy sight : before whom no man living shall be justified, for thou chargest even thine angels with folly.

How much more sinful man, who dwelleth in a house of clay : and drinketh iniquity like water.

Who is pure from defilement, of them that are polluted : not one of them ; even though his life be but of one day upon the earth, and his months such as may be numbered.

Truly of them that are born, there is none that sinneth not : neither is there any righteous man on the earth who doth not commit iniquity.

But with thee is forgiveness, although thou art very terrible : thou art my hope, O Lord God, and my soul trusteth in thee.

My soul doth wait for thee; in thy word is my trust : for there is mercy with thee, and with thee is plenteous redemption.

This I know, that thou wilt not reject me for ever : but thou, who didst cast me out, wilt again pity me according to the multitude of thy mercies.

Loving and merciful art thou, O Lord God : thou wilt not turn thy face away from us, if we shall have returned to thee.

For thou, O Lord God, art true and patient : and in mercy thou orderest all things.

The fountains of thy bounty flow forth abundantly : and thy grace never fails.

All thy ways are mercy and truth : to them that seek thy covenant and thy testimonies.

As gentle as a father is to his sons, so gentle art thou, O Lord, to them that fear thee : of the abundance of thy mercy thou indulgest our infirmities.

Thou dost acknowledge thine handiwork; thou rememberest of what kind we are : thou art mindful that we are but flesh, and of no constancy.

Thou forgettest not that this world is filled with injustice and impiety : and lieth altogether in wickedness.

But thou art gracious and merciful, long suffering and of great kindness : and repentest thee of the evils of men.

Have mercy upon me, O Lord God of my salvation, for the glory of thy name : set me free, and be merciful to my sins for thy name's sake.

O righteous Father, consider not the multitude of mine iniquities, but look on the face of thy holy Child Jesus : who did no sin, but bare our sins in his own body on the wood of the cross.

Turn thy face from my sins : and blot out all mine iniquities.

Make me a clean heart, O God : and renew a right spirit within me.

Cast me not away from thy presence : and take not thy Holy Spirit from me.

Give me joy of thy salvation : and strengthen me with thine Almighty Spirit.

Make my heart tender, O Lord God, that I may return to thy paths : for I have walked too long in the paths of unrighteousness.

Turn thou me to thee, and I shall be turned : for thou art he that formed me; but I am clay, and the work of thine hands.

Turn not away thy face from me : nor cast thy servant away in displeasure.

O be thou my helper : leave me not, neither forsake me, O Lord, my God, and my salvation. Amen.

Psalm II.

For the forgiveness of sins.

O MOST mighty God of spirits and of all flesh : whose judgments are unsearchable, and wisdom most deep.

Hear the prayers of thy servant : and turn not away from the petitions of thine handmaid.

For as long as I live I will call unto thee, and will not keep silence : while my spirit ruleth these limbs.

Unto thee do I lift up my soul : unto thee do I direct mine eyes.

Let thine anger be turned away from me,

I pray : and grant that I may find favour in thine eyes.

According to the greatness of thy mercy : forgive me all my sins.

Deliver me from all my wickedness, and heal my soul which hath sinned against thee : free me from the guilt of my transgressions, for I acknowledge my faults, and am sorry for my sins.

I have forsaken thy way : and though I knew thy commandments I have done all things contrary unto them.

I have made of no account the covenant which I had made with thee : and I have neglected to keep thy law.

Verily I have sinned against thee, O Lord God : and the stain of my sin abideth with me even until now.

I have forsaken thee, O God my Creator, I have gone back from thee my Saviour : and as a bull which refuseth the yoke, even so have I rebelled against thee.

I have hardened my heart against thee : and I have spoken with a stiff neck after my transgressions.

I have put my trust in a lie, for craftiness I have been unwilling to know thee : I have followed the wiliness of my heart.

My vain glory hath deceived me : and the boldness of my heart hath led me astray.

These things have I done in my thoughts and imaginations : these are the thoughts of man's heart which are evil continually.

My soul is far from peace : my forgetfulness of the law hath confounded me.

The burden of my transgressions is heavy upon me : it is as a weight about my neck too heavy to be borne.

Thou spakest unto me, and I would not hear; thou calledst me, I did not answer : I believed not thy words, nor endured thy counsel.

Thy word was a reproach unto me : neither put I my faith in thy commandments.

Thou smotest me, and I felt no sorrow : thou didst correct me, but I would not receive thy teaching.

I thought in my heart : that thou wast not mindful of mine offences.

With my mouth and my lips I glorified thee : but my heart was far from thee.

Even as Adam hid his sin, so have I hidden my transgressions : that I might conceal mine iniquity in secret places.

I asked not counsel of thy mouth : and I would not hear thy law.

In thy sight have I gone astray : and my soul hath lost her steadfastness.

I have forsaken thee, the fountain of living waters : that I might dig for myself wells full of mire, and which have no water.

In all these things I have not returned unto thee, nor have come before thy face with prayer : that I might depart from my evil ways.

Behold, O Lord, and consider how I am brought very low : all my beauty hath consumed away, and I am able no more to look up to thee.

And yet there was no cause wherefore I should forsake thee: and as a vain person, should seek after vanity.

O Lord, have mercy upon me and hear my prayers, for thou art my God: and there is no Saviour beside thee.

Let thine anger be turned aside from me: neither destroy me on account of the sins of my youth.

Forgive me, O Lord, I earnestly entreat thee, forgive me: for thy great mercy's sake.

O Lord God of Hosts, if thou be minded to save, who shall be able to gainsay thee: if thou stretch forth thine hand, who shall turn thee aside.

For thou canst deal with me as a potter's vessel: behold, I am in thine hand, even as clay in the hand of the potter.

Correct me, O Lord, but in mercy, not in thine anger, lest thou bring me to nothing: that I may understand and know how dangerous a thing it is to forsake thee, my Lord God, and to put thy fear far from me.

There is no man who can heal me, and give medicine to my sickness: there is none who can set me free, except thee, O Lord, who givest wounds and healest them, who bringest down and liftest up.

My destruction cometh upon me from myself: only in thee is my help and my salvation.

For there is none who is like unto thee:

great art thou, and great is the name of thy mightiness.

Turn thou me, O Lord, unto thee, and I shall be turned : take from me a deceitful heart, that thy law may bear fruit in me.

Be mindful of me, on account of my goodness, O Lord : and of thy perfect love towards me.

Alas, O Lord God, behold thou art he who madest heaven and earth by thy great wisdom, and by thy stretched out arm : and nothing is difficult with thee.

Thou art that great and mighty God whose name is the Lord of Hosts : great and wonderful in thy counsels.

Thou art he at whose word all things were created : by thy command they exist, and thy word returneth not unto thee empty.

O Lord God, thou hast mercy on all men, because thou canst do all things : thou puttest away the sins of men when they repent.

For thou lovest all things that are, and hatest nothing that thou hast made : not in hatred hast thou made anything or ordained it.

Thou sparest all, because all things are thine : O thou lover of souls.

Thou doest mercy, equity, and justice upon earth : for thou hast a delight therein.

Righteous and good art thou, O Lord, but I have offended thy countenance : I have transgressed thy covenant, I have dealt deceitfully towards thee.

Thou hast seen, O Lord, my sins, undertake thou my cause : remember how I am brought low, look upon my shame and consider it.

In the time of reconciliation hear me : have mercy upon me in the day of thy salvation.

Have mercy upon me, have mercy upon me, for I have no help beside thee : whose will nothing may resist, if thou hast determined to save.

Hear me when I call unto thee in my misery : give me confidence in thy name, and free me with thy hand.

Look down from heaven, O Lord, behold from thine holy habitation : and from the throne of thy glory.

Bow me not down with the burden of mine iniquity : neither forget thou my grief and misery.

Be not angry with me any more, O Lord : nor remember any longer mine iniquity.

O let my prayer come unto thee : say unto my soul, I am thy salvation. Amen.

Psalm III.

For the forgiveness of sins.

O GOD eternal, just, and holy : who keepest covenant and mercy with them that love thee, and keep thy commandments ;

Look upon me, and pity me, for I have sinned against thee : and have done evil in thy sight.

Pour upon me the abundance of thy mercy : that thy servant may find a heart for praying to thee.

I lay not my prayers before thy presence in justification of myself : but trusting to thy great mercies.

To thee, O Lord, are justice, pity, and atonement : but to me confusion of face because of mine iniquities.

Even from the beginning have I dealt proudly with thee : committing iniquity and ceasing not.

Thou hast redeemed me, O Lord; but I have spoken falsehoods against thee : and my heart hath not been right towards thee.

Thou hast taught me, and hast strengthened mine arm, and I have imagined evil against thee : having become as a broken bow.

Vain-glory hath appeared in my countenance, mine iniquity hath come up before me : I seek thee, O Lord, I hope to find thee; thou art parted from me, for I have gone greedily after vanity.

But I will reprove my sins before thee : until thou have pity upon me, and receive me into thy favour.

Be it far from me to go back again from thee : and not to seek the fulfilment of thy promises.

I will not hold my peace, I will not keep

silence : until thou confirm thy covenant with me, which thou hast made of old.

For as the righteousness of the righteous shall not deliver him, in the day wherein he hath sinned : even so the wickedness of the wicked shall not hurt him, in the day wherein he shall have turned from his evil way.

Herein will I look unto thee, O Lord God, for thou art good unto them that trust in thee : even unto the soul that seeketh thee.

Thou keepest truth for ever : and that which goeth out of thy lips shall not come to nought.

Destroy me not, O Lord, for mine iniquities : neither keep thou evil against me for ever.

Open thine eyes and behold the greatness of my distress : for mine iniquity is grievous in thy sight, and my sins have come up before me.

O let me not consume away and perish, neither forsake me in my sins : for thou art a God of mercy and kindness.

May it repent thee of the evil which thou hadst determined against me, and do thou according to thy name : although my sins and my transgressions are many.

O Lord, thou art my God, and I am called by thy name : leave me not in the deep of my troubles.

Thou hast taught many, and hast strengthened the weary hands : thy words have raised the faltering, and thou hast made firm the bended knees.

And therefore will I seek thee, O Lord God : for thou hast done great and many things, and beyond man's understanding.

Thou hast raised the poor from the dust : thou hast exalted the lowly by thy help.

For thou art he that deliverest the poor in his distress from the pit of destruction : where no bottom is.

Thou art merciful and liberal, for thou pitiest them that have not yet come into the world : and art exceeding merciful unto them that walk in thy law.

Thou art long-suffering unto them that have sinned : thou grantest them time and place, that they may be changed from their malice.

Hear me in mine unhappiness, when I call unto thee : for in thee, and in thy name, have I put my trust.

Help thou thy servant for good : and let me not be confounded in my hope.

Return, O Lord, and save my soul : cast me not away, whom thou hast redeemed by thy mighty arm.

Look not upon the hardness of my heart nor upon my transgressions : but pardon me of thy bounteous mercy.

Hear, O Lord, and forget thine anger : give ear, O Lord, and do according to thy great name.

I wait for thy salvation, O Lord : all the day long is my meditation in it.

For thy mercies are infinite : and thy loving-kindness without measure.

Hear me in thy good pleasure : withhold not any more thy pity from me.

In the faith of thy judgment I will await thee : unto thy name and unto thy remembrance is the desire of my soul.

Incline my heart to do thy commandments : and make my way ever straight in thy sight.

O let me not go wrong from thy paths : nor leave me in the deep of my sins.

Withdraw not thine eyes from me : but teach me to do that which is well-pleasing in thy sight, O Lord.

Make a covenant with me for good, and put thy fear in my heart : that I may not fall away from thee, all my days.

Withdraw not from me thy kindness for ever : nor cause thy truth to fail.

Do good unto me in thy compassion : for thou art merciful, and keepest not thine anger for ever.

Remember me in thy good pleasure : and visit me with thy salvation.

I know that thou, O God, art merciful and gracious : long-suffering, and of great kindness.

Thou art good and righteous : keeping covenant and mercy with thy servants, who walk before thee with their whole heart.

There is none other God beside thee, O God : who takest thought for all.

Great hath ever been thy mercy towards me : thou hast rescued my soul from the nethermost hell.

May thy goodness, O Lord, ever be with me : for in thee is all my hope.

In the time of trouble, I call upon thee, O Lord : for thou art nigh unto them that call upon thy holy name.

Succour me, O Lord, show the light of thy countenance upon me : my soul trusteth in thee, my heart hath rejoiced in thee.

Let my prayer come up before thy throne : incline thine ear to my supplication.

Hear me when I repent, O Lord : for with patience hast thou mercifully waited for my repentance, even until now.

O God, my life have I laid before thee, save me for thy name : for in thee hath been my hope.

What remaineth to me upon earth : this one thing only I need, that I may find favour in thy sight.

Wherefore, O Lord God, I beseech thee, deliver me from this sorrow : or lighten thou it by thy counsel, or consolation, or howsoever shall seem good unto thee. Amen.

Psalm IV.

Complaint of the soul oppressed and overcome by sin.

O LORD God our Governor, gentle and long-suffering : patient and of great mercy and truth;

Who, for thy tender love, and for thy great mercy's sake : hast delivered us from the power of darkness ;

And hast saved us, by the washing of regeneration, and renewing of the Holy Ghost : whom thou hast shed on us abundantly, through Jesus Christ our Saviour ;

If I have found favour in thy sight, permit me to speak a word with thee : and be not angry with me.

Wherefore dost thou forget me for ever : and forsakest me in the midst of my distress ?

Where is thy zeal and thy might : where is the multitude of thy mercies, and of thy compassion.

He that hath fallen, O Lord, shall not he arise : he that is turned aside from the way, shall he not return ?

Shall my sorrow endure for ever : shall my grievous sickness never be healed ?

Wherefore am I gone astray for ever : my transgression hath waxed more and more, and I cannot return.

For it is not given to man to direct his paths : and to make his steps perfect before thee.

In thine hand is the life of every living thing : and the spirit of all human flesh.

Thou showest mercy on whom thou wilt have mercy : thou art long-suffering to those whom thou regardest.

Thou givest death, and thou givest life : thou bringest down to the gates of hell, and thou bringest back.

Thine eyes are over all our ways : and thou searchest the hearts of men.

There is no darkness, nor shadow of night: wherein they may hide themselves who do iniquity.

Neither shall any man hide himself in secret, but thou regardest him : for thou fillest the heaven and the earth.

Wherefore hast thou cast me away from thy countenance : as though I were thine enemy?

Wherefore hast thou laid the burden of my sins upon my head : for no man can endure thy wrath?

Wherefore showest thou thy power against the downcast : wherefore destroyest thou me for the sins of my youth?

If I have sinned, what shall I do unto thee : if mine iniquities have been multiplied, what shall I offer unto thee?

If I shall have wrought righteousness, what shall I give thee : if mine iniquities have been multiplied, what wilt thou receive at my hand?

My disobedience will bring evil upon me : and my righteousness will betray me.

The life of man upon earth is but temptation : and if I shall have sinned, as all men sin, what can I do?

Will man be pure before thee : or will the son of man be blameless in his works?

What is mortal man that he shall be pure in thy sight : what righteousness is there in him that is born of a woman?

Remember, I beseech thee, O Lord, that

thou hast made me of clay : and thou wilt bring me into the dust of death again.

My days are consumed away like smoke, they vanish daily : my life passeth swiftly, like the wind, nor seeth good.

But a little while ago was I born, and soon shall I sink in death : I never continue in one stay.

Short are the days of my life : thou hast set me a bound, which I shall not pass.

Naked came I from my mother's womb, and naked shall I return thither : surely every man living is altogether vanity.

Take pity, O Lord, upon the sorrowful : and despise not thou the works of thine own hands.

For if we have sinned, we are thine, knowing thy greatness : and if we have not sinned, verily we are reckoned by thee.

O Lord my God, let thine anger cease from me : and cast all my sins behind thy back.

Remove from me thy visitation : I have fainted by reason of thy heavy hand.

For when thou chastenest man for sin : thou makest him to consume away.

All his beauty perisheth in him : like as when a moth fretteth a garment.

O that some one would protect me for awhile, until thine anger be turned aside : or that thou wouldst appoint unto me a season, wherein thou wilt remember me.

I am cast away from the sight of thine eyes : shall I never behold thy face any more for ever ?

My soul is melted within me : the days of my sorrow have taken hold upon me.

The water-floods of tribulation compass me about : and the waves of thy wrath are gone over me.

I cry unto thee, O Lord God, and thou hearest not : I seek pity, but thou receivest not my prayer.

Wherefore rejectest thou the unhappy from thy presence : wherefore hast thou so long forsaken me?

Wherefore takest thou not away mine iniquity : and the disobedience of my heart?

Arise, withdraw not thyself any more, O Lord : stir up thyself, nor drive me away for ever.

Remember me, I beseech thee : for fear taketh hold upon me, and trembling, and I am altogether afraid.

But I will not keep still silence : I will speak to thee in the grief of my heart.

O turn thou thine indignation from me : and rescue my soul, for a little while, from its sad state.

I am a stranger here : even as all men living are.

What is man, that thou art angry with him : or the children of corruption, that thou art so bitter against them?

Wilt thou add sorrow to sorrow : I labour in spirit, and find no rest.

Ere I take my food, my sorrow vexeth me : my sighs rise up within me, and cease not.

As though my bones were out of joint, even so is it, when mine enemies reproach me : saying unto me daily, Where is now thy God?

Wherefore hidest thou thy face at these things, O Lord : and takest no account of my sorrow?

I pour forth my supplications daily in thy presence : even before thee I make mention of my grief.

My spirit is vexed within me : and my heart within me is desolate.

Art thou minded, O Lord : to reject the work of thine own hands?

O deliver my soul, lest it go down to corruption : and my life see not the light.

What shall it profit me that I was ever born, if I shall soon be destroyed for ever : since the dead praise not thee, neither all they that go down into hell.

I have sinned; what shall I do unto thee? wherefore hast thou set me as an adversary against thee : and I am become a trouble unto myself.

Wherefore weighest thou mine iniquity so strictly : since there is no man that can deliver me out of thine hand.

If I should say that I am righteous : thou wouldest justly condemn me to eternal fire.

But I confess that I am a sinner : and mine heart I bring low in thy sight.

Verily if any man shall strive with thee in judgment : not one shall answer for a thousand.

Hence cometh it that I fear for all my works: for I know that thou sparest not a sinner.

If I shall look unto thy power, O how mighty art thou: if I shall appeal unto thy judgment, who will plead my cause?

Unto thee do I cry, O Lord: unto thee do I make my supplication, O my God.

Let thine anger cease from me: that I may understand that thy mercy is greater than my sins.

What is my strength, that I may endure: or what is the end, that my soul may patiently wait for it?

My righteousness is not as a wall of stone: neither my flesh like unto gates of brass.

Seest thou not, how that there is no help in me: and my pride hath departed from me?

But though thou hidest these things in thine heart: yet know I that thou wilt remember me.

For thou art true and just, O Lord God, and condemnest not unjustly: but repayest to every man according to his work.

All this hath happened unto me, that I have forgotten thee: and have behaved myself frowardly in thy covenant.

My heart hath turned backward: and I have gone after the lusts of my flesh.

This hast thou searched out and known: for thou knowest the secrets of the heart.

Lay not to mine account, O Lord, the sins of my youth: neither keep thou mine old offences in remembrance.

L

The sorrow which I have daily hath overwhelmed me : and sadness hath filled mine heart.

I seek for peace, but I find it not : I seek for healing, and sickness cometh upon me.

When the tempest of thy wrath hath passed by, let thy mercy come unto me : for mine unhappiness increaseth ever more and more.

Woe is me that I have sinned : therefore is mine heart grieved, and my joy hath ceased.

How am I left desolate; how hath confusion covered my face : for I have forsaken thy law.

Death is come up into our windows : and is entered into the innermost parts of mine heart.

I keep silence with myself daily, I commune with my soul : my life draweth nigh unto hell.

Who will give me rest from my sorrows : I will leave the way of men, and will be far off.

Who will give water to my head, and to mine eyes a fountain of tears : that I may weep day and night for my sins?

I will tarry for him that can save me : and can rescue me from the wrath to come.

There is no confidence within me of living nor of dying : I fear thy judgment, O God, and the vengeance prepared for the wicked.

The dread of sin disquieteth me : and my heavy conscience weigheth me down.

O God, who lovest mankind, thou most just Judge : spare me, I pray thee, while there is time.

Forgive me that which I fear, blot out that whereof I am afraid : before I go hence, and am no more seen.

My sins torment me above measure : they are more than I am able to endure.

Alas, for my contrition, and for the grief of my sickness : surely this is of mine iniquity, I will meditate thereupon, and will bear it. Amen.

Psalm V.

For imploring the gift of Divine wisdom.

O LORD God of mercy, who hast made all things by thy word : and by thy wisdom hast ordained man;

O eternal God, who knowest that which is hidden : who knowest all things before they are made;

Open my lips and my mouth : that I may declare thy praise.

Make me a clean heart, and renew a right spirit within me : and put far from me every evil desire.

I am foolish, O Lord, and ignorant : and thy knowledge is not within me.

I know not, nor understand, for mine

eyes are darkened : and mine heart regardeth it not.

I am ignorant, even as it were a child before thee : neither know I my going out, and my coming in.

I am a man of polluted lips, and I have but a short time to live : and I cannot understand thy law.

Give, I beseech thee, a teachable heart to thy servant : that I may know what is acceptable in thy sight.

Send from heaven the spirit of thy wisdom : and fill mine heart with a knowledge of her.

Thy wisdom giveth true understanding : and counsel and learning from thy mouth.

Thy wisdom openeth the mouth of the dumb : and maketh eloquent the tongue of babes.

If any man seemeth perfect among the sons of men : yet if thy wisdom have forsaken him, he shall be of none account.

Thy wisdom is a treasure unto men that never faileth : and they who use her become the friends of God.

O how happy is the man who hath understanding : and who hath obtained a soul endued with wisdom.

What man is he that can know thy counsel : or who can think what the will of the Lord is ?

Who can understand thy mind, unless thou give him wisdom : and instruct him by thy Holy Spirit ?

For the thoughts of mortal men go astray in many things : and our devices are but uncertain.

For the corruptible body presseth down the soul : and the earthy tabernacle weigheth down the mind that museth upon many things.

Above are counsel and happiness : there also are prudence and righteousness.

With thee are riches and glory : incorruptible wealth and holiness.

He who findeth thee, findeth life : and he that loveth not thee, cleaveth unto death.

O Lord God, touch thou my lips, that mine iniquity may depart : dwell thou in mine heart, that my sins may be cleansed.

Into a malicious soul wisdom entereth not : neither will she abide in a body, which is given over to sin.

Teach me, O Lord my God, lest mine ignorance be increased : and my sins be multiplied.

Let thy Spirit teach me what things be well-pleasing in thy sight, and lead me into the right way : for I have wandered too long in the path of unrighteousness.

Let wisdom be established in my soul : and write thou thy law in mine heart.

Above all things that are lovely and beautiful, desire I wisdom : I esteem riches as nothing in comparison of her.

How do I love thy wisdom, O Lord : how constant is my meditation on her.

How sweet are thy words unto mine heart : sweeter than honey unto my lips.

Thy word is a lantern unto my feet : and a light unto my path.

Thy wisdom pleaseth me more : than thousands of gold and silver.

I have more delight in the ways of thy wisdom : than in great multitude of riches.

O that my ways were made so direct : that I might learn thy wisdom and thy words.

Thy word kindleth, even as the fire : therefore doth my soul desire it.

Happy is the man whom thou teachest, O Lord : whom thou makest learned in thy law.

His soul shall muse upon wisdom : and his tongue shall speak of judgment.

The law of his God shall be written in his heart : and his footsteps shall not slide.

O Lord God of my salvation, hear my prayer : and my tongue shall tell of thy mercies.

Give me wisdom that sitteth by thy throne : that I may be able to know good from evil, and may learn thy secrets.

Enlighten mine eyes : that I may see the wondrous things of thy law.

O be mindful of thy word unto thy servant that calleth upon thee : for in thee have I put my trust.

Make known unto me the path of wisdom : and hide not thine understanding from me.

Deal with me according to thy loving-kindness : and let me not be disappointed of my hope.

Teach me to be wise and to understand : for my whole desire is unto thy wisdom.

Put thy word in my mouth : and thy wisdom in mine heart.

Let thy wisdom rule all mine imaginations : that they may be well-pleasing in thine eyes for ever.

Marvellous are thy words : therefore doth my soul delight in them.

Thy wisdom is perfect, thine understanding is clear : and giveth light unto the eyes.

More to be desired than gold and precious stones : sweeter even than honey and the honeycomb.

Thy wisdom is pure, and giveth comfort to the soul : thy word is true, and teacheth wisdom to the simple.

When will he that wandereth in spirit understand : and he that is ignorant, when will he learn knowledge?

When shall thy Spirit be poured forth from on high : when shall the heart of the fool learn discipline? when shall the stammering tongue be eloquent?

I am poor and simple, O Lord : O let thy strong hand be a help unto me.

I know that thou canst do all things : and nothing is difficult with thee.

Thou art great and past finding out : and of thy wisdom there is no end.

I have laid my cause before thee : do unto thy servant according to thy great mercy.

Look thou upon me, and pity me : that I may accomplish that which in faith I believe I can do through thee.

Make the way of thy wisdom known unto me : and fill mine heart with understanding of her.

Hear my voice according to thy mercy, O Lord : do thou unto me according to thy will.

Give glory to thy name, O Lord : for thou art good and gracious, neither is there any Saviour beside thee.

Hear me, O Lord, according to thy name : and withhold not thy mercy from me.

My lips shall declare thy praise : when thou shalt have taught me thy wisdom.

Then shall I sing of thy marvellous acts : that others may be converted unto thee.

And that they may bless thy holy name : even for ever and ever. Amen.

Psalm VI.

That we may be heard by God.

O LORD, hear my prayer : and let my cry come unto thee.

Turn not away thy face from me : in the day of my trouble.

Whensoever I call upon thee : give ear unto me, O Lord my God.

For thou art great and dost wondrous things : thou art God alone.

SIXTH PSALM OF PRAYER.

Great also are thy works : thy thoughts are very deep.

Incline thine ear unto me, and hear me : for I am poor and in misery.

Have mercy upon me, O Lord : for unto thee do I fly when trouble is nigh at hand.

Make thou the soul of thy servant to rejoice : for I lift up my soul unto thee.

For thou, O Lord, art good and gracious : and of great mercy unto all them that call upon thee.

Give ear unto my prayer : and graciously receive my supplication.

In thee do I put my trust, O Lord my God; O let me not be confounded : deliver me in thy righteousness.

Hearken unto the voice of my complaint, my King and my God : for unto thee do I make my prayer.

Hear my voice, when I cry unto thee : have mercy upon me, and save me.

My prayer do I make unto thee, O Lord, if ever thine acceptable time may come : hear me, O my God, in the multitude of thy mercy, even in the truth of thy salvation.

Hear me, O Lord, for thy loving-kindness is comfortable : look upon me, according to thy great pity.

Be not thou far from me : hasten to mine assistance, O my God.

May my words be well-pleasing unto thee : may the meditation of my heart be acceptable in thy sight.

O turn not away thy face from thy servant : sorrow compasseth me about on every side, O be thou my help.

My heart longeth after thee, my soul doth desire thee : I long for thy countenance.

Turn not away thy face from me, cast not thy servant away in displeasure : thou hast been my succour, forsake me not in my distress, O Lord my God.

Unto thee do I cry daily : depart not from me, neither be thou deaf unto me.

Let my prayer come up before thee : let my cry be heard in thy presence.

Hear me, O Lord : for I lift my soul to thy holy temple.

Give me help in trouble : for vain is the help of man.

I long for thine assistance, O Lord : and my delight is in thy commandments.

Look upon me, and pity me : for I am poor and in misery.

O Lord God of hosts, if thou wilt, thou canst help me : for nothing can surpass thy might.

My God, my God, forsake me not in my distress : for the sake of thy great name.

Haste thee, O God, to deliver me : make haste to help me, O God.

Deliver me, I beseech thee : for in thee do I put my trust, O Lord my God.

Behold, there is no help in me : neither is there any that looketh to my need.

I am afflicted and in sore distress : and my strength hath departed from me.

Raise up thyself, O Lord : and let thy glory be shown unto thy servant.

Let thy salvation come unto me : that all mine enemies may be put to shame.

Thine arm is mighty : and when thou wilt, all things are subject unto thee.

The heavens are thine, the earth is thine : thou hast made the round world, and the fulness thereof.

O let thy mercy be showed upon me, that I may be comforted : for thy love is better than life.

I cleave unto thy testimonies, O Lord : O let me never be confounded.

Out of the deep I cry unto thee, O Lord : Lord, hear my voice.

O let thine ears consider well : the voice of my complaint.

If thou lay my sins to my charge : O Lord, how can I expect thy favour?

But thy mercy surpasseth all things : thy truth is higher than the heavens.

Therefore doth my soul look up unto thee : unto thee doth she make her prayer.

Hold not thy peace, O God, keep not still silence : for thine own sake, let not thine holy name be defiled.

Give thy loving-kindness unto them that call upon thee : and thy righteousness unto them that seek thee.

I have laid my burden upon thee; O do thou sustain me : neither let the waterfloods go over him that trusteth in thee.

My soul seeketh after thee : let thy right

hand be a defence unto me against the power of mine enemies.

Hear me, O Lord, and deliver me : incline thine ear unto my prayers, and save me.

For I am in need, O Lord, do thou regard me : thou art my Saviour, and my Guardian, O Lord God.

O God, holy and righteous is thy way : who is so great a God as thou, O our God?

It is thou that doest great things, thy name is Jehovah : thou alone art the most highest above all the earth.

O be thou reconciled unto thy servant : and hide not thy face from me any more.

Do good unto me in thy kindness : that I may make my boast of thee, all the days of my life.

My lips rejoice to sing praises unto thee : and so doth my soul whom thou hast redeemed.

My heart shall meditate upon thy righteousness : when they are confounded who seek to do me evil.

And I will keep the way of thy commandments : when thou hast set my heart at liberty. Amen.

Psalm VII.

For a right guidance of life.

UNTO thee, O Lord my God : do I lift up my soul.

In thee do I put my trust, O Lord : let me not be confounded, neither let mine enemies triumph over me.

Make known unto me thy ways, O my God : teach thou my feet to walk in thy paths.

Direct me in thy truth, and instruct me, for thou art God my Saviour : all the day long do I wait for thee.

Thou art good and righteous, O God : therefore dost thou bring back sinners to thy way.

Thou guidest the meek in thy judgment : thou teachest the gentle thy testimonies.

Thou healest the broken in heart : and givest ease unto their sickness.

Thou raisest up them that are fallen : and liftest up all that are down.

Thou givest sight to the blind : thou loosest the prisoners.

Thou art nigh unto all them that call upon thee : if they call upon thee in truth.

Thou showest kindness unto them that fear thee : thou hearest their prayer, and savest them.

Have mercy upon me, O God, have mercy upon me : for my soul trusteth in thee.

Truly my soul waiteth for thee : for thou art my salvation, my glory, and the might of my strength.

For thine own sake, O Lord God : lay not my sins to my charge.

I understand not all my sins, I am compassed about by evils without number : my transgressions have taken such hold upon me, that I cannot look up.

Let thine hand be for an help unto me : to direct me in all my doings.

Make my steps perfect in thy ways : that mine iniquity may not gain the mastery over me.

Place a guard upon my mouth : and keep the door of my lips.

May the words of my mouth and the meditation of my heart : be always acceptable in thy sight.

Let not the word of truth depart from my mouth : neither let malice dwell within my heart.

O Lord, deliver my soul from lying lips : and from a deceitful tongue.

Put the word of truth and holiness in my mouth : and the words of idleness keep far from me.

Save me from the evil speeches of men : and govern me according to thy wisdom.

Turn away mine eyes, lest they behold vanity : and make them steadfast in thy way.

Remove far from me fornication and impurity : and let not the lust of the flesh beguile me.

SEVENTH PSALM OF PRAYER.

Deliver my soul from pride, lest it get the dominion over me : and thus shall I be innocent of the great offence.

Guard my feet from every evil way : lest my footsteps go astray from thy paths.

Mine eyes look unto thee, O Lord; for thou art near : and all thy paths are truth.

Manifold are thy mercies, O Lord : happy is the man that trusteth in thee.

For when I said, my feet are moved : thy mercy, O Lord, held me up continually.

Teach me to do thy will : and lead me in the right way, for thou art my God.

O Lord, I beseech thee, deliver my soul : and redeem me from the power of darkness.

Make thy face to shine upon thy servant : for unto thee have I fled, O Lord my God.

Look upon me, and have mercy upon me : for I am poor and in misery.

Keep thou my soul, and deliver me, that I may never be confounded : for in thee have I put my trust.

Leave me not, O Lord my God : though I have done no good thing before thee.

Of thy goodness grant unto me : that I may at least begin to live after thy commandments. Amen.

Psalm VIII.

For protection against our enemies.

DELIVER me from mine enemies, O Lord of Hosts : defend me by the mightiness of thy power.

Keep thou my soul, for thou art holy : O save thy servant, who putteth his trust in thee.

For mine enemies assault me daily : and seek after my soul to destroy it.

O God, be thou my helper : save me, O Lord, from them that rise up against me.

Haste thee, O Lord, to deliver me : make haste to help me, O Lord.

Be thou a protection unto me, and my house of defence : that thou mayest save me.

For thou art my strength and my refuge : O lead me, and direct me, for the sake of thy name.

O my God, deliver me from the hand of mine enemies, and cast me not away in the time of trouble : for all my strength is gone out of me.

Help me, O Lord my God : and save me for thy mercy's sake.

Have mercy upon me, O Lord God of my salvation : deliver me in thy righteousness,

From the assault of them that persecute me : from the malice of the foes who compass me about on every side.

Let them be confounded, and brought to

shame, that are against my soul : let them be covered with shame and dishonour that wish me evil.

Let them be turned back with shame that say : God hath deserted him, let us persecute him and take him, for there is none to deliver him.

O God, draw nigh unto my soul; and comfort me : deliver me from mine enemies.

Scatter them abroad with thy power : and break their strength.

Lest they say one to another : we have overcome him and cast him down.

Save me, O Lord my God, for I have trusted in thee : say unto my soul, Fear not, for I am with thee.

My life is in thine hand, deliver me from mine enemies : for they cease not to trouble me.

Their malice increaseth daily, and the multitude of the mighty cometh in upon me : and keep not thee in their sight.

But thou, O Lord God, art merciful and righteous : long-suffering, patient in goodness and in truth.

Look upon me, and have mercy upon me, give thy strength unto thy servant, for I call upon thee : and pour forth my prayers in thy presence.

Mine enemies rejoice, because I have fallen : and my heart hath turned aside from thy way.

But I put my trust in thy mercy : and my heart rejoiceth in thy salvation.

For thou art good, and thy mercy endureth for ever : and thy truth from generation to generation.

Let all those that seek thee be joyful and glad in thee : and let them that love thy salvation say always, The Lord be praised.

Psalm IX.

Against our enemies.

BEHOLD, O Lord, how many are they that trouble me : many are they that rise up against me.

Many are they that say of my soul : that there is no hope for him in his God.

In thee, O Lord God, have I put my trust : save me from all them that persecute me, and deliver me.

Lest they tear my soul in pieces : and there be none to deliver it.

Have pity upon me, O Lord, look upon mine affliction : which I suffer from mine enemies.

O deliver not thy poor to forgetfulness : let not the expectation of the oppressed perish for ever.

Put them to flight, let them fail in their counsels : cast them down according to their iniquity, for they have rebelled against thee.

Let their strength be consumed and

NINTH PSALM OF PRAYER.

perish : and let their perversity descend upon their own head.

Let the wicked be turned into hell : let them be taken in the pit which they have digged.

But I will hope in thee : who savest them that put their trust in thy name.

Thou forgettest thine own, say they : thou hidest away thy face, and thou seest not their affliction.

Through their pride do we suffer persecution : and in our trouble do they greatly rejoice.

How long, O Lord, wilt thou remain afar off : and hide thyself in the needful time of trouble?

How long shall the wicked despise thee : and say in their heart that thou regardest not?

Arise, O Lord, lay to thine hand : and forget not them that are oppressed.

Smite thou the strength of the malicious : that they may perish with their iniquity.

Let thine anger come upon them : hot thunderbolts and the breath of the whirlwind, this shall be their portion.

Prevent me in the day of mine affliction : and deliver thou me from my distress.

Have mercy upon me, for I am compassed about on every side : and my strength is brought low in mine iniquity.

I have become a shame among mine enemies : they lay in wait to destroy my soul.

The pains of death compass me about : the floods of iniquity make me afraid.

The bands of hell get hold upon me, the snares of death surround me : and in the path where I would go, I find but stumbling.

Raise thou me up, O Lord, and punish the perverse people : deliver me from my deceitful enemies.

Hear me in the day of my trouble : let thy great name be my defence.

For thou art my defender and my glory : thou healest all mine infirmity.

Save me, O Lord, I beseech thee : that mine enemies may not prevail against me.

Pour out thine indignation upon them : and let the fierceness of thy wrath consume them.

Let them be confounded for ever : let them tremble, and come to an end together.

Let them fall into the deep pit : let them never rise up any more.

That they may know that thy name is the Lord of Hosts : who alone art mighty and exalted for ever and ever. Amen.

Psalm X.

When the enemy cometh on so fast that he cannot be endured.

HAVE mercy upon me, O God, for the enemy oppresseth me : he is daily fighting and troubling me.

He desireth to devour me for ever : and many are they that insult me proudly.

They keep themselves together and hide themselves : they secretly mark my footsteps, when they lay wait for my soul.

They are like unto a lion that is greedy for his prey : even like a young lion, that lieth in wait in secret places.

They set themselves about my path : and turn their eyes on my misery.

They have spread a net abroad for my feet : they have digged a deep pit for my soul.

Strengthen me, O God, in thy righteousness : make my way perfect in thy sight.

Keep thou my goings in the right way : lest haply my footsteps slide.

I am afflicted above measure : help me because of mine adversaries.

Show forth thy marvellous loving-kindness in me : and deliver me out of their hands.

Hide me from the assembly of wicked doers : from the company of them that do iniquity.

Quicken me according to thy mercy : lest I be cast down, when the enemy rageth against me.

O send forth thy light and thy truth that they may lead me : and bring me unto thy holy hill and to thy dwelling.

Make mine hands ready for battle : strengthen mine arms even like a brazen bow.

Arm me with strength unto the battle : lay low them that rise up against me.

Teach me in the way wherein I shall walk : and guide me with thine eye.

Slay mine enemies before my face : and put to shame all them that hate me.

O let not mine adversary overcome me : neither let the company of the mighty overwhelm me.

Make my feet firm, O Lord : and make thou my paths straight, I beseech thee.

In my trouble they rejoice, they are gathered together against me : they take counsel privily how they may kill me in the way.

All the day long do they curse my words : every thought of their hearts is evil continually.

My soul is, as it were, in the midst of raging lions : whose teeth are as spears and arrows, and their tongue a sharp sword.

Who will stand with me against all such : or who will take my part against the evildoers?

At thy rebuke, O Lord, they will flee : at the voice of thy thunder they will be afraid.

For thou lookest upon the earth, and it quaketh to its foundations : thou touchest the mountains, and they smoke.

Judgment cometh forth from thy presence : thine eyes take account of equity.

Keep me, O Lord, from mine enemies : protect me under the shadow of thy wings.

Give sentence upon them that trouble

me : fight thou against them that fight against me.

Let them fall away backward who persecute me : let them be ashamed who imagine mischief against me.

Let them be even as the dust before the wind : and let the angel of the Lord scatter them.

Even as the smoke vanisheth, so let them flee away : and as the wax melteth in the heat of the fire, so let them perish in thy presence, O God.

Let them be overthrown, so that they may not be able to stand : withhold not thine hand until thou hast destroyed them.

Let their ways be dark and slippery : and let the angel of the Lord persecute them.

And thou, O Lord God, have pity upon me : raise thou me up, and I shall resist them.

For I am poor and in misery : O let thy salvation hold me up.

Let thy right hand chasten and correct me : and give me not over unto the will of mine enemies.

My soul is very full with the derision of them that hate me : and with the despitefulness of the proud.

My spirit is vexed within me, my heart within me is desolate : but I will hope in thee, and will thank thee for thy salvation.

Help me for thy truth, O thou that art my salvation : and the hope of all the ends of the earth, and of the boundless sea ;

Who rulest by thy power from all eternity : and thine eyes behold all things.

What God is there beside thee : who is like unto the most mighty Lord?

Under the shadow of thy wings shall be my refuge : until this tyranny be overpast.

In thee is my strength and my safety : from everlasting unto everlasting. Amen.

Psalm XII.

On trust in God.

O LORD, my light and my salvation : of whom shall I be afraid?

O Lord, the strength of my life : in whom I shall always put my trust.

For as the hart desireth the waterbrooks : even so longeth my soul after thee, O God.

My soul thirsteth for thee : for with thee is the well of life, and refreshment in trouble.

Here is labour and sorrow : trouble and misery upon earth.

Daily is there fighting with our enemies : there is no rest nor peace in our life.

But whoso putteth his trust in thy help : shall be safe under thy protection for ever.

He shall say unto thee, Thou art my defence and my refuge : my God, in thee will I put my trust.

Thou shalt deliver me from the snare of the hunters : and from the attempts of them that persecute me.

Under thine arms shalt thou overshadow me : I shall be safe beneath thy wings.

Thy truth shall surround me with a shield : there shall no evil come nigh unto me.

Therefore if mine enemies make war against me, to swallow me up : I will in no wise be afraid.

Though the camp of the enemy stand up against me, yet shall not I fear : though the terrors of death come upon me, I shall be safe in thee.

Thou shalt hide me in thy dwelling-place, even in the secret place of thy tabernacle shalt thou hide me in the time of trouble : thou shalt set my feet upon a rock.

Thou shalt raise me up above mine enemies that compass me about : from their hands shalt thou deliver me.

Though I walk in the midst of trouble, yet shalt thou keep me : thou shalt stretch forth thine hand against mine adversaries, and with thy right hand shalt thou save me.

Thou, O Lord, shalt perform all things for me : my God, thy mercy endureth for ever, despise not thou the works of thine own hands.

Draw me forth out of the net, which mine enemies have spread for me : and deliver me from their snare.

How great are the blessings, which thou givest unto them that fear thee : which thou showest unto them that trust in thee, even before the sons of men.

Thou hidest them in the secret place of thy countenance from the tumult of the enemy : and from the strivings of them that hate them.

How precious is thy goodness, O Lord : and the sons of men shall put their trust under the shadow of thy wings.

They shall be satisfied from the plenteousness of thine house : thou shalt give them to drink of the well of pleasure.

Of the fountain of life shall they drink with thee : and in thy light shall they see light.

Thy righteousness is like the high mountains : and thy thoughts are very deep.

Thy mercy reacheth unto the heavens : and thy truth unto the clouds.

O God, thou hast been our refuge : from generation unto generation.

Before the foundations of the earth were laid : thou art God from everlasting unto everlasting.

My God, thou hast been my helper from my youth up until now : and even unto gray hairs wilt thou not forsake me.

All my strength will I ascribe unto thee : for thou art my defender, O my God, and my Saviour.

Therefore whensoever I shall be afraid : I will put my trust in thee.

Whensoever I shall call upon thee : I know that thou art my God.

O let thy loving-kindness be ever upon me : and may thy covenant abide faithful with me for ever.

If I shall have forsaken thy law : and shall not have walked in thy judgments ;

If I shall have neglected thy statutes : and gone astray from thy commandments ;

Then visit thou my sins with thy rod : and my wickedness with thy scourge.

But withdraw not thou thy mercy from me : and make not thou my faith to be in vain.

Break not the covenant which thou hast made with us : and change not that which is gone out of thy lips.

For in thee, O God, is our salvation, and our glory : thou art our helper, in whom is all our hope.

And this we know indeed : that they who trust in thee shall not be confounded.

For who ever trusted in thee, and was confounded : or who ever called upon thee, and thou didst not regard him ?

For thy name's sake, O Lord, thou forgivest our sins : even though they are many and great.

Thou art a support unto them that fear thee : and thou showest them thy covenant.

Unto thee, O Lord, do I cry for help : I believe that thou wilt save me, for thy great mercy's sake.

In peace shalt thou redeem my soul from wrath : which shall come to pass in the latter day.

I will offer unto thee the sacrifice of praise : and I will pay my vows unto the Most Highest.

The wicked lie in wait to destroy me : but I put my trust in thy mercy.

Thou, O God, art my defence, and my buckler : my might, the horn also of my salvation, and my refuge.

I wait for thy salvation, O Lord : blessed is the man that putteth his trust in thee.

O what great things hast thou reserved for me in heaven, O Lord : so that there is nothing upon earth that I desire in comparison with thee.

Unto thee will I cleave with all my strength : in thee will I put my confidence.

Into thy hands I commend my spirit : O redeem me from the powers of the darkness of this world. Amen.

Psalm XIII.

If God delays his assistance for a while.

MY God, my God, why hast thou forsaken me : wherefore lookest thou not upon my need ?

Will thy loving-kindness be clean gone for ever : wilt thou not be gracious any more ?

How long wilt thou be angry, O Lord : wilt thou let thy wrath burn like fire for ever ?

When wilt thou turn thee at the last and

deliver my soul : my darling from the power of the enemy?

Shall I cry for ever, and wilt thou not hear : shall I make my complaint unto thee when I suffer violence, and wilt thou not save?

O Lord God of Hosts : how long wilt thou be angry with thy servant that prayeth?

Return unto me, O God my Saviour : neither let thine indignation burn any more toward me.

Turn thee, O God, and restore all things : and he who was before sorrowful shall come again with joy.

Let thine hand be upon the creature of thy right hand : even upon the son of man whom thou madest so strong for thyself.

Mine enemies live and are mighty : they increase daily who trouble me.

All that they do is to abuse my counsel : because I have set God ever as my hope, before my face.

They say unto me daily, Thou trustedst in God that he would deliver thee : let him save thee if he hath a favour unto thee.

They leap upon me like dogs, the company of the wicked barketh around me : they have wounded my hands and my feet.

O Lord, be not thou far from me : thou art my strength, O haste thee to help me.

O deliver my soul from destruction : turn away my steps from the power of the dog.

Save me from the mouth of the lion : rescue me from the pit of destruction.

Thou art holy and strong, and none may resist thee : when thine anger burneth like fire.

Who is he, O Lord, who doth not fear thee : who of the princes will not obey thee?

At the breath of thine indignation the earth doth tremble : and the heathen shall not endure thy vengeance.

Help me, O God my Saviour, and deliver me for the glory of thy name : and be not angry with me for ever.

For I confess my sins unto thee : and mine iniquity vexeth me sore.

Arise, O Lord, to my help : and redeem me in thy mercy.

O God, my refuge, and my strength : thou art found to be a very present help in trouble.

Thou didst take me from my mother's womb : thou wast my help, when I hanged yet upon my mother's breast.

On thee have I been laid, ever since I was born : thou art my God even from my mother's womb.

Withdraw not thou far from me, for trouble is now nigh at hand : and there is none to deliver me.

Mine enemies compass me about : mine adversaries surround me on every side.

And I am weak and brought very low : I mourn in the disquietness of my heart.

I am poured out like water, my strength faileth me : I am become like a broken vessel.

Have mercy upon me, O Lord, have mercy

upon me : impute not unto me my sins, which I have committed in my foolishness.

Remember not thou my former sins : let them be covered by thy mercy, for I am very miserable.

I am brought into so great sorrow and heaviness : that I go mourning all the day long.

And now, O Lord, what is my hope : surely my soul doth trust in thee.

O show thy loving-kindness unto me : and withhold not thy salvation from me.

My soul is full of sorrow : she hath drawn nigh unto hell.

I am poor and needy : and my heart is vexed within me.

Cast me not away in the time of trouble : when my strength faileth me, fail thou not me, O Lord.

O deliver me from mine enemies : make me not a reproach to them that triumph over me.

Save me from the lions roaring after their prey : from the hands of them that seek my soul.

Unto thee do I cry, O Lord, for thou art my hope : and my portion in the land of the living.

Bring thou my soul out of prison : and set my feet in an ample place.

Turn not away thy face from me : lest I be like unto them that go down into the pit.

O give ear unto my supplication : for my heart doth sink within me.

Deliver me from them that persecute me : for they are too strong for me.

Hear me, O Lord, and that quickly : that my spirit faint not within me.

Bring my soul out of trouble : and in thy mercy scatter all mine enemies.

And destroy all them that seek to destroy me : for I am thy servant, O Lord. Amen.

Psalm XIIII.

In which we thank God that our enemies have not prevailed against us.

I WILL magnify thee, O Lord my God : for thou hast lifted me up, and hast not allowed mine enemies to triumph over me.

O Lord God of hosts, I cried unto thee : and thou didst save me.

Thou hast brought my soul out of hell : thou hast upheld me, that I might not fall into the pit of destruction, whence is no return.

Thou hast not shut me up into the hands of mine enemies : but hast set my feet in a large place.

I sought thee, and thou didst hear me : and didst deliver me from all my troubles.

Thou hast turned my sorrow into joy : thou hast banished my grief, and hast surrounded me with gladness.

Thou hast showed forth thy salvation unto

thy servant : thou hast had pity on me in mine afflictions.

My mouth shall tell of thy righteousness : and of thy kindnesses which have always been unto me, so many that I cannot count them.

I will give thee thanks, until death come upon me : I will sing unto thee as long as I have any being.

I will rejoice, and be glad in thy mercy : for thou hast looked upon my necessities, and hast known my soul in trouble.

Thou hast been a sure refuge unto me : and the strength of my confidence.

I will bless thee, O Lord, for thine eternal kindness : and for thy mercy which is infinite.

Thou hast been my consolation in the evil day : my God, thou hast been gracious unto me, and hast turned aside the malice of mine enemies.

In the multitude of my thoughts within me : thy consolations have rejoiced my heart.

Thou hast given me joy for the days wherein I was afflicted : for the years wherein I suffered adversity.

Thou hast remembered the reproach of thy servant : and how the adversary persecuted me in his madness.

O Lord God of hosts, who is like unto thee : O most mighty God, thou art great and highly to be praised.

Thou art exalted high above all the earth : thou art a great God above all gods.

Glory and honour are before thy countenance : holiness and magnificence are in thy sanctuary.

Righteousness and judgment are the foundation of thy throne : mercy and truth go before thy face.

Blessed art thou, O Lord : who hast not kept back thy loving-kindness from thy servant.

I waited for thee, O Lord, and thou didst give ear unto me : and didst hear my cry.

Thou broughtest me out of the pit of destruction, and out of the miry clay : thou didst set my feet upon a rock, and didst order my ways.

Thou gavest me my desire : I saw the joy of thy countenance.

Thou hast smitten all mine adversaries : and hast broken their strength in pieces.

Thou didst rebuke the multitude of the gainsayers : and didst take me out of their hands.

Thou didst cast them into their own snare : in the net which they hid for me are their feet taken.

Mine enemies are turned back and fallen : and have perished from thy presence.

Thou hast been a strength to the poor : a helper in time of need, and in tribulation.

Thou hast executed judgment for me : and hast pleaded my cause against mine accusers.

Though thy wrath burned for a moment : yet didst thou turn and refresh me.

I thought within myself: that I was altogether cast out from thy presence.

But thou didst hear my prayer: and in the abundance of thy mercy, didst receive me to thy favour.

O Lord, thou hast given strength to my soul, in thy good pleasure: when thou didst hide away thy face, how was I troubled.

Unto thee did I cry in my trouble, and thou didst answer me: when my soul was disquieted within me, I remembered thee, O Lord.

I tasted and saw how sweet thou art: thy counsels which are to usward are without example, and are greater than I can tell.

Thine is the glory, the honour, and the power, for thou hast created all things: and for thy pleasure they are, even now.

Blessed be thy name, O Lord: from henceforth and for evermore. Amen.

Psalm XV.

In which the Divine goodness is praised.

O LORD, our God, how wonderful is thy majesty over all the earth: thou hast set thy praise over all the heavens.

What is man, that thou raisest him thus: or the son of man, that thou so regardest him?

Thou art great and wonderful, O Lord: and much to be praised upon thy holy mountain.

Unto thee do we sing, O God: unto thee shall the vow be performed in all time.

I will confess the mightiness of thy works: thy righteousness endureth for ever.

Thou, O Lord God, hast done great and marvellous things: in the works that thou doest none is like unto thee.

True and just are all thy ways: there is none but will fear thee and praise thy name.

I thank thee, O Lord God, from my whole heart: I will sanctify thy name for ever.

Thou art my strength, and my praise, O Lord: thou hast brought down mine enemies, thou art judge from everlasting.

Thy right hand is very strong: thy right hand bringeth mighty things to pass.

Powerful is the arm of thy might: thou hast supported mine infirmity with thy kindness.

I will confess thy name which is great and terrible: for I know that it is holy.

Though I fall I shall not be destroyed: for thou hast raised up mine hand.

I showed my way unto thee and put my trust in thee: and thou hast done all my desire.

Thou hast broken the head of mine enemies: and hast brought low the pride of them that go on still in their wickedness.

Thou subduest their power, and when they are naughty in their ways, thou restrainest them : and scatterest them with the arm of thy might.

In thy name will I always rejoice : and in thy loving-kindness is all my hope.

Thou lovest righteousness and judgment : the earth is full of thy mercy.

Thine eye is upon them that fear thee : and upon them that trust in thy mercy.

There shall no good thing be wanting unto them that seek thee : there shall be no need unto them that fear thee.

For thou directest their ways : and thine ear is open to their cry.

That thou mayest rescue their souls from death : and mayest comfort their sorrows in the day of woe.

For thou art present to the broken in heart : and with thine hand dost thou support the contrite in spirit.

Thou redeemest the souls of thy servants : and all they that hope in thee shall not be destitute.

Therefore shall my tongue sing of thy praise, O Lord God : I will confess unto thee for ever.

I will love thee, O Lord my strength : O Lord, thou art my foundation, my strength, my saviour, and my refuge;

My God, and my defender : my shield, the horn of my salvation, and my comforter.

After that I called upon thee and praised thy name : thou savedst me from mine enemies.

When I was in trouble, I called upon

thee : thou didst hear my voice from thine holy temple, and my cry went up even to thine ears.

Thou hast preserved me from mine enemies who rose up against me : thou hast saved me from my bitter foes.

Thou hast delivered me from the company of evil doers : and mine eye hath seen my desire upon mine enemies.

Wherefore when I go through the valley of the shadow of death, I will fear no evil; for thou shalt be with me : thy rod and thy staff shall comfort me.

Thou shalt be a refuge for me in time of trouble : thou shalt keep me from them that seek to destroy me.

Mine eyes look unto thee, O Lord : for thou shalt bring my feet out of the net.

Unto thee, O Lord, do I pay my vows : I will give thee thanks for ever and ever. Amen.

Psalm XV.

Thanks to God for his loving-kindness.

MY soul praiseth thee, O God : and all that is within me doth praise thy holy name.

My soul giveth thanks unto thee : and will never forget thy benefits.

Who makest atonement for all my sins : and healest all mine infirmities.

Who redeemest my soul from death : and showest thy grace and mercy upon me.

Who satisfiest my soul with good things : and restorest my youth unto me.

Thou hast been merciful unto me always : and hast avenged thyself upon mine enemies.

Thou hast been my castle, O Lord : and the strong rock of my salvation.

Thou hast been a leader to me by thy counsel : and in pity hast thou taken me up.

Thou hast multiplied upon me thy mercy : and after thine anger thou hast turned and comforted me.

Thou hast showed me many and evil tribulations : but at length thou hast brought me out of the bottomless deep.

Thou hast made known unto me thy ways : thou hast not hid thy counsels from me.

Thou art gracious and merciful, O Lord God : slow to anger and of great goodness.

Thou keepest not thine anger for ever : neither withholdest thou thy mercies in thy wrath.

Thou renderest not unto us according to our sins : nor visitest us according to our iniquities.

As high as the heaven is in comparison of the earth : so great is thy mercy unto us.

As far as the east is from the west : so far hast thou put our sins from us.

Even as a father hath pity on his children :

even so hast thou had pity upon us, O Lord our God.

Thou hast not forgotten the work of thine hands : thou rememberest that every man living is but flesh ;

And that the age of man is but as grass : for he flourisheth as a flower of the field.

As soon as the wind goeth over him, he is gone : and his place is no more found.

But thy mercy, O Lord, is everlasting toward them that fear thee : and thy righteousness endureth for ever.

If we keep thy covenant : and think upon thy commandments to do them.

O Lord, thou hast set thy throne in the heavens : and by thy power thou rulest all things.

I will magnify thee, O God, and will praise thy name for ever : even for ever and ever.

I will give thanks unto thee, and will make thy name to be honoured : unto all generations.

Great art thou, O Lord, and greatly to be praised : there is no end of thy greatness.

Generation unto generation shall declare thy works : and shall tell of thine ancient righteousness.

They shall praise the greatness of thine holy glory : and the remembrance of thy loving-kindness.

For thou art good unto all : and thy mercy is over all thy works.

The eyes of all wait upon thee : that

thou mayest give them their meat in due season.

Thou openest thine hand : and fillest all things living with plenteousness.

Righteous art thou, O Lord, in all thy ways : and holy in all thy works.

Thou keepest all that love thee : and there shall no torment touch them.

My mouth shall tell of thy praise : and let everything that is living praise thy holy name for ever.

Praise the Lord, O ye angels of his, ye that excel in strength : ye that do his commands, and are obedient unto the voice of his word.

Praise the Lord, all ye his hosts : ye servants of his that do his pleasure.

Magnify the Lord with me : and let us exalt his name for evermore.

Praise the Lord, all ye his saints : for his name only is excellent, and his praise above heaven and earth.

Praise the Lord, all ye his works : in every place of his dominion.

Let everything that hath breath : praise thee, O Lord. Amen.

THE PSALMS OF THE PASSION.

PSALM XXII. *Deus, Deus meus.*

The description of the Passion of our Saviour Christ, and of his advancement and kingdom.

MY God, my God, look upon me; why hast thou forsaken me : and art so far from my health, and from the words of my complaint?

O my God, I cry in the day-time, but thou hearest not : and in the night-season also I take no rest.

And thou continuest holy : O thou worship of Israel.

Our fathers hoped in thee : they trusted in thee, and thou didst deliver them.

They called upon thee, and were holpen : they put their trust in thee, and were not confounded.

But as for me, I am a worm, and no man : a very scorn of men, and the outcast of the people.

All they that see me laugh me to scorn : they shoot out their lips, and shake their heads, saying,

He trusted in God, that he would deliver him : let him deliver him, if he will have him.

But thou art he that took me out of my mother's womb : thou wast my hope, when I hanged yet upon my mother's breasts.

I have been left unto thee ever since I was born : thou art my God even from my mother's womb.

O go not from me, for trouble is hard at hand : and there is none to help me.

Many oxen are come about me : fat bulls of Basan close me in on every side.

They gape upon me with their mouths : as it were a ramping and a roaring lion.

I am poured out like water, and all my bones are out of joint : my heart also in the midst of my body is even like melting wax.

My strength is dried up like a potsherd, and my tongue cleaveth to my gums : and thou shalt bring me into the dust of death.

For many dogs are come about me : and the council of the wicked layeth siege against me.

They pierced my hands and my feet; I may tell all my bones : they stand staring and looking upon me.

They part my garments among them : and cast lots upon my vesture.

But be not thou far from me, O Lord : thou art my succour, haste thee to help me.

Deliver my soul from the sword : my darling from the power of the dog.

Save me from the lion's mouth : thou hast

heard me also from among the horns of the unicorns.

I will declare thy name unto my brethren : in the midst of the congregation will I praise thee.

O praise the Lord, ye that fear him : magnify him, all ye of the seed of Jacob, and fear him, all ye seed of Israel;

For he hath not despised, nor abhorred, the low estate of the poor : he hath not hid his face from him, but when he called unto him he heard him.

My praise is of thee in the great congregation : my vows will I perform in the sight of them that fear him.

The poor shall eat and be satisfied : they that seek after the Lord shall praise him; your heart shall live for ever.

All the ends of the world shall remember themselves, and be turned unto the Lord : and all the kindreds of the nations shall worship before him.

For the kingdom is the Lord's : and he is the Governor among the people.

All such as be fat upon earth : have eaten, and worshipped.

All they that go down into the dust shall kneel before him : and no man hath quickened his own soul.

My seed shall serve him : they shall be counted unto the Lord for a generation.

They shall come, and the heavens shall declare his righteousness : unto a people that shall be born, whom the Lord hath made.

PSALM LXIX. *Salvum me fac.*

The complaint of Christ and his Church in their great adversities: a fervent prayer for deliverance: the adversaries of God are cursed: a hearty thanksgiving for help obtained.

SAVE me, O God : for the waters are come in, even unto my soul.

I stick fast in the deep mire where no ground is : I am come into deep waters, so that the floods run over me.

I am weary of crying; my throat is dry : my sight faileth me for waiting so long upon my God.

They that hate me without a cause are more than the hairs of my head : they that are mine enemies, and would destroy me guiltless, are mighty.

I paid them the things that I never took : God, thou knowest my simpleness, and my faults are not hid from thee.

Let not them that trust in thee, O Lord God of hosts, be ashamed for my cause : let not those that seek thee be confounded through me, O Lord God of Israel.

And why? for thy sake have I suffered reproof : shame hath covered my face.

I am become a stranger unto my brethren : even an alien unto my mother's children.

For the zeal of thine house hath even eaten me : and the rebukes of them that rebuked thee are fallen upon me.

I wept, and chastened myself with fasting : and that was turned to my reproof.

I put on sackcloth also : and they jested upon me.

They that sit in the gate speak against me : and the drunkards make songs upon me.

But, Lord, I make my prayer unto thee : in an acceptable time.

Hear me, O God, in the multitude of thy mercy : even in the truth of thy salvation.

Take me out of the mire, that I sink not : O let me be delivered from them that hate me, and out of the deep waters.

Let not the water-flood drown me, neither let the deep swallow me up : and let not the pit shut her mouth upon me.

Hear me, O Lord, for thy loving-kindness is comfortable : turn thee unto me according to the multitude of thy mercies.

And hide not thy face from thy servant, for I am in trouble : O haste thee, and hear me.

Draw nigh unto my soul, and save it : O deliver me, because of mine enemies.

Thou hast known my reproof, my shame, and my dishonour : mine adversaries are all in thy sight.

Thy rebuke hath broken my heart; I am full of heaviness : I looked for some to have pity on me, but there was no man, neither found I any to comfort me.

They gave me gall to eat : and when I was thirsty they gave me vinegar to drink.

Let their table be made a snare to take themselves withal : and let the things that should have been for their wealth be unto them an occasion of falling.

Let their eyes be blinded, that they see not : and ever bow thou down their backs.

Pour out thine indignation upon them : and let thy wrathful displeasure take hold of them.

Let their habitation be void : and no man to dwell in their tents.

For they persecute him whom thou hast smitten : and they talk how they may vex them whom thou hast wounded.

Let them fall from one wickedness to another : and not come into thy righteousness.

Let them be wiped out of the book of the living : and not be written among the righteous.

As for me, when I am poor and in heaviness : thy help, O God, shall lift me up.

I will praise the name of God with a song : and magnify it with thanksgiving.

This also shall please the Lord : better than a bullock that hath horns and hoofs.

The humble shall consider this, and be glad : seek ye after God, and your soul shall live.

For the Lord heareth the poor : and despiseth not his prisoners.

Let heaven and earth praise him : the sea, and all that moveth therein.

For God will save Sion, and build the cities of Judah : that men may dwell there, and have it in possession.

The posterity also of his servants shall inherit it : and they that love his name shall dwell therein.

PSALM LXXXVIII. *Domine Deus.*

Complaint of the righteous much troubled with sickness and persecutions, and without comfort.

O LORD God of my salvation, I have cried day and night before thee : O let my prayer enter into thy presence, incline thine ear unto my calling.

For my soul is full of trouble : and my life draweth nigh unto hell.

I am counted as one of them that go down into the pit : and I have been even as a man that hath no strength.

Free among the dead, like unto them that are wounded, and lie in the grave : who are out of remembrance, and are cut away from thy hand.

Thou hast laid me in the lowest pit : in a place of darkness, and in the deep.

Thine indignation lieth hard upon me : and thou hast vexed me with all thy storms.

Thou hast put away mine acquaintance far from me : and made me to be abhorred of them.

I am so fast in prison : that I cannot get forth.

My sight faileth for very trouble : Lord, I have called daily upon thee, I have stretched forth my hands unto thee.

Dost thou show wonders among the dead :

or shall the dead rise up again and praise thee?

Shall thy loving-kindness be showed in the grave : or thy faithfulness in destruction?

Shall thy wondrous works be known in the dark : and thy righteousness in the land where all things are forgotten?

Unto thee have I cried, O Lord : and early shall my prayer come before thee.

Lord, why abhorrest thou my soul : and hidest thou thy face from me?

I am in misery, and like unto him that is at the point to die : even from my youth up thy terrors have I suffered with a troubled mind.

Thy wrathful displeasure goeth over me : and the fear of thee hath undone me.

They came round about me daily like water : and compassed me together on every side.

My lovers and friends hast thou put away from me : and hid mine acquaintance out of my sight.

PSALM II.   *Quare fremuerunt gentes?*

The rage of the people against Christ: Christ is ordained a king by his Father: rulers are exhorted to godly knowledge.

WHY do the heathen so furiously rage together : and why do the people imagine a vain thing?

The kings of the earth stand up, and the rulers take counsel together : against the Lord and against his Christ.

Let us break their bonds asunder : and cast away their cords from us.

He that dwelleth in heaven shall laugh them to scorn : the Lord shall have them in derision.

Then shall he speak unto them in his wrath : and vex them in his sore displeasure.

Yet have I set my King : upon my holy hill of Sion.

I will preach the law, whereof the Lord hath said unto me : Thou art my Son, this day have I begotten thee.

Desire of me, and I shall give thee the heathen for thine inheritance : and the utmost parts of the earth for thy possession.

Thou shalt bruise them with a rod of iron : and break them in pieces like a potter's vessel.

Be wise now therefore, O ye kings : be learned, ye that are judges of the earth.

Serve the Lord in fear : and rejoice unto him with reverence.

Kiss the Son, lest he be angry, and so ye perish from the right way : if his wrath be kindled, (yea, but a little,) blessed are all they that put their trust in him.

PSALM LIX. *Eripe me de inimicis.*

The prayer of Christ for himself and for his brethren, against his persecutors.

DELIVER me from mine enemies, O God : defend me from them that rise up against me.

O deliver me from the wicked doers : and save me from the blood-thirsty men.

For lo, they lie waiting for my soul : the mighty men are gathered against me, without any offence or fault of me, O Lord.

They run and prepare themselves without my fault : arise thou therefore to help me, and behold.

Stand up, O Lord God of hosts, thou God of Israel, to visit all the heathen : and be not merciful unto them that offend of malicious wickedness.

They go to and fro in the evening : they grin like a dog, and run about through the city.

Behold, they speak with their mouth, and swords are in their lips : for who doth hear?

But thou, O Lord, shalt have them in derision : and thou shalt laugh all the heathen to scorn.

My strength will I ascribe unto thee : for thou art the God of my refuge.

God showeth me his goodness plenteously : and God shall let me see my desire upon mine enemies.

Slay them not, lest my people forget it : but scatter them abroad among the people, and put them down, O Lord, our defence.

For the sin of their mouth, and for the words of their lips, they shall be taken in their pride : and why? their preaching is of cursing and lies.

Consume them in thy wrath, consume them, that they may perish : and know that it is God that ruleth in Jacob, and unto the ends of the world.

And in the evening they will return: grin like a dog, and will go about the city.

They will run here and there for meat: and grudge if they be not satisfied.

As for me, I will sing of thy power, and will praise thy mercy betimes in the morning: for thou hast been my defence and refuge in the day of my trouble.

Unto thee, O my strength, will I sing: for thou, O God, art my refuge, and my merciful God.

¶ *Any of these Psalms of the Passion may be used as a separate Office with one of the* PRAYERS OF THE PASSION, *p.* 218.

THE PASSION

OF

Our Saviour Jesus Christ.

WRITTEN BY SAINT JOHN.

The Betrayal.

JESUS went forth with his disciples over the brook Cedron, where was a garden, into the which he entered, and his disciples. And Judas also, which betrayed him, knew the place: for Jesus ofttimes resorted thither with his disciples. Judas then, having received a band of men and officers from the chief priests and Pharisees, cometh thither with lanterns and torches and weapons. Jesus therefore, knowing all things that should come upon him, went forth, and said unto them, Whom seek ye? They answered him, Jesus of Nazareth. Jesus saith unto them, I am he. And Judas also, which betrayed him, stood with them. As soon then as he had said unto them, I am he, they went backward, and fell to the ground. Then asked he them again, Whom seek ye? And they said, Jesus of Nazareth. Jesus answered, I have told you that I am he: if therefore ye seek me, let these go their way: that the saying might be fulfilled, which he spake, Of them which thou gavest me have I lost none. Then Simon Peter having a sword drew it, and smote the high priest's servant, and cut off his right ear. The servant's name was Malchus. Then said Jesus unto Peter, Put up thy sword into the sheath: the cup which my Father hath given me, shall I not drink it? Then the band and the captain and officers of the Jews took Jesus, and bound him: and led him away to Annas first; for he was father in law to Caiaphas, which was the high priest that same year. Now Caiaphas was he, which gave counsel to the Jews, that it was expedient that one man should die for the people.

Before the High Priest.

AND Simon Peter followed Jesus, and so did the other disciple: that disciple was known unto the high priest, and went in with Jesus into the palace of the high priest. But Peter stood at the door without. Then went out that other disciple, which was known unto the high priest, and spake unto her that kept the door, and brought in Peter. Then saith the damsel that kept the door unto Peter, Art not thou also one of this man's disciples? He saith, I am not. And the servants and officers stood there, who had made a fire of coals; for it was cold:

and they warmed themselves: and Peter stood with them, and warmed himself. The high priest then asked Jesus of his disciples, and of his doctrine. Jesus answered him, I spake openly to the world; I ever taught in the synagogue, and in the temple, whither the Jews always resort; and in secret have I said nothing. Why askest thou me? ask them which heard me, what I have said unto them: behold, they know what I said. And when he had thus spoken, one of the officers which stood by struck Jesus with the palm of his hand, saying, Answerest thou the high priest so? Jesus answered him, If I have spoken evil, bear witness of the evil: but if well, why smitest thou me? Now Annas had sent him bound unto Caiaphas the high priest. And Simon Peter stood and warmed himself. They said therefore unto him, Art not thou also one of his disciples? He denied it, and said, I am not. One of the servants of the high priest, being his kinsman whose ear Peter cut off, saith, Did not I see thee in the garden with him? Peter then denied again: and immediately the cock crew.

Trial before Pontius Pilate.

THEN led they Jesus from Caiaphas unto the hall of judgment: and it was early; and they themselves went not into the judgment hall, lest they should be defiled; but that they might eat the passover. Pilate then went out unto them, and said, What accusation bring ye against this man? They answered and said unto him, If he were not a malefactor, we would not have delivered him up unto thee. Then said Pilate unto them, Take ye him, and judge him according to your law. The Jews therefore said unto him, It is not lawful for us to put any man to death: That the saying of Jesus might be fulfilled, which he spake, signifying what death he should die. Then Pilate entered into the judgment hall again, and called Jesus, and said unto him, Art thou the King of the Jews? Jesus answered him, Sayest thou this thing of thyself, or did others tell it thee of me? Pilate answered, Am I a Jew? Thine own nation and the chief priests have delivered thee unto me: what hast thou done? Jesus answered, My kingdom is not of this world: if my kingdom were of this world, then would my servants fight, that I should not be delivered to the Jews: but now is my kingdom not from hence. Pilate therefore said unto him, Art thou a king then? Jesus answered, Thou sayest that I am a king. To this end was I born, and for this cause came I into the world, that I should bear witness unto the truth. Every one that is of the truth heareth my voice. Pilate saith unto him, What is truth? And when he had said this, he went out again unto the Jews, and saith unto them, I find in him no fault at all. But ye have a custom, that I should release unto you one at the passover: will ye therefore that I release unto you the King of the Jews? Then cried they all again, saying, Not this man, but Barabbas. Now Barabbas was a robber.

The Condemnation.

THEN Pilate therefore took Jesus, and scourged him. And the soldiers platted a crown of thorns, and put it on his head, and they put on him a purple robe; and said, Hail, King of the Jews! and they smote him with their hands. Pilate therefore went forth again, and saith unto them, Behold, I bring him forth to you, that ye may know that I find no fault in him. Then came Jesus forth, wearing the crown of thorns, and the purple robe. And Pilate saith unto them, Behold the man! When the chief priests therefore and officers saw him, they cried out, saying, Crucify him, Crucify him. Pilate saith unto them, Take ye him, and crucify him: for I find no fault in him. The Jews answered him, We have a law, and by our law he ought to die, because he made himself the Son of God. When Pilate therefore heard that saying, he was the more afraid; and went again into the judgment hall, and saith unto Jesus, Whence art thou? But Jesus gave him no answer. Then saith Pilate unto him, Speakest thou not unto me? knowest thou not that I have power to crucify thee, and have power to release thee? Jesus answered, Thou couldest have no power at all against me, except it were given thee from above: therefore he that delivered me unto thee hath the greater sin. And from thenceforth Pilate sought to release him: but the Jews cried out, saying, If thou let this man go, thou art not Cæsar's friend: whosoever maketh himself a king speaketh against Cæsar. When Pilate therefore heard that saying, he brought Jesus forth, and sat down in the judgment seat in a place that is called the Pavement, but in the Hebrew Gabbatha. And it was the preparation of the passover, and about the sixth hour: and he saith unto the Jews, Behold your King! But they cried out, Away with him, away with him, crucify him. Pilate saith unto them, Shall I crucify your King? The chief priests answered, We have no king but Cæsar. Then delivered he him therefore unto them to be crucified.

The Way of Sorrows and the Crucifixion.

AND they took Jesus, and led him away. And he, bearing his cross, went forth into a place called the place of a skull, which is called in the Hebrew, Golgotha: where they crucified him, and two other with him, on either side one, and Jesus in the midst. And Pilate wrote a title, and put it on the cross; and the writing was, JESUS OF NAZARETH THE KING OF THE JEWS. This title then read many of the Jews: for the place where Jesus was crucified was nigh to the city: and it was written in Hebrew, and Greek, and Latin. Then said the chief priests of the Jews to Pilate, Write not, the King of the Jews; but that he said, I am the King of the Jews. Pilate answered, What I have written, I have written. Then the soldiers, when they had crucified Jesus, took his garments, and made four parts, to every soldier a part; and also his coat: now the coat was without seam, woven from the top throughout. They said therefore among themselves, Let us not rend it, but cast lots for it, whose it shall be: that the Scripture might be fulfilled, which saith, They parted my raiment among them, and for my vesture they did cast lots. These things therefore the soldiers did. Now there stood by the cross of Jesus, his mother, and his mother's sister, Mary the wife of Cleophas, and Mary Magdalene. When Jesus therefore saw his mother, and the disciple standing by, whom he loved, he saith unto his mother, Woman, behold thy son. Then saith he to the disciple, Behold thy mother. And from that hour that disciple took her unto his own home. After this, Jesus, knowing that all things were now accomplished, that the Scripture might be fulfilled, saith, I thirst. Now there was set a vessel full of vinegar: and they filled a spunge with vinegar, and put it upon hyssop, and put it to his mouth. When Jesus therefore had received the vinegar, he said, It is finished: and he bowed his head, and gave up the ghost.

The Piercing.

THE Jews therefore, because it was the preparation, that the bodies should not remain upon the cross on the sabbath-day, (for that sabbath-day was an high-day,) besought Pilate that their legs might be broken, and that they might be taken away. Then came the soldiers, and brake the legs of the first, and of the other which was crucified with him. But when they came to Jesus, and saw that he was dead already, they brake not his legs. But one of the soldiers with a spear pierced his side, and forthwith came thereout blood and water. And he that saw it bare record, and his record is true: and he knoweth that he saith true, that ye might believe. For these things were done that the Scripture should be fulfilled, A bone of him shall not be broken. And again, another Scripture saith, They shall look on him whom they pierced.

The Burial.

AND after this Joseph of Arimathæa, being a disciple of Jesus, but secretly for fear of the Jews, besought Pilate that he might take away the body of Jesus: and Pilate gave him leave. He came therefore and took the body of Jesus; and there came also Nicodemus, who at the first came to Jesus by night, and brought a mixture of myrrh and aloes, about an hundred pound weight. Then took they the body of Jesus, and wound it in linen clothes with the spices, as the manner of the Jews is to bury. Now in the place where he was crucified, there was a garden; and in the garden a new sepulchre, wherein was never man yet laid. There laid they Jesus therefore, because of the Jews' preparation day; for the sepulchre was nigh at hand.

CONTEMPLATION OF THE CROSS.

I.

WHAT man is this whom I behold all bloody, with skin torn and with the marks of stripes inflicted upon him, hanging down his head for weakness towards his shoulders, crowned with a wreath of thorns which pierce through his skull even to the brain, and nailed to the cross? What fault could he have done so grievous as to deserve it? What judge could be so cruel as to inflict so awful a punishment? What executioner could have so brutal a mind as to deal thus cruelly with him? Now I bethink myself, I know him. It is Christ.

Art thou he that excellest all the children of men in beauty? Art thou he, on whose lips grace was shed most plentifully; yea, even with God's own hand? Where then is that beauty of thine? Where is that grace of thy lips? I find it not. I see it not. Fleshly eyes conceive not so great a mystery. Open thou the eyes of my soul.

Bring thy divine light nearer unto me, and give me power to look more earnestly upon thee.

I see it is Jesus, the Son of God, the spotless Lamb without sin, without fault, without offence, who took my wickedness upon himself; to the intent that I, being set free from sin, might be brought again into God's favour, might rise again from my fall, return home again from banishment, and attain the end for which I was created. That which I deserved, he suffered; and that to which I never could have attained, he giveth.

O my Redeemer, Deliverer, and Saviour, draw me to thee; that, being alway mindful of thy death, trusting in thy goodness, and being thankful for thine unspeakable benefits, I may be made partaker of so great a reward, and not be separated from thy body through mine own ingratitude, so that thou shouldest have been born in vain in respect of me, and in vain have suffered so many torments, yea even the most bitter death, of thine own free will, for my sake. Amen.

II.

MY mind beholdeth thy body crucified for my soul. O that thou wouldest also crucify me with thee, so that I might live, yet not I but thou, my Lord Christ, in me! How shall I find grace to die with thee, that I may rise again with thee to life everlasting? Thou didst die for me, that I might live through thee. Thy flesh is crucified, O Christ: crucify thou the power of sin which reigneth in me, that having put off the old Adam I may be transformed into thee the second Adam, to lead a new life by forsaking all wickedness, unbelief, and the tyranny of Satan.

Let thy yoke become sweet, and thy burden light to me through thy cross, that I, following thee willingly and cheerfully, may come to the same place where thou art, even to thy most blessed and eternal Father, from whom nothing may ever separate us hereafter. Amen.

III.

O PERFECT and wonderful obedience, whereby thou didst submit thyself to innumerable torments, yea, even to a most bitter and reproachful death, because it seemed good in thy Father's sight. O noontide of fervent love and sunshine never drawing towards eventide, show us where thou feedest thy sheep in the midst of the day, and where thou dost shelter them from the cold. O would to God that we might be transformed into that cross of thine, that thou mayest dwell in our hearts by faith, that we being rooted and grounded in love, may with all thy holy ones, comprehend the length, and breadth, and depth, and height of thy cross, which exceed all the might and wisdom of the world. Amen.

IV.

I SEE a marvellous kind of love. The high and holy One boweth down the head, to the intent that we should hope to be heard, and should be heard indeed. Thou offerest the kiss of peace and of atonement, yea, and that of thine own accord, who art thyself grieved and wronged, unto us who have done the wrong.

Thou reachest out thine arms to embrace us. Thou stretchest out thy pierced hands, to give us all things abundantly, without holding anything back. Thy side is open unto thy heart to receive us in thither, if we will enter in at the open door. Thy feet are fast nailed, to the intent that we may know that thou wilt never depart from us, if we depart not from thee.

O Lord and heavenly Father, thou seest the hardness of our hearts, and the dulness of our souls. It is not enough for us to be allured and called so gently, so sweetly, and so lovingly, but thou must be fain to draw us with cords of love to thee. Create a new and obedient heart within us, in the place of our old and stony heart, which feeleth no gentleness, nor is moved by any hope of the good things which are promised. Amen.

V.

O LORD Jesu Christ, the everlasting delight and triumph of them that love thee, exceeding all joy and all desire, thou Saviour and Lover of repentant sinners, who yearnest ever towards the children of men, and therefore, in the fulness of time, becamest man, for the sake of men; remember all the foretaste and grief of sorrow which thou didst endure, even from the instant of thy conception in the human nature during thine earthly life, but especially at the time when thy passion was at hand, according to the eternal ordinance which God had purposed in his mind before the worlds were made. Remember the bitterness and anguish which thou feltest in thine heart, even by thine own record, when thou saidst, "My soul is exceeding sorrowful even unto death," and at such time as thou gavest thy body and thy blood to thy disciples at thy last supper, didst wash their feet, and with tender words of comfort toldest them of thy passion which was at hand.

Remember the agony which thou didst endure in thy body before thy suffering on the cross; when after thrice praying thou didst sweat water like blood, wast betrayed by one of thine own disciples, apprehended by thine own chosen people, accused by false witnesses, condemned wrongfully by three judges in thy chosen city at the time of the Passover, in the youth of thy body, and being guiltless wast delivered to the Gentiles, wast spit upon, stripped of thine own garment, clothed in mockery, buffeted, blindfolded, struck with fists, tied to a post, flogged, and crowned with thorns.

O most beloved Jesu, make me, I beseech thee, mindful of these thy pains and sufferings which thou didst endure for my sins, that I might be set free from them, and that my atonement might be made with thy Father through thy chastisement. Make me to abhor my sins which could not be put away but by thy grievous punishment. Make me to be heartily sorry for my impurity, and to eschew mine offences which caused so great torments to thee. Make me mindful of thy great love to me and to all mankind; and let the remembrance of it kindle in me an unfeigned love towards thee and to my neighbour. Let this thine infinite goodness produce in me a willing mind, and a desire to suffer all things patiently for thy sake and for the truth of thy gospel; and let it cause in me a contempt for all worldly and earthly things, and an earnest longing for the heavenly inheritance, for the purchase of which for me and my attainment thereunto thou hast endured these and all other thy most bitter and intolerable torments.

Wherefore, I beseech thee, grant me true repentance, amendment of life, perseverance in all goodness, a steadfast faith, and a happy death, through the merits of thy sufferings, that I may be made partaker of thy blessed resurrection. Amen.

VI.

O LORD Jesu, joy of the Angels, paradise of delight, remember the fear and grief which thou didst endure, when all thine enemies compassed thee around like wild beasts on every side, and vexed thee with buffetings and blows, and assailed thee with bitter and reproachful words. I beseech thee, O Lord, for thine own sake, and for thine exceeding great mercies' sake which caused thee to endure these things for our redemption, deliver me from all mine enemies, visible and invisible; and grant that I may find both protection in this life, and endless happiness in the life to come, beneath the shadow of thy wings. Amen.

VII.

O JESU, Maker and Creator of the world, whom no measure can comprehend within bounds, and who holdest the earth in thine hand, call to mind the most bitter pain which thou didst endure when they nailed thy holy hands to the cross, and pierced thy tender feet, making thy wounds more and more painful because thou wast not agreeable to their fancy, and so straining and drawing out thy body to the length and breadth of the cross, that they loosened all the sinews of thy limbs.

I beseech thee to grant that my continual minding of this thy most holy and bitter pain upon the cross may cause me to stand in awe of thee, and also to love thee. Amen.

VIII.

O JESU, heavenly Physician, remember the anguish, pain, and grief which thou didst suffer by the rending and tearing of all thy members when thou wast lifted up and nailed to the cross, insomuch that no one of them remained whole and sound, so that no sorrow was ever like unto thy sorrow, for there was not any part of thee left whole, from the sole of the foot to the crown of the head; and yet even then, mindful of all thy pains, thou didst pray meekly to thy Father for thine enemies saying, "Father, forgive them, for they know not what they do."

I beseech thee by thy loving-kindness and mercy which caused thee to suffer these pains for my sake, let thy passion be the full pardon of all my sins. Amen.

IX.

O JESU, mirror of eternal brightness, and fountain of infinite love, who hanging upon the cross didst thirst for the salvation of mankind: I beseech thee, kindle in us the desire of all good works, quench in us the thirst of all carnal lusts, and destroy the inordinate affections of worldly delight. Amen.

X.

O JESU, our Lord and King, the strength and joy of our souls, who for our sakes didst suffer such anguish of heart that the bitterness of thy death and the exclamation of the Jews upbraiding and reviling thee, made thee cry out with a loud voice, "My God, my God, why hast thou forsaken me?" I beseech thee, forsake me not in my distress, but be at hand to comfort and deliver me, especially in the hour of death. Amen.

XI.

O JESU, fathomless sea of all mercy, I beseech thee by thy deep wounds which pierced through thy flesh even to thy heart, draw me from the gulf of my sins, and hide me in the holes of thy wounds from the sight of thy Father's just wrath, until his displeasure be overpast. Amen.

XII.

O JESU, the standard of unity and the bond of love, remember thine innumerable wounds wherewith thou wast smitten from head to foot by the wicked Jews, so that thou wast reddened with thy blood thus shed, which torment thou didst suffer in thy chaste body for our sakes, O most meek Jesu, leaving nothing undone on thy behalf which might be for our benefit. I beseech thee, write all thy wounds in my heart with thy most precious blood, that in them I may read thy great love towards me. Let the remembrance of them be laid up continually in the chamber of my heart, that the sight of the pains and grief which thou sufferedst for my sake in thy Passion may make me love thee more and more, and never cease until I be come unto thee, the treasure of all goodness and all joy, which I beseech thee to grant me for thine own sake, O most loving Jesu. Amen.

XIII.

O JESU, the only-begotten Son of the heavenly Father, and the brightness and image of his substance, remember thy commending of thy spirit into thy Father's hands, when, with body racked with pain, and heart full of anguish, having first shown the loving-kindness of thy mercy, thou gavest up the ghost. I beseech thee, for the sake of this thy precious death, O King of Saints, give me strength to withstand the devil, the world, and the flesh, that being dead unto sin, I may live to thee only. And when my soul, having accomplished her journey, shall depart hence, do thou receive her home, I beseech thee, into the hands of thy mercy. Amen.

XIV.

O JESU, the true and faithful vine, remember the abundant shedding of thy blood as from grapes pressed in the winepress, when thou didst tread the wine-press alone, and didst begin to us the cup of water and wine by the piercing of thy side by the soldier. I beseech thee, O most loving Jesu, by this bitter death of thine, and by the shedding of thy most precious blood, wound my heart with such repentance for my sins and joy in thy love, that my tears may be my food day and night. Turn thou me wholly unto thee, that my heart may dwell with thee continually, and my conversation may be acceptable unto thee. And let my life be such through thy goodness, that I may praise thee for ever with all thy saints in the life to come. Amen.

XV.

¶ *May be said as the* COLLECT *of the* SIXTH HOUR.

O LORD Jesu Christ, Son of the Living God, who for the salvation of the world drankest vinegar and gall upon the cross; even as thou didst commit thy soul into thy Father's hands when thou didst give up the ghost after thou hadst finished all things, so do I commit my soul into thy merciful hands, beseeching thee both to preserve it here from all sin, and in the end to receive it in peace into the company of thy departed saints, that with them I may praise thee everlastingly, who livest and reignest with the Father and the Holy Ghost, ever one God, world without end. Amen.

PRAYERS OF THE PASSION

OF

Our Saviour Christ.

Blessed be the Father, and the Son, and the Holy Ghost.

Let us praise him and magnify him above all for ever.

ALMIGHTY God, our heavenly Father, thy mercy and goodness is infinite and without measure. It was thy mercy, and no goodness that was in us, which moved thee to send into the world thine only-begotten and eternal Son, to take our nature upon him, and therein to work the mystery of our redemption and salvation; according as thou hadst appointed, and hadst spoken before, by the mouths of all thy prophets which were from the beginning. Also it was by thy blessed will, thy mercy and goodness towards us, that thy heavenly Son did suffer persecution, trouble, and adversity; was betrayed by his own friend and disciple Judas;

was traitorously taken and carried away to be falsely accused and unjustly condemned, to be beaten and to be scourged; and finally with scornful rebukes to be put to the most painful and shameful death that could have been devised. All this, O heavenly Father, was done, through thy mercy and blessed will, for our sakes; not only to answer and satisfy thy just wrath and anger which we had deserved for the offences of our first parents, and yet daily do deserve, by transgressing thy holy commandments; but also to restore us again unto thy grace and favour, and to endue us with thy heavenly gifts, that we may serve thee in holiness and righteousness, all the days of our life; and finally to make us, by the free benefit of thy dearly beloved Son's passion and the price of his most precious blood, partners with him of his infinite and unspeakable glory and bliss in heaven. Wherefore, O heavenly Father, we beseech thee, pour upon us thine Holy Spirit, and make us, in our hearts, clearly to see, and stedfastly to believe, this thine infinite goodness, shown and given unto us by thine own Son our Saviour Jesus Christ; and, with this belief, make us to put all our confidence and hope of salvation in him, whom thou hast appointed to be our only Redeemer and Saviour. Make us ever to render unto thee most humble and hearty thanks for thine incomprehensible goodness and mercy towards us. Finally make us to profess the death of thy dearly-beloved Son in renouncing and forsaking all sin; that we may rise with him in newness of life, in righteousness, innocence, and all true holiness; and after this life may reign with him in everlasting glory. Hear us, our heavenly Father, for our Lord Jesus Christ's sake. Amen.

ALMIGHTY God, our heavenly Father, we humbly beseech thee to grant that, as thine only-begotten and dearly beloved Son, our Saviour Jesus Christ, according to his blessed will, suffered willingly death and bitter passion for our redemption and salvation, having thereof foresight and certain knowledge; So in like manner, whensoever it shall be thy pleasure to lay like cross and affliction on us, we may also willingly and patiently bear it, in the trial of our faith for the latter day, unto thine everlasting glory. Hear us, our heavenly Father, for our Lord Jesus Christ's sake. Amen.

OUR Saviour and Redeemer, Jesu Christ, who in thy last Supper with thine Apostles, didst deliver thy blessed BODY and BLOOD under the form of bread and wine: Grant us, we beseech thee, ever steadfastly to believe, and kindly to acknowledge thine infinite and almighty power, thine incomprehensible love towards us, and that we may always worthily receive the same blessed Sacrament according to thy holy ordinance, that thereby we may obtain increase of all goodness, in unity of Spirit with thee our head, and by thee and thy Spirit with all the company of them that are truly thine, who are thy spiritual and mystical body, and our spiritual and Christian brethren. Hear us, our Saviour Christ, for thy Name's sake, who livest and reignest, with the Father and the Holy Ghost, One God, world without end. Amen.

ALMIGHTY God, our heavenly Father, who didst suffer thine Apostle Peter, presuming on his own power, miserably to fall, not only in the denial of his Master Christ for fear of an handmaid, but also in swearing that he knew him not: Grant to us, we beseech thee, merciful Father, that we may never presume on our own might and power, but being in our hearts humble and lowly, acknowledging our own infirmity, frailty, and weakness, may ever, in all our affairs, receive at thy mighty hand strength and comfort, to the due performance of thy holy and blessed will. Hear us, our heavenly Father, for our Lord Jesus Christ's sake. Amen.

O BLESSED Saviour Jesu Christ, who in that great heaviness of thy soul and intolerable anguish which thou sustainedst before thy passion, didst fall down upon thy face in prayer unto thy heavenly Father: Give us grace and the aid of thy Holy Spirit, that we likewise, in all heaviness of mind and troubles of this world, may seek evermore, by most humble and earnest prayer, the aid and comfort of our heavenly Father. Hear us, our Saviour Christ, for thy name's sake, who livest and reignest with the Father and the Holy Ghost, One God, world without end. Amen.

ALMIGHTY God, Eternal Father, we do remember that in the condemnation of thine own dearly beloved Son, that most innocent lamb, our Saviour Jesus Christ, the judge did sit, witnesses were brought, Christ was presented and condemned, and all truth there was trodden underfoot, all unrighteousness did reign, and innocence was condemned. O most gracious Lord and Father, grant unto our heads and rulers, that they may ever in all their judgments judge according to true justice and equity, without corruption, partiality, and wicked time-serving; that their service may tend to the suppression of heresy, and to the maintenance of thine everlasting truth, justice, honour, and glory. Hear us, O heavenly Father, for our Lord Jesus Christ's sake. Amen.

PRAYERS.

IN THE MORNING.

O LORD God Almighty to whom and before whom all things are manifest and plain, who sufferest not a sparrow to fall to the ground without thy providence, and who in times past, by thy Holy Spirit, didst guide our forefathers, Abraham, Isaac, and Jacob, in thy paths and ways; and for the journey of young Tobias into a strange country, didst provide thy Holy Angel and messenger to be his guide; Grant unto me, a sinner, whom by thy word thou dost encourage to call upon thee, in all times of need and of necessity, that I may have thy Holy Spirit so to direct my paths and ways, this day, that I may walk according to thy will and pleasure, to the profit of my neighbour and the glory of thy Name; through Jesus Christ our Lord. Amen.

ANOTHER FOR THE MORNING.

O LORD Jesu Christ, who art the very bright Sun of the world, ever rising, never setting, who with thy glad look, dost engender, preserve, nourish, and make joyful all things that are in heaven and earth: Shine favourably, I beseech thee, into my spirit; that, the night of sin and mists of error being driven away by thine inward light, I may walk all my life without stumbling and offence, seemly, as in the daytime, being pure from the works of darkness. Grant this, O Lord, who livest and reignest with the Father and the Holy Ghost, One God, world without end. Amen.

ANOTHER FOR THE MORNING.

O LORD, our heavenly Father, I thank thee that thou hast vouchsafed to keep me this night through thy great mercy, and hast spared me to work in thy service through another day. And I beseech thee, of thine infinite loving-kindness, to give me grace so to pass the day now coming in all lowliness, meekness, chastity, charity, patience, goodness, fear, and wariness, that my service may please thee through him who shall come to judge both the quick and the dead and the world by fire. Keep and preserve me from all evil, from all stumbling and giving of offence, from all wilful sin, and from all the crafts and assaults of mine enemies both ghostly and bodily, both seen and unseen; and lead me, O Lord, by the safe guidance of thy Holy Spirit, that I may come at last to the joy of thy heavenly kingdom, through Jesus Christ our Lord. Amen.

AT NIGHT.

O LORD our only God, true, gracious, and merciful, who commandest them that love thy name to cast fear and care from them and to cast it upon thee, promising most mercifully to be their protector from their enemies, their refuge in danger, their governor in the day, their light in darkness, and their guardian in the hours of night; never to sleep, but to watch continually over thy faithful people: I beseech thee, of thy bountiful goodness, O Lord, to forgive me wherein I have offended thee, this day, and to receive me under thy protection, this night, that I may rest in quietness both of body and of soul. Grant to mine eyes sleep, but let my heart ever watch perpetually unto thee, that the weakness of the flesh cause me not to offend the Lord. Let me at all times feel thy goodness toward me, that I may be at all times stirred to praise thee: late, and early, and at midday, may thy praise be in my mouth; and at midnight, Lord, instruct me in thy judgments, that all the course of my life being spent in holiness and purity, I may be led in at last to the everlasting rest which thou hast promised, by thy mercy, to them that obey thy word, O Lord: to whom be honour, praise, and glory, for ever and ever. Amen.

ANOTHER FOR THE NIGHT.

O ETERNAL God, the very God of peace and of all consolation, who broughtest again from death our Lord Jesus, the great Shepherd of the sheep through the blood of the everlasting covenant, make us fruitful in all good works to do thy will, and work in us that which is acceptable in thy sight: Sanctify us wholly; keep our whole spirit, soul, and body faultless unto the coming of thy dear Son our Lord Jesus Christ. Thou art faithful, O Father, who hast promised this, who also shalt bring it to pass. To thee therefore be given everlasting praise, honour and glory, though Jesus Christ our Lord. Amen.

ANOTHER FOR THE NIGHT.

ALMIGHTY Father, everlasting God, I thank thee that thou, of thine infinite goodness, hast guarded me thine unworthy servant in safety and peace through this day, and hast protected me from the snares of the enemies both of my body and of my soul. And I pray thee that whatsoever sin I have committed to-day against thy precepts and commandments, by thought, by word, or by deed, this thou wilt wholly remit and pardon of thy Fatherly kindness. Moreover, I pray and implore thee that thou wilt protect me through this night too under the shadow of thy wings, and that of the same thy goodness and grace thou wilt mercifully defend and keep me from all danger of body and of soul, that mine eyes may sleep in peace, my body may rest in safety, and my soul may ever watch for thee; through Jesus Christ thy Son our Lord. Amen.

BEFORE GOING TO SLEEP.

TAKE me into thy protection, O Lord Jesu Christ, our defender; and grant that, while my body sleepeth, my soul may wake in thee, and cheerfully and joyfully behold the happy and gladsome heavenly life, wherein thou reignest with the Father and the Holy Ghost, and the angels and holy souls of men are most blessed fellow-citizens, for ever and ever. Amen.

PRAYER OF ERASMUS BEFORE RECEIVING THE HOLY COMMUNION.

WHAT tongue or what heart can worthily give thee thanks, O Lord Jesu, for thine unspeakable love towards us, who to redeem mankind forlorn didst vouchsafe to become Man, and to take all the miseries of our state upon thee; insomuch that in the end thou, being a pure and spotless Lamb, wast content to be made a sacrifice for us upon the altar of the Cross, and to undergo the punishment due for our sins, that thou mightest reconcile us to thy Father. Both in life and in death thou didst spend, give, and bestow thyself wholly upon us and for us.

Yet thy lovingkindness was not herein satisfied. For, lest at any time we might forget thy so great love, or our trust in thee might fail at any time, thou even now reigning in heaven dost refresh our souls from time to time with the food of thy Body, and dost cheer them with the holy cup of thy Blood.

Wherefore I beseech thee let thy Spirit cleanse my heart, that I may not come unworthily to that heavenly feast and to the Table whereat even the angels tremble; but that by thy shedding of thyself into my body I may grow manly in thee and become stronger by spiritual increase; so that I may continue to the end in the blessed fellowship of thy mystical body whom thou willest to have all one with thee, even as thou art one with the Father by the union of the Holy Ghost, to whom be praise and glory for evermore. Amen.

PRAYER OF THE DYING S. JEROME BEFORE RECEIVING THE HOLY COMMUNION.

WHAT am I, O my Lord Jesus Christ, that thou shouldest vouchsafe to come under my roof? Can a sinful man deserve such grace? Truly, O Lord, I am not worthy. Am I better than all my fathers were? Thou wouldest not show thyself to Moses, even for a moment, and how then doth it come to pass that thou humblest thyself so much as to come down to a man that is a publican and a sinner? And thou vouchsafest not only to eat with him, but also to give thyself to be eaten by him. Hail, O Bread of Life which camest down from heaven, and which givest life to as many as receive thee worthily! Verily, whoso receiveth thee worthily, although his soul be severed from his body by temporal death, yet shall he not die for ever, inasmuch as that separation is not a death but a passing from life unto life; by reason whereof he that eateth thee worthily beginneth to live with thee for ever when he dieth in this world. Thou art the Bread of the angels: the very sight of thee refresheth and glorifieth the angels. Thou art food for the soul and not for the body. Thou nourishest the mind and not the flesh.

He that eateth thee is turned into thee, that by partaking of thee he may become God: and yet thou art not changed into his substance as other bodily meats are. But woe be to them that receive thee unworthily, O most holy food; by the eating whereof aright a man becometh God, is set free from all evil, is filled with all goodness, and is made immortal. O sacred provision of our pilgrimage, whereby we pass out of this troublesome world to the company of heaven!

Come therefore, thou believing soul, rejoice and be of good courage, for thou shalt not die. Feed upon these dainties, and hesitate not. Take thy fill of this feast, wherein the Body of thy Saviour is set before thee to feed on. Man fell from God by eating the food of the forbidden tree, but by this food he is raised again to eternal glory, through Jesus Christ our Lord. Amen.

THANKSGIVING AFTER RECEIVING THE HOLY COMMUNION.

O MOST merciful Father, we render unto thee all praise, thanks, honour, and glory, for that it hath pleased thee of thy great mercies to grant to us miserable sinners so excellent a gift and treasure as to receive us into the fellowship and company of thy dear Son Jesus Christ our Lord; whom thou hast delivered to death for us, and hast given to us as a necessary food and nourishment unto everlasting life. And now, we beseech thee also, O heavenly Father, to grant us this petition, that thou never suffer us to become so unkind as to forget such infinite benefits, but that thou wilt imprint them so clearly on our hearts, that we may grow and increase daily more and more in true faith, which continually is exercised in all manner of good works; and do thou, O Lord, strengthen and confirm us in these perilous days, that when Satan rages against us we may stand and continue steadfast in thee, to the advancement of thy glory, who art God over all things, blessed for ever. Amen.

ON SUNDAY MORNING.

O LORD Jesu Christ, who on the first day of the week didst rise from the dead and break in sunder the gates of hell, we beseech thee to look upon us thy servants and to pour thy grace into our hearts, that being loosed from the bands of our sins we may keep this day holy unto thee, and that what we learn in church we may carry out in our daily lives throughout the week, ever looking unto thee who livest and reignest with the Father and the Holy Spirit, one God, world without end. Amen.

FOR TRUST IN GOD.

THE beginning of the fall of man was trust in himself. The beginning of the restoration of man was distrust in himself and trust in God. O most gracious and most wise guide our Saviour Christ, who leadest in the right way to immortal blessedness those who, truly and unfeignedly trusting in thee, commit themselves unto thee; Grant that as we are blind and feeble indeed, so we may take and repute ourselves, that we presume not of ourselves to see ourselves, but so far to see that we may ever have thee before our eyes, to follow thee who art our guide; to be ready to obey thy call most obediently, and to commit ourselves wholly unto thee; that thou, who only knowest the way, mayest lead us by the same way, unto our heavenly desires; to whom with the Father and the Holy Ghost be all honour and glory for ever and ever. Amen.

FOR PATIENCE IN TROUBLE. Ps. lx.

HOW hast thou, O Lord, humbled me and brought me down! I dare scarcely venture to make my prayers unto thee, for thou art angry with me, but not without my deserving. I have sinned, O Lord, I confess it; I will not deny it. But, O my God, pardon my trespasses, release me from my debts, render now thy grace again unto me, heal my wounds, for I am vexed by means of thy heavy hand. Yet, Lord, I abide, waiting for relief at thy hand, and not without hope; for I have received a token of thy favour and grace towards me, even the word of promise concerning Christ, who for me was offered upon the Cross for a ransom, a sacrifice, and a price for my sins. Wherefore, according to thy promise, defend me, O Lord, by thy right hand, and give a gracious ear to my requests. O be thou my help in trouble, for vain is the help of man. Tread down therefore mine enemies, by thine own power, who art mine only aider and protector, O Lord God Almighty, through Jesus Christ our Lord. Amen.

FOR CONCORD OF CHRIST'S CHURCH.
Ps. lxviii.

ARISE, O Lord, and let thine enemies be scattered: let them also that hate thee flee before thee. But let the righteous and Christ's disciples be glad and rejoice: let them sing praises and be joyful before thee. Let them magnify thy greatness; let them extol thy majesty. Let thy glory increase, let the kingdom of Christ from heaven among the redeemed be enlarged: be thou the Father of the fatherless, the judge of the widows, and the protector of them especially whom the world forsaketh, whose consciences are troubled, whom the world persecuteth for Christ's sake, who are needy and full of misery. In thine house, O Lord, let us dwell in peace and concord; give us all one heart, one mind, one true interpretation of thy word. Take off the bands no less from the consciences than the bodies of the miserable captives, and of them also who are compassed by the toils of death, and unadvisedly strive against grace. How thirsty, Lord, is the flock of thine inheritance! Pour down abundantly, I beseech thee, the showers of thy grace, that a more plenteous fruitfulness may come, and that thy people may be strengthened by thy Spirit. Grant to us, O Lord, thy word abundantly, that there may be many preachers of thy gospel who may work with godly unity in thy service. Let thy Church, the spouse of Christ, divide large spoils of the conquered Satan. Let all who believe in thee through Christ, O Lord God of our salvation, sing praises unto thee and magnify thy name. We are entered upon the voyage of salvation: be thou our guide into the haven, that, being delivered by thee from death, we may escape and lay hold on eternal life. Finish the thing which thou hast begun in us: make us to go on from faith to faith: leave us not to our own will and choice, which is ever ready to stumble and fall. To the thunderbolts of thy word give might, O Lord, that we may give the glory to thee alone. Give unto thy people courage and power to withstand sin, and to obey thy word in all things, O God most glorious and excellent over all, through Jesus Christ, our Lord. Amen.

AGAINST THE ENEMIES OF CHRIST'S TRUTH. Ps. cxl.

DELIVER me, O Lord, from the evil men; for thou seest how they imagine mischief in their hearts, and stir up strife all the day long. They have sharpened their tongues like a serpent, and adders' poison is under their lips. But, O merciful Lord, let me not fall into their hands, lest they do with me even as they list. Thou only art my God; hear thou the voice of my prayers. Thou, O Lord God, art the strength of my health: cover thou my head in the day of battle, whensoever the ungodly shall assault me, suffer not the wicked to have his desire, O Lord, lest he revile thee in his pride. Avenge the cause of the poor, and rid me of these daily grievances, that I may give thanks unto thy name with joy, and may continue in thy sight for ever, through the merits and mediation of thine only Son, Jesus Christ our Lord. Amen.

TO THE HOLY GHOST.

COME, Holy Spirit, the only consolation of the distressed, sanctifier and giver of life, true teacher of divine truth. O joy and glory of the souls which trust in Christ, fill the hearts of thy faithful ones with heavenly comfort. Kindle within us the fire of thy love; that the deceits, the perversity, and the selfishness of our flesh may be burnt away, and the rich gifts and rewards of divine grace may be imparted to us miserable men, whereby we may by thine assistance acknowledge Christ Jesus our Lord, and his redemption, and leading the new and true life in him may with all steadfastness persevere unto the end, and receive from him the prize of everlasting bliss for ever and ever, through Jesus Christ our Lord. Amen.

ANOTHER TO THE HOLY GHOST.

COME, Holy Spirit, our only consolation, true teacher of divine truth, and burning fire of heavenly love, kindle the hearts of all who call upon thee, that they may pray with murmurings which cannot be uttered, and by their supplications may obtain grace from thee to acknowledge God the Father, and his only Son our Lord, and evermore to increase in this knowledge, until they behold the unfading glories of the heavenly kingdom; through the same Jesus Christ our Lord. Amen.

TO KEEP THE TONGUE, AND AVOID THE INFECTION OF THE WORLD. Ps. cxli.

UNTO thee do I cry, O Lord, hear me speedily: let my prayer be set forth in thy sight as the incense, and let the lifting up of my hands be as an evening sacrifice. Set thou a watch about my mouth, guard my lips and my tongue, that they speak nothing amiss; but that they may call heartily upon thee and praise thy name. Let not mine heart be inclined to evil nor be occupied with sinners in ungodly works, lest I be a partaker in the sins which please them. Let me not live as they would have me live, but rather as shall best please thee: let me not approve either their counsels or their deeds, though they show a fair face to the world. Let me not hearken to the allurements of the ungodly who entice me to unclean things, but rather let me listen to the righteous man though he sharply correct and chide me. Let mine eyes look ever unto thee, O Lord, that I may trust in thee alone, and go to thee for assistance. O cast not out my soul, neither suffer it to perish. Keep me from the snares of the ungodly, and save me from the designs of the wicked. Defend me, O Lord, through thy grace, for there is none whom we can trust but thee; and this we beg through the merits and mediation of thine only Son, Jesus Christ our Lord. Amen.

PRAYER OF ANY CAPTIVE, ACCORDING TO THE FORM OF DAVID, WHEN HE WAS HIDDEN IN THE CAVE. Ps. cxlii.

WITH my voice do I cry unto thee, O Lord; even unto thee do I make my supplication: to the bosom of thy love I disclose the secrets of my heart, and show thee of my trouble. Thou knowest all my ways, O Lord, and thou seest how the ungodly have laid their snares for me. Lo, I cast mine eyes on this side and that, but I see that there is no man who will help me. I have no place to flee unto, so laden am I with the fetters of misery. O Lord my Maker and Father, now unto thee do I cry: thou art mine only anchor, my defence, and my help. Thou art my hope and my portion in the land of the living; yea, I have none other possession but thee alone. Unto thee therefore do I cling, knowing certainly that nothing can go amiss with me if thou be near. Consider then my complaint; behold how I am brought low by my persecutors, who are stronger than I. Defend me and deliver me from this prison of sin and death, that I may give thanks unto thy name. All the saints, angels, and men make suit for me, desiring thee for my comfort. They shall not cease until they obtain their request; even until thou forgive me my sins, and send me comfort in this distress, together with patience and longsuffering. If I shall obtain this, the righteous shall resort unto my company, and shall not cease to give thee thanks when they behold how thou deliverest me from these dangers, to the praise of thy name. O Lord, be merciful unto us, and aid us: then shall we magnify thy glorious name for ever; through Jesus Christ our Lord. Amen.

IN GREAT TROUBLE OF CONSCIENCE.
Ps. cxliii.

HEAR my prayer, O Lord, and consider my desire: hearken unto me for thy truth and righteousness' sake. Enter not into judgment with thy servant, for in thy sight shall no man living be justified: yea, not one of thy saints shall appear guiltless at thy bar, unless thou grant him thy gracious pardon; for the very stars are not pure and faultless before thee, and even the angels thou chargest with folly. Mine enemies are persecuting my soul: they smite my life down to the ground; they lay me in the darkness as the men that have been long dead. My spirit is vexed within me: my heart within me is desolate; unto thee I stretch forth my hands, imploring mercy of thee. For as the thirsty land longeth for a shower of rain, even so my soul longeth for thine help and succour. Hear me, O Lord, speedily; for my spirit waxeth faint. Hide not thy face from me, lest I be like unto them that go down into the pit of damnation. After the passing of this night of misery, let the pleasant morning of consolation shine brightly on me, that I may hear and feel thy loving-kindness betimes, for in thee is my trust. Show thou me the way that I should walk in; for if thou be not my guide, I must wander and stray from the way. To thee, O Lord, I lift up my soul; deliver me, I beseech thee, from the hand of mine enemies. Thou alone art my succour and defence: teach me to do the thing that pleaseth thee, for thou art my God. Let thy good Spirit conduct me into the land of the living: quicken my spirit for thy Name's sake; from all these troubles, for thy righteousness' sake, deliver me. Of thy goodness towards me slay mine enemies, and destroy all them that vex my soul; for I am thy servant, and for thy sake I suffer this dishonour. As thou art God, so help thou me, through Jesus Christ our Lord. Amen.

A PRAYER OF THE CHURCH AGAINST SIN. Wisd. xv. 1—4.

THOU, O God, art gracious and true, long-suffering, and in mercy ordering all things. For if we sin we are thine, knowing thy power: but we will not sin, knowing that we are counted thine. For to know thee is perfect righteousness: yea, to know thy power is the root of immortality. Amen.

IN WARS, THE PRAYER OF KING ASA. 2 Chron. xiv. 11.

O LORD, it is nothing with thee to help them that have need, whether with many or with them that have no power: help us, O Lord our God; for we rest on thee, and in thy name we go against this multitude. O Lord, thou art our God: let not man prevail against thee. Amen.

THE PRAYER OF MANASSES KING OF JUDAH. 2 Chron. xxxvi.

O LORD, Almighty God of our fathers, Abraham, Isaac, and Jacob, and of their righteous seed; who hast made heaven and earth, with all the ornament thereof; who hast bound the sea by the word of thy commandment; who hast shut up the deep, and sealed it by thy terrible and glorious name; whom all men fear, and tremble before thy power; for the majesty of thy glory cannot be borne, and thine angry threatening towards sinners is terrible: but thy merciful promise is immeasurable and unsearchable; for thou art the most high Lord, of great compassion, longsuffering, very merciful, and repentest of the evils of men. Thou, O Lord, according to thy great goodness hast promised repentance and forgiveness to them that have sinned against thee: and of thine infinite mercies hast appointed repentance unto sinners, that they may be saved. Thou therefore, O Lord, that art the God of the just, hast not appointed repentance to the just, as to Abraham, and Isaac, and Jacob, which have not sinned against thee; but thou hast appointed repentance unto me that am a sinner: for I have sinned above the number of the sands of the sea. My transgressions, O Lord, are multiplied: my transgressions are multiplied, and I am not worthy to behold and see the height of heaven for the multitude of mine iniquities. I am bowed down with many iron bands, that I cannot lift up mine head, neither have any release: for I have provoked thy wrath, and done evil before thee: I did not thy will, neither kept I thy commandments: I have set up abominations, and have multiplied offences. Now therefore I bow the knee of mine heart, beseeching grace of thee. I have sinned, O Lord, I have sinned, and I acknowledge mine iniquities: wherefore, I humbly beseech thee, forgive me, O Lord, forgive me, and destroy me not with mine iniquities. Be not angry with me for ever, by reserving evil for me; neither condemn me into the lower parts of the earth. For thou art the God, even the God of them that repent; and in me thou wilt show all thy goodness: for thou wilt save me, that am unworthy, according to thy great mercy. Therefore I will praise thee for ever all the days of my life: for all the powers of the heavens do praise thee, and thine is the glory for ever and ever. Amen.

THE PRAYER OF JOB IN HIS ADVERSITY AND DISTRESS. Job i. 21.

NAKED came I out of my mother's womb, and naked shall I return thither: the Lord gave, and the Lord taketh away; blessed be the name of the Lord. Amen.

PRAYER OF JEREMIAH. Jer. xvii. 14.

HEAL me, O Lord, and I shall be healed: save me and I shall be saved: for thou art my praise. Be not a terror unto me: thou art my hope in the day of evil. Let them be confounded that persecute me, but let not me be confounded: let them be dismayed, but let not me be dismayed: bring upon them the day of evil, and destroy them with double destruction. Amen.

PRAYER OF JEREMIAH. Jer. xxxi. 18.

O LORD, thou hast chastised me and I am chastised: turn thou me and I shall be turned, for thou art the Lord my God. Surely after that I was turned, I repented; and after that I was instructed, I smote upon my breast: I was ashamed, yea, even confounded, because I did bear the reproach of my youth.

PRAYER OF SOLOMON FOR A COMPETENT LIVING. Prov. xxx. 7.

TWO things have I required of thee: deny me them not before I die. Remove far from me vanity and lies: give me neither poverty nor riches; feed me with food convenient for me: lest I be full and deny thee and say, Who is the Lord? or lest I be poor and steal, and take the name of my God in vain.

PRAYER FOR OBTAINING OF WISDOM. Wisd. ix. 1.

O GOD of my fathers, and Lord of mercy, who hast made all things with thy word, and ordained man through thy wisdom, that he should have dominion over the creatures which thou hast made, and order the world according to equity and righteousness, and execute judgment with an upright heart: give me wisdom that sitteth by thy throne; and reject me not from among thy children: for I thy servant and son of thine handmaid am feeble, and of a short time, and too young for the understanding of judgment and laws. For though a man be never so perfect among the children of men, yet if thy wisdom be not with him, he shall be nothing regarded. O send thy wisdom out of thy holy heavens, and from the throne of thy glory, that being present she may labour with me, that I may know what is pleasing unto thee. For she knoweth and understandeth all things, and she shall lead me soberly in my doings, and preserve me in her power. So shall my works be acceptable. Amen.

THE PRAYER OF JESUS THE SON OF SIRACH IN NECESSITY, AND FOR WISDOM. Ecclus. li.

I WILL thank thee, O Lord and King, and praise thee, O God my Saviour: I do give praise unto thy name: for thou art my defender and helper, and hast preserved my body from destruction, and from the snare of the slanderous tongue, and from the lips that forge lies, and hast been mine helper against mine adversaries: and hast delivered me according to the multitude of thy mercies and greatness of thy name, from the teeth of them that were ready to devout me, and out of the hands of such as sought after my life, and from the manifold afflictions which I had; from the choking of fire on every side, and from the midst of the fire which I kindled not; from the depth of the belly of hell, from an unclean tongue, and from lying words. By an accusation to the king from an unrighteous tongue my soul drew near even unto death, my life was near to the hell beneath. They compassed me on every side, and there was no man to help me: I looked for the succour of men, but there was none. Then thought I upon thy mercy, O Lord, and upon thy acts of old, how thou deliverest such as wait for thee, and savest them out of the hands of the enemies. Then lifted I up my supplication from the earth, and prayed for deliverance from death. I called upon the Lord, the Father of my Lord, that he would not leave me in the days of my trouble, and in the time of the proud, when there was no help. I will praise thy name continually, and will sing praise with thanksgiving; and so my prayer was heard: for thou savedst me from destruction, and deliveredst me from the evil time: therefore will I give thanks, and praise thee, and bless thy name, O Lord. When I was yet young, or ever I went abroad, I desired wisdom openly in my prayer. I prayed for her before the temple, and will seek her out even to the end. Even from the flower till the grape was ripe hath my heart delighted in her: my foot went the right way, from my youth up sought I after her. I bowed down mine ear a little, and received her, and gat much learning. I profited therein, therefore will I ascribe the glory unto him that giveth me wisdom. For I purposed to do after her, and earnestly I followed that which is good; so shall I not be confounded. My soul hath wrestled with her, and in my doings I was exact: I stretched forth my hand to the heaven above, and bewailed my ignorance of her. I directed my soul unto her, and I found her in purity: I have had my heart joined with her from the beginning, therefore shall I not be forsaken. My heart was troubled in seeking her: therefore have I gotten a good possession. The Lord hath given me a tongue for my reward, and I will praise him therewith. Draw near unto me, ye unlearned, and dwell in the house of learning. Wherefore are ye slow, and what say ye of these things, seeing your souls are very thirsty? I opened my mouth, and said, Buy her for yourselves without money. Put your neck under the yoke, and let your soul receive instruction: she is hard at hand to find. Behold with your eyes, how that I have had but little labour, and have gotten unto me much rest. Get learning with a great sum of money, and get much gold by her. Let your soul rejoice in his mercy, and be not ashamed of his praise. Work your work betimes, and in his time he will give you your reward.

PRAYER TO SPEAK THE WORD OF GOD BOLDLY. Acts iv. 24.

Specially useful for these present times.

LORD, thou art God, who hast made heaven, and earth, and the sea, and all that in them is: who by the mouth of thy servant David hast said, Why did the heathen rage, and the people imagine vain things? The kings of the earth stood up, and the rulers were gathered together against the Lord, and against his Christ. For of a truth against thy holy child Jesus, whom thou hast anointed, both Herod and Pontius Pilate, with the Gentiles, and the people of Israel, were gathered together, for to do whatsoever thy hand and thy counsel determined before to be done. And now, Lord, behold their threatenings: and grant unto thy servants, that with all boldness they may speak thy word, by stretching forth thine hand to heal; and that signs and wonders may be done by the name of thy holy child Jesus. Amen.

PRAYER OF ERASMUS FOR THE PEACE OF THE CHURCH.

O LORD Jesu Christ, who of thine almighty power hast made all creatures, both visible and invisible; who of thy godly wisdom governest and rulest all things in goodly order; who of thine unspeakable goodness dost keep, defend, and further all things; who of thy great mercy restorest the decayed, renewest the fallen, raisest the dead: Vouchsafe, we pray thee, to cast thy countenance upon thy well-beloved spouse the Church; even that loving and merciful countenance wherewith thou dost reconcile all things in heaven, in earth, and whatsoever is above heaven and under the earth. Vouchsafe to cast on us those tender and pitiful eyes with which thou didst once behold Peter, that great shepherd of thy church, who forthwith remembered himself and repented: even the eyes with which thou didst once behold the scattered multitude, and wast moved with compassion, in that, for lack of a good shepherd, they wandered as sheep dispersed and scattered abroad. Thou seest, O good Shepherd, that many sorts of wolves have broken into thy sheepfold, of whom every one crieth, "Here is Christ, there is Christ;" so that if it were possible even the elect would be deceived. Thou seest by what winds, by what waves, by what storms thine holy ship is tossed, even thy ship wherein thy little flock is in peril of being drowned: and what is now left but that it utterly sink and we all perish? Yet for this tempest and storm we may thank our own wickedness and sinful lives. We see it well, and we confess it. We see thy righteousness, and bewail our own unrighteousness; but we appeal to thy mercy which, according to the psalm of thy prophet, is over all thy works. We have now suffered much punishment, being plunged in so many wars, vexed by spoiling of our goods, scourged by so many diseases and forms of pestilence, shaken by so many floods, frightened by so many strange sights from heaven: and yet appeareth there nowhere any haven or port unto us who are weary, amidst so many evils, but every day yet more grievous punishments seem to hang over our heads. We complain not of thy severity, most tender Saviour, but herein we see thy mercy to us who have deserved more grievous plagues of thee. But, O most merciful Jesu, we beseech thee, that thou wilt not consider nor weigh what is due for our deservings, but rather what beseemeth thy mercy, without which not even the angels in heaven can stand before thee, much less we poor vessels of clay. Have mercy on us, O Redeemer, who art easy to be entreated. We are not worthy of mercy, but give thou this glory unto thine own name. Suffer not that the Jews, Turks, and heathen who have not known thee, or who envy thy glory, should continually triumph over us and say, "Where is their God, where is their Redeemer, where is their Saviour, where is their Bridegroom of whom they boast?" These reproachful words and upbraidings fall upon thee, O Lord, while by our misfortunes men weigh and esteem thy goodness; for they think that we are forsaken, when they see that thou helpest us not. Once when thou didst sleep in the ship and a tempest suddenly arising threatened death to all in the ship, thou didst awake at the cry of a few disciples, and straightway at thine Almighty word the waves subsided, the winds fell, the storm was suddenly turned into a great calm: the dumb waters knew their Maker's voice.

Now in this far greater tempest, wherein not the mere bodies of a few men bé in danger but innumerable souls, we beseech thee, at the cry of thy holy Church which is in danger of drowning, that thou wilt awake. So many thousands of men do cry, "Lord, save us, we perish:" the tempest is past man's control: yea, we see that the endeavours of them that would help it are altogether vain. It is thy word that must do the deed, O Lord Jesu; only say then with the word of thy mouth, "Cease, thou tempest," and forthwith shall the desired calm appear. Thou wouldest have spared so many thousands of wicked men, if in the city of Sodom had been found but ten righteous. Now that there be so many thousands of men who love the glory of thy name, who sigh for the beauty of thy house, wilt thou not at these men's prayers let go thine anger, and remember thine accustomed and ancient mercies? Wilt not thou with thy heavenly power turn our folly into thy glory? Wilt thou not turn the evils of the wicked to the good of thy Church. For thy mercy is wont then most of all to succour when the thing is with us past remedy, and neither the might nor wisdom of man can help it. Thou alone bringest into order again that which is involved in disorder: thou art the only author and maintainer of peace. Thou didst frame that old confusion which we call chaos, wherein without order, without form, confusedly lay the discordant seeds of things;

and thou didst ally with wonderful order, and knit in a perpetual bond, the things that of nature fought together. But how much greater confusion is this, where is no charity, no fidelity, no bonds of love, no reverence either of laws or of rulers, no agreement of opinions, but, as in a misordered choir, every man singeth a contrary note. Among the heavenly planets is no dissension: all four elements keep their place, all do their own office whereunto they be appointed. And wilt thou suffer thy spouse, for whose sake all things were made, thus by continual discords to perish and go to wreck? Wilt thou suffer the evil spirits, authors and workers of discord, to bear the sway in thy kingdom unchecked? Wilt thou suffer that mighty captain of mischief, whom thou once overthrewest, again to invade thy tents and to spoil thy soldiers? When thou wast a man here, conversant with men, at thy voice fled the devils. Send forth, we beseech thee, O Lord, thy Spirit, which may drive away, out of the hearts of all them that profess thy name, the wicked spirits, masters of riot, of covetousness, of vainglory, of carnal lust, of mischief and of discord. Create in us, O our God and King, a clean heart, and renew thy Holy Spirit in our souls. Take not thy Holy Spirit from us. Give unto us the joy of thy salvation, and with thy free Spirit strengthen thy spouse and the herdsmen thereof. By this Spirit didst thou reconcile the earthly to the heavenly: by this thou didst fashion and reduce so many tongues, so many nations, so many different sorts of men, into the one body of the Church, which body by the same Spirit is knit to thee its head. This Spirit if thou wilt vouchsafe to renew in all men's hearts, then shall also these miseries from without cease to vex us: or, if they cease not, they will turn to the profit and avail of them that love thee. Stay this confusion, set in order this horrible chaos, O Lord Jesu; let thy Spirit move upon these waters of evil wavering opinions. And because thy Spirit, as the prophet saith, conceiveth all things and hath the knowledge of speaking, cause that, as to all them that are of thine house is one law, one baptism, one God, one hope, one Spirit, even so they may have also one voice, one note and song, professing one catholic truth. When thou didst ascend to heaven triumphantly, thou sentest down from above thy precious things, thou gavest gifts to men, thou dealtest sundry rewards of thy Spirit. Renew again from above thine old bounty: give unto thy Church, now fainting and sinking downward, that which thou gavest her when she rose up at the first beginning. Give unto princes and rulers the grace to stand in awe of thee, and that they may guide the state as men who must shortly give account unto thee who art King of kings. Give wisdom to accompany their footsteps ever; that, whatsoever is best to be done, they may perceive it with their minds and pursue it in their deeds. Give to thy bishops the gift of prophecy, that they may declare and interpret Holy Scripture, not of their own brain but of thine inspiring. Give them the threefold charity, which thou once didst demand of Peter, when thou didst deliver unto him the charge of thy sheep. Give to thy priests the love of soberness and chastity. Give to thy people a good will to follow thy commandments, and a readiness to obey such persons as thou hast appointed over them. Thus shall it come to pass, if through thy gift thy princes shall command that which thou requirest, if thy pastors and herdsmen shall teach the same and thy people obey them both, that the old dignity and tranquillity of the Church shall return again to a goodly order, unto the glory of thy name. Thou didst spare the Ninevites, who were given over to destruction, as soon as they turned to repentance. And wilt thou despise thy spouse falling down at thy feet, who instead of sackcloth hath sighs, and instead of ashes tears? Thou hast promised forgiveness to such as turn unto thee, but it is thy gift that a man shall turn with his whole heart unto thee, to the intent that all our goodness may redound to thy glory. Thou art the Maker: repair thy work, which thou hast fashioned. Thou art the Redeemer: save that which thou hast bought. Thou art the Saviour: suffer not them to perish who hang upon thee. Thou art the Lord and Owner: challenge thy possession. Thou art the Head: help thy members. Thou art the King: give us reverence of thy laws. Thou art the Prince of Peace: breathe upon us brotherly love. Thou art the God: have pity on thy humble beseechers. Be thou all in all of us, to the intent that the whole choir of thy Church, with agreeing minds and harmonious voices, for mercy obtained at thy hands, may give thanks to the Father, Son, and Holy Ghost, that most perfect example of concord, in that they are distinct in property of persons, and one in nature; to whom be praise and glory, for ever and ever. Amen.

FOR THE KEEPING OF A GOOD NAME.

THE wise man who knew thy secrets, O heavenly Father, taught us that an honest name is a treasure most precious, when he said, "Better it is to have a good name than precious ointments." But this so excellent and good a thing we neither can get nor keep, but by thy help; for the well and fountain of a good name is a faultless life. This therefore in especial we demand and crave of thee, O Lord Almighty; yet forasmuch as often innocence and faultless living is not enough, neither yet a sure buckler and defence against such as have the poison of serpents under their lips, yea, and oftentimes it happeneth that when we suppose ourselves to be among our true friends, we dwell with Ezekiel among scorpions and venomous serpents; we cry with thy holy prophet, " O Lord, deliver my soul from lying lips and a deceitful tongue." But if, nevertheless, it seemeth good to thee to try thy servants with this affliction, to the intent that they may the better be brought to godliness and perfection, grant, we pray thee, that with Paul thy valiant champion, we may through reproach and glory, through infamy and good name, abide still in thy commandments, through Jesus Christ, who also himself, when he walked here on earth, was reviled, slandered, evil spoken of, and called to his teeth a Samaritan, a wine-bibber, a deceiver of the people, and one that had a devil. The same now reigneth in glory with thee and the Holy Ghost for ever and ever. Amen.

AGAINST WORLDLY CAREFULNESS.

O MOST dear and tender Father, our defender and nourisher, endue us with thy grace that we may cast off the great blindness of our minds and carefulness of worldly things, and may give our whole care to keeping of thy holy law; and that we may labour and travail for our necessities in this life, like the birds of the air and the lilies of the field, without care. For thou hast promised to be careful for us, and hast commanded that upon thee we should cast all our care, through Jesus Christ our Lord, who liveth and reigneth with thee and the Holy Ghost, one God, world without end. Amen.

AGAINST PRIDE AND UNCHASTITY.

O THOU Lord, Father, and God of my life, set me free from the assaults of pride: turn away from me all impure desires. Take from me the lust of the body; let not the desires of uncleanness take hold upon me; give me not over to an irreverent and obstinate mind, through Jesus Christ our Lord. Amen.

AGAINST PRIDE.

O LORD Jesu Christ, in most mighty power most meek, and in greatest excellence most lowly, yea of thine own will most humble, give unto me thy mind and spirit, that I may acknowledge my weakness, leavened and infected by sin; that through thine example I may become humble and meek, who have no cause to boast myself. Things of the world are uncertain, lent for a short use. The body is fading, frail, and feeble; the mind is blind and froward. Whatsoever I have of my own, it is naught: if I have any goodness, it is of thee and not of me. Knowing this feebleness of myself, why should I magnify myself, and especially since thou, Lord of heaven and earth, being of such wonderful excellence, didst humble thyself to the lowest estate of man, grant me true humility, that I may be exalted to thine everlasting glory, who livest and reignest with the Father and the Holy Ghost for ever and ever. Amen.

AGAINST ENVY.

O LORD, the Creator and Maker of all things and the disposer of the gifts which thou bestowest of thy bounty, giving to each man more than he deserveth, so that we have no cause of grudge or envy towards thee, who givest unto all men of thine own, even to such as deserve it not, and to each man sufficiently towards the attainment of thy heavenly joys; grant to us that we be not envious, but quietly content with thy judgment and the disposing of thy gifts and benefits. Grant us to be thankful for that which we receive, and not to murmur secretly with ourselves against thy judgment and blessed will in bestowing thy free benefits; but rather to love and praise thy bountiful goodness, and always to magnify thee, O Lord, the fountain of kindness and of love. To thee be honour and glory for ever and ever. Amen.

AGAINST ANGER.

O LORD Jesu Christ, who saidst that whosoever is angry with his brother shall be guilty of the judgment; who also dost reserve from time to time all vengeance and displeasure to thy secret and just judgment: Grant to us of thy mercy that we may never fall into intemperance of word or of speech through anger or desire of revenge, but that remembering thy commandment which chargeth us to do well to them that hate us and to pray for them that say evil of us, we may ever bear in mind thy holy example who didst pray for them that crucified thee; to whom, with the Father and the Holy Ghost, be glory for ever and ever. Amen.

IN ADVERSITY.

O LORD God, without whose will and pleasure not even a sparrow falleth to the ground, seeing it is of thy will and permission that I am in this misery and adversity, and that thou punishest me with trouble, not to destroy me and cast me away, but to call me to repentance and to save me (for whom thou lovest thou chastenest); and forasmuch as affliction and adversity teach us patience, and whosoever patiently beareth tribulation is made like unto the Saviour Christ our Head: finally, seeing that in all tribulation and adversity I am in assurance of comfort at thy gracious hand, for thou hast commanded me to call upon thee in the time of sorrow, and hast promised to hear and succour me; Grant me therefore, O Almighty God and merciful Father, in all trouble and adversity to be quiet without impatience and murmuring, without discouragement and despair, to praise and to magnify thee, to put my whole trust and confidence in thee, who never forsakest them that trust in thee, but workest all for the best to them that love thee and seek the glory of thy holy name; hear me, O merciful Father, for Jesus Christ's sake thy Son our Lord. Amen.

IN PROSPERITY.

I GIVE thee thanks, O God Almighty, who not only hast endued me with the gifts of nature, as reason, power, and strength, but also hast plentifully given me the substance of this world. I acknowledge, O Lord, that these are thy gifts, and I confess that there is no perfect or good gift but it cometh of thee, O Father of lights, who givest freely and castest no man in the teeth. Gold, O Lord, is thine, and silver is thine, and to whom it pleaseth thee thou givest it: to the godly that they may be thy disposers and distributors thereof, and to the ungodly to increase their damnation. Wherefore, my most merciful God, I humbly beseech and desire of thee to frame in me, with thy Holy Spirit, a faithful heart and a ready hand, to distribute these thy gifts according to thy will and pleasure; that I treasure not up here, where thieves may rob and moths corrupt, but may treasure up that reward which thou hast promised in thy heavenly kingdom, where neither thief may steal nor moth corrupt, in the everlasting rest before the glory of thy presence; to whom with the Son and the Holy Ghost be all honour and praise, world without end. Amen.

PRAYER OF S. THOMAS AQUINAS,

To be said at all times.

O MERCIFUL God, grant me to covet, with a fervent mind, those things which may please thee, to search them wisely, to know them truly, and to fulfil them perfectly, to the praise and glory of thy name. Order my living so that I may do that which thou requirest of me; and give me grace that I may obtain those things which are best for my soul. O Lord, make my way sure and straight to thee, so that I fall not between prosperity and adversity, but that in prosperity I may give thee thanks, and in adversity be patient, so that I be not lifted up by the one nor depressed by the other: and that I may rejoice in nothing but that which moveth me to thee, nor be sorry for aught but for that which draweth me from thee; desiring to please nobody, nor fearing to displease any, beside the Lord. Let all worldly things be vile unto me, for thee: let me not be glad with the joy that is without thee, and let me desire nothing besides thee. Let that labour delight me which is for thee, and let all other labour weary me which is not in thee. Make me to lift up my heart ofttimes to thee, and when I fall make me to think on thee, and to be sorrowful with a steadfast purpose of amendment. My God, make me humble without dissimulation, cheerful without lightness, serious without mistrust, sober without dulness, true without duplicity, fearing thee without despair, trusting thee without presumption, obedient without arguing, patient without grudging, and pure without corruption. My most loving Lord and God, give me a waking heart, that no curious thought withdraw me from thee; let it be so strong that no unworthy affection draw me backward; so stable that no tribulation break it. My God, grant me wisdom to know thee, diligence to seek thee, conversation of life to please thee, and finally, hope to embrace thee; for the sake of the precious blood of that immaculate Lamb, our only Saviour Jesus Christ; to whom with the Father and the Holy Ghost, three Persons and One God, be all honour and glory, world without end. Amen.

PRAYER OF S. BERNARDINE. *O bone Jesu.*

O GOOD Jesu, O beloved Jesu, O Jesu Son of the pure Virgin Mary, full of grace and truth; O beloved Jesu, after thy great mercy have pity upon me. O loving Jesu, I pray thee, by the same precious blood which for us miserable sinners thou wast content to shed upon the altar of the Cross, that thou wilt put away all my sins and despise me not in mine humble suit, calling upon this thy most holy name of Jesus. This name Jesus is a beloved name. This name Jesus is the name of health. For what else is Jesus, but Saviour? O good Jesu, who hast created me, and with thy precious blood hast redeemed me, suffer me not to be lost whom thou hast made of nought. O good Jesu, let not my wickedness destroy me, whom thine almighty goodness made and formed. O good Jesu, consider what is thine in me, and take thou away that which draweth me from thee. O good Jesu, have mercy upon me, while the time serveth to have mercy, lest thou destroy me in the time of thy dreadful doom. O good Jesu, although I, a miserable sinner, have justly deserved everlasting punishment for my grievous sins by thy rightful justice, yet I appeal from thy righteousness, and steadfastly trust in thine unspeakable mercy, and therefore pity thou me, as a loving Father and merciful Lord. O good Jesu, what profit is there in my blood, since I must go down into corruption? For the dead praise not thee, O Lord, neither they that go down into the pit. O most merciful Jesu, have mercy upon me. O most beloved Jesu, deliver me. O loving Jesu, have mercy upon me a sinner. O Jesu, admit me a miserable sinner into the number of thy chosen. O Jesu, the health of them that trust in thee: O Jesu, the welfare of them that believe in thee, have pity upon me. O beloved Jesu, the propitiation of all my sins; O Jesu, Son of the pure Virgin Mary, endue me with thy grace, wisdom, charity, chastity, and humility: and in all mine adversities give me holy patience, that I may be able to bear my cross with thee, to love thee, and to glory and delight in thee for ever and ever. Amen.

TO BE SAID AT THE HOUR OF DEATH.

O LORD Jesu, who art the only health of all men living, and the everlasting life of them that die in thy faith, I a wretched sinner give and submit myself wholly unto thy most blessed will, and being sure that the thing cannot perish which is committed unto thy mercy, I willingly now leave this frail and wicked flesh in hope of the Resurrection which in better wise shall restore it to me again. I beseech thee, most merciful Lord Jesu Christ, that thou wilt by thy grace strengthen my soul against all temptations, and that thou wilt cover and defend me with the shield of thy mercy against all the assaults of the devil. I see and acknowledge that there is in myself no help of salvation; but all my confidence, hope, and trust is in thy most merciful goodness. I have no merits nor good works which I may allege before thee; of sins and evil works, alas, I see a great multitude; but through thy mercy I trust to be in the number of them to whom thou wilt not impute their sins, but that thou wilt take and accept me for righteous and just, and to be the inheritor of everlasting life. Thou, merciful Lord, wast born for my sake. Thou didst suffer both hunger and thirst for my sake. Thou didst preach and teach; thou didst suffer most grievous pains and torments for my sake; and finally, thou gavest thy most precious body to die, and thy blood to be shed on the Cross for my sake. Now, most merciful Saviour, let all these things profit me, which thou hast freely given me, who hast given THYSELF for me: let thy blood cleanse and wash away the foulness of my sins. Let thy righteousness hide and cover mine unrighteousness. Let the mercies of thy passion and thy blood be the satisfaction for my sins. Give me, Lord, thy grace, that my faith and salvation in thy blood waver not in me, but be ever firm and constant; that the hope of thy mercy and life everlasting never decay in me; that charity wax not cold in me; finally, that the weakness of my flesh be not overcome by the fear of death. Grant to me, merciful Saviour, that when death hath closed the eyes of my body, yet that the eyes of my soul may still behold and look upon thee; that when death hath taken away the use of my tongue and speech, yet my heart may cry and say unto thee, "*In manus tuas, Domine, commendo spiritum meum;* O Lord, into thy hands, I give and commit my soul." "*Domine Jesu, accipe spiritum meum:* Lord Jesu, receive my soul unto thee." Amen.

GENERAL CONFESSION OF SINS TO GOD.

O MOST merciful Lord God, and most dear and tender Father, vouchsafe, I heartily beseech thee, to look down with thy fatherly eyes of pity upon me, a most miserable sinner, who lie here prostrate in heart before the feet of thy mercy; for I have sinned against the throne of thy glory, and before thee, O Father, insomuch that I am no more worthy to be called thy son. Nevertheless, forasmuch as thou art the God and Father of all comfort, and desirest not the death of a sinner, but, as a good Samaritan, takest thought of my poor wounded soul, make me, I pray thee, by pouring the precious oil of thy comfort into my wounds, joyfully to find rest with the lost son in the bosom of thine everlasting pity. For lo, thou art my hope and trust, in whom alone I repose myself, having full confidence and faith in thee, and therefore I say with faithful heart, trusting in thy mercy, I believe in thee, O God the Father; in thee, O God the Son; and in thee, O God the Holy Ghost, three Persons and one true and very God; beside whom I acknowledge none other God in heaven above, nor in earth beneath; yea, and I, a poor sinner, do accuse myself unto thee, dear Father, that I have often and grievously offended thine Almighty goodness and majesty, in the committing of my manifold sins; for I have not kept the least of thy holy commandments, as thy righteousness may require and demand of me. I have not honoured thee as my God, nor dreaded thee as my Lord, nor loved thee as my Father, nor trusted in thee as my Creator and Saviour. Thy holy and dreadful name, to which all glory and honour belongeth, have I used in vain. I have not sanctified the holy days with works which be acceptable unto thee, nor instructed my neighbour in virtue accordingly. I have not honoured my parents, nor been obedient unto them; through whom, as by an instrument, thou hast wrought my coming into this world. The high powers and rulers, who take their authority of thee, I have not been willingly obedient unto. I have not kept my heart pure and clean from murder: yea, had not thy grace and mercy defended me, I should have committed the deed also. I am not pure from theft, nor from adultery, nor from bearing false witness, but I have in my heart and mind desired my neighbour's goods and things. I have followed the great prince of this world, Satan, who is a liar from the beginning, in concupiscence of the flesh, in pride of living, in lying, in deceitfulness, in lust, in hatred, and envy, in malice, in despair, and in unbelief. My fine senses have I misused and mis-spent, in hearing, seeing, smelling, tasting, and in feeling, which thou hast given me to use to thy honour and glory, and to the honour and edification of my neighbour. But in what manner soever I have offended and sinned against thine eternal majesty, (for no man knoweth thoroughly his sins, nor how oft he offendeth,) whether it hath been by day or by night, yea, even from my childhood unto this day, whether in words, works, or thoughts, secretly or openly;

O my merciful God, I am sorry for it, even from the very bottom of my heart; yea, and my soul mourneth for sorrow, most merciful Father, that I am not a thousand times more sorry than I am. And now, in token of great repentance, though all hearts be known unto thee, I beat my breast, and say in bitterness of heart and soul—O Lord God, the Father, have mercy: O Lord God, the Son, have mercy: O Lord God, the Holy Ghost, have mercy. Spare me, of thine infinite mercy, dear Lord, now, and all the days of my life; and impart to me thine abundant grace, that I may change my sinful life, and put off the old man with his evil lusts: that I may die unto the world, and that the world may be unto me a cross, and I may advance in a new life. Strengthen me, O Lord, in true humility of heart; in perfect love, hope, and trust in thee. Give my soul the grace to desire thee only, in thee only to rejoice and repose myself, that I may utterly renounce and forsake my vain affiance on this world; so that thou mayest find me ready, with the good servant, in the midnight of my death, which shall suddenly steal upon me, as a thief, ere I am aware of it. Be thou unto me, at that time of need, O Lord, a tower of strength, a place of refuge, and a defending God, against the face of the fiend who, as a roaring lion, will be then most ready to devour me, and against desperation, which will then be busy to grieve me. Let then thy comfort cleave fast unto me; let thy mercy keep me, and thy grace guide me. Take then again, O Lord my God and Father, that which thy powerful might hath shaped: take then again, O Lord the Son, that which thou hast so wisely governed, and hast bought with thy precious blood: take then again, O Lord the Holy Ghost, that which thou hast kept and preserved so lovingly in this region of sin and vale of misery; Three Persons and One very God, unto whom be praise and honour for ever and ever. Amen.

FOR THE DESIRE OF THE LIFE TO COME.

THIS my body is the dark and gloomy prison of the soul: this world is an exile and a banishment: this life is care and misery; but where thou art, O Lord, there is the true country of liberty and everlasting blessedness. Stir our minds continually to remember so great felicity. Pour into our hearts a desire of things so precious and so infinitely to be desired. Give quietness unto our minds; and grant that we may have some taste of the everlasting joys, whereby these things of the world may seem of small account to us, and those things which we seek for so earnestly, and embrace so greedily, and retain so surely, may be refused and despised by us; so that we may most fervently desire the sweetness of thy familiarity, wherein all goodness is contained. To thee be honour and glory for ever and ever. Amen.

METRICAL LITANIES.

NIGHT LITANY.

GOD the Father, God the Son,
   Holy Ghost the Comforter,
Ever-blessed Three in One,
  Spare us, Holy Trinity.

Jesu, hear us, Lord of all,
As the shades of evening fall,
Hear thy servants when they call,
  Hear us, Holy Jesu.

Jesu born in hour of night,
Lord of Glory infinite,
God of God, and Light of Light,
  Hear us, Holy Jesu.

Thou who on the stormy deep
'Mid the tempest-din didst sleep,
In the gloom thy servants keep;
  Hear us, Holy Jesu.

Thou whose path was on the wave
When the winds at night did rave,
Save us, Master, Jesu, save!
  Hear us, Holy Jesu.

Thou whose voice consoling said
O'er the lifeless maiden's bed,—
"She but sleeps; she is not dead,"
  Hear us, Holy Jesu.

Thou who saidst—"I go to end
The sleep of Lazarus our friend,"
Us too waking thus attend,
   Hear us, Holy Jesu.

Thou who standing by the bier
Bad'st the mother dry her tear,
Ere the dead thy voice might hear,
   Hear us, Holy Jesu.

By the vigil kept by thee
In the dark Gethsemane,
When thine own slept wearily:
   Hear us, Holy Jesu.

Guardian of the soul opprest,
Who with still voice murmurest—
"Sleep on now and take thy rest,"
   Hear us, Holy Jesu.

By thy slumber in the cave,
In the deep sleep of the grave,
Guard us sleeping, Jesu, save:
   Hear us, Holy Jesu.

Through the grave and gate of death
When the faint soul travaileth,
Shelter her thine arms beneath:
   Hear us, Holy Jesu.

Lord, have mercy upon us.
   Christ, have mercy upon us.
Lord, have mercy upon us.
Our Father, &c.

℣. I will lay me down in peace and take my rest.
℟. For it is thou, Lord, only that makest me dwell in safety.

Let us pray.

GRANT, O Lord, that as we are baptized into the death of thy blessed Son our Saviour Jesus Christ, so by continual mortifying our corrupt affections we may be buried with him; and that through the grave, and gate of death, we may pass to our joyful resurrection; for his merits, who died, and was buried, and rose again for us, thy Son Jesus Christ our Lord. Amen.

COMMENDATORY LITANY.

¶ *May be sung after any of the Dirge Hours.*

GOD the Father, God the Son,
Holy Ghost, the Comforter,
Ever-blessed Three in One;
Hearken to our humble prayer:
    Hear us when we call to thee,
    Spare us, Holy Trinity.

Child of Mary, who didst bear
Mortal flesh, for man to die;
Child of sorrow, toil, and care,
Grant *him* rest eternally:
    Lord of life and love, we pray,
    Grant *him* mercy in that day.

Dweller in the vale of Death,
Second Adam, Source of Life,
Wearer of the thorny wreath,
Victor in the deadly strife:
    Lord of life, &c.

Thou who didst let fall the tear
On the grave of Bethany;
Who at Nain didst stay the bier,
That lone mother's tear to dry:
    Lord of life, &c.

Thou whose Voice could wake the dead—
"Maid! I say to thee, arise!"
Who didst bow thy dying head
On the day of Sacrifice:
    Lord of life, &c.

Thou who passedst through the gloom
Which enshrouds the Vale of death,
Guide *his* footsteps through the tomb,
Shelter *him* thine arms beneath:
   Lord of life, &c.

By thy Flesh with scourges torn,
By thy suffering human Soul,
By the Crown of woven thorn,
By the mocking title-scroll:
   Lord of life, &c.

By thy 𝔉irst 𝔚ord on the Rood—
"Pardon, Father, through the flow
Of thy Son's Atoning Blood,
For they know not what they do:"
   Lord of life, &c.

By that 𝔖econd 𝔚ord from thee,
Which gives light to dying eyes—
"Thou shalt be to-day with me
In the joys of Paradise:"
   Lord of life, &c.

By thy 𝔗hird 𝔚ord on the Cross—
"Mother, now behold thy Son!"
Word of love in earthly loss,
Last bequest unto thine own:
   Lord of life, &c.

By thy 𝔉ourth 𝔚ord—"O my God,
Why hast thou forsaken me?"
When thy Spirit felt the rod
Of our chastisement on thee:
   Lord of life, &c.

By thy 𝔉ifth 𝔚ord full of toil,
Offered for the world accurst,
Loosening Adam's sin-parched soil,
When the God-man said, "I thirst:"
   Lord of life, &c.

By the **Sixth Word** sounding forth,
In the hour of triumph won,
" It is finished!" and for earth
Is the work in heaven begun:
   Lord of life, &c.

By thy **Last and awful Word**—
"Father, I commend my soul
To thine hands:" O God and Lord,
By thy Manhood pure and whole:
   Lord of life, &c.

By the quiet rock-hewn cave,
Where thy Body slept so well,
When thy spirit, through the grave,
Entered to the realms of hell:
   Lord of life, &c.

By thy preaching of the Christ
To the souls in prison bound,
When was rolled away the mist
Which had hung their vision round:
   Lord of life, &c.

By the joyous Easter morn
When thou brak'st the bars of death,
God Incarnate, Virgin-born,
Robed in garb of Nazareth:
   Lord of life, &c.

By thy bright Ascension hour,
When thou wentest up on high,
Unto God's right hand of power
Captor of captivity:
   Lord of life, &c.

By th' Eternal Sacrifice
Which thou pleadest at the throne,
Only gift which can suffice,
For that gift is all thine own:
   Lord of life, &c.

T

By the Offering which we plead,
One with thine in heaven above
By the Lamb whose Five Wounds bleed
To fill full our Cup of Love:
   Lord of Life, &c.

In the fell and fearful day,
Day of fury and of ire,
When the earth shall melt away
In the thunder-blast of fire:
   Lord of life, &c.

When to hear the doom are met
Saints and sinners, quick and dead,
And the great White Throne is set,
And the books are open spread:
   Lord of life and love, we pray,
   Who didst tread the narrow way,
   Ransom for *his* soul to pay,
   Let *him* not be cast away,
   Grant *him* mercy in that day.

Lord, have mercy upon us,
   Christ, have mercy upon us.
Lord, have mercy upon us.
Our Father, &c.

℣. I heard a voice from heaven saying unto me,
℟. Blessed are the dead which die in the Lord.

Let us pray.

O ALMIGHTY God, who hast knit together thine elect in one communion and fellowship, in the mystical Body of thy Son Christ our Lord: Grant us grace so to follow thy blessed Saints in all virtuous and godly living, that we may come to those unspeakable joys which thou hast prepared for them that unfeignedly love thee; through Jesus Christ our Lord. Amen.

LITANY OF THE ASCENSION.

RISEN Lord, enthroned on high,
  Now the toils of life are o'er,
Hear thy Church's daily cry
Rising heavenward evermore—
  Lord, to save us make good speed,
  Jesu, help us in our need.

Now the battle-strife is done
Which the Victor fought so well,
For the crown of life is won
From the vanquished king of hell—
  Lord, to save us, &c.

Breaker of the bonds of death,
Captor of captivity,
One in power with him who saith,
All things doth he give to thee—
  Lord, to save us, &c.

Virgin-born, to thee we kneel,
Gifts for man who didst receive—
Human soul and flesh, to heal
The death-tainted sons of Eve—
  Lord, to save us, &c.

Second Adam, from whose Side,
In the tranquil sleep of death,
Issued forth the heavenly Bride,
Mother to the sons of Seth—
  Lord, to save us, &c.

Bruiser of the serpent's head,
Thou the Serpent on the Tree,
Healer of the souls half-dead,
All who fainting look to thee—
  Lord, to save us, &c.

Judah's Lion, from whose might
Honey-sweet distils the power

Which lays low the beast of night,
Seeking whom he may devour—
   Lord, to save us, &c.

Lamb of God, who tak'st away
Of our sin the guilty stain,
Ransom thou for man to pay
On the Altar as if slain—
   Lord, to save us, &c.

When in worship low we bend,
Master, leave us not alone;
Let the Holy Ghost descend
From the Father's central throne—
   Lord, to save us, &c.

Fill the shrine whence loud and long
Swells the pleading litany,
Matin chant and Evensong,
To the feet of God on high—
   Lord, to save us, &c.

Lord, have mercy upon us.
   Christ, have mercy upon us.
Lord, have mercy upon us.
Our Father, &c.

℣. Set up thyself, O God, above the heavens.
℞. And thy glory above all the earth.

Let us pray.

O GOD the King of Glory, who hast exalted thine only Son Jesus Christ with great triumph unto thy kingdom in heaven; We beseech thee, leave us not comfortless; but send to us thine Holy Ghost to comfort us, and exalt us unto the same place whither our Saviour Christ is gone before, who liveth and reigneth with thee and the Holy Ghost, One God, world without end. Amen.

HORARIUM

SEU LIBELLUS

PRECATIONUM

LATINE EDITUS.

ANTE OMNES HORAS DICENDÆ ORATIONES.

IN nomine Patris, et Filii, et Spiritûs Sancti. *Amen.*

DOMINE Pater et Deus meus, benedictum nomen tuum in sæcula. Imbue cor meum, aperi labia, et Sancto tuo Spiritu dirige me ad veram omnium peccatorum meorum confessionem, ut oratio mea a te audiatur in nomine Filii tui Jesu Christi. *Amen.*

PATER noster qui es in cœlis : Sanctificetur nomen tuum. Adveniat regnum tuum. Fiat voluntas tua, sicut in cœlo, et in terrâ. Panem nostrum quotidianum da nobis hodie. Et dimitte nobis debita nostra, sicut et nos dimittimus debitoribus nostris. Et ne nos inducas in tentationem, sed libera nos a malo. Amen.

HORARIUM.

Ad Matutinum.

℣. Domine, labia mea aperies.

℟. Et os meum annuntiabit laudem tuam.

℣. Deus, in adjutorium meum intende.

℟. Domine, ad adjuvandum me festina.

Gloria Patri, et Filio: et Spiritui Sancto.

Sicut erat in principio, et nunc, et semper : et in sæcula sæculorum. Amen.

Alleluia.

PSALMUS XCV.

Canticum excitans ad laudandum Deum.

VENITE, exultemus Domino, jubilemus Deo salutari nostro : præoccupemus faciem ejus in confessione, et in psalmis jubilemus ei.

Quoniam Deus magnus Dominus, et rex magnus super omnes deos: quoniam non repellet Dominus plebem suam, quia in manu ejus sunt omnes fines terræ, et altitudines montium ipse conspicit.

Quoniam ipsius est mare et ipse fecit illud; et aridam fundaverunt manus ejus : venite adoremus et procidamus ante Deum, ploremus coram Domino, qui fecit nos; quia ipse est Dominus Deus noster, nos autem populus ejus, et oves pascuæ ejus.

Hodie si vocem ejus audieritis, nolite obdurare corda vestra, sicut in exacerbatione, secundum diem tentationis in deserto: ubi tentaverunt me patres vestri, probaverunt, et viderunt opera mea.

Quadraginta annis proximus fui generationi huic, et dixi, Semper hi errant corde; ipsi vero non cognoverunt vias meas: quibus juravi in irâ meâ, Si introibunt in requiem meam.

Gloria Patri, et Filio: et Spiritui Sancto;

Sicut erat in principio, et nunc et semper: et in sæcula sæculorum. Amen.

Hymnus.

JAM, lucis orto sidere,
  Deum precemur supplices,
Ut, in diurnis actibus,
Nos servet a nocentibus:

Linguam refrænans temperet,
Ne litis horror insonet:
Visum fovendo contegat,
Ne vanitates hauriat:

Sint pura cordis intima,
Absistat et vecordia:
Carnis terat superbiam
Potûs cibique parcitas:

Ut, quum dies abscesserit,
Noctemque sors reduxerit,
Mundi per abstinentiam
Ipsi canamus gloriam. Amen.

𝔄ntiphona. Salvare in perpetuum.

PSALMUS VIII.

De laude, honore, et gloriâ Christi.

DOMINE Dominus noster : quam admirabile est nomen tuum in universâ terrâ!

Quoniam elevata est magnificentia tua : super cœlos.

Ex ore infantium et lactentium perfecisti laudem propter inimicos tuos : ut destruas inimicum et ultorem.

Quoniam videbo cœlos tuos, opera digitorum tuorum : lunam et stellas quæ tu fundasti.

Quid est homo, quod memor es ejus? aut filius hominis quoniam visitas eum?

Minuisti eum paulominus ab angelis, gloriâ et honore coronasti eum : et constituisti eum super opera manuum tuarum.

Omnia subjecisti sub pedibus ejus, oves et boves universas : insuper et pecora campi.

Volucres cœli, et pisces maris : qui perambulant semitas maris.

Domine Dominus noster : quam admirabile est nomen tuum in universâ terrâ!

Gloria Patri. Sicut erat.

PSALMUS XIX.

De gloriâ Dei, quæ in creaturis elucet, et de lege Sacrosanctâ.

CŒLI enarrant gloriam Dei : et opera manuum ejus annuntiat firmamentum.

Dies diei eructat verbum : et nox nocti indicat scientiam.

Non sunt loquelæ, neque sermones : quorum non audiantur voces eorum.

In omnem terram exivit sonus eorum : et in fines orbis terræ verba eorum.

AD MATUTINUM.

In sole posuit tabernaculum suum : et ipse tanquam sponsus procedens de thalamo suo.

Exsultavit ut gigas ad currendam viam : a summo cœlo egressio ejus :

Et occursus ejus usque ad summum ejus : nec est qui se abscondat a calore ejus.

Lex Domini immaculata, convertens animas : testimonium Domini fidele, sapientiam præstans parvulis.

Justitiæ Domini rectæ, lætificantes corda : præceptum Domini lucidum, illuminans oculos.

Timor Domini sanctus; permanet in sæculum sæculi : judicia Domini vera, justificata in semetipsa.

Desiderabilia super aurum et lapidem pretiosum multum : et dulciora super mel et favum.

Etenim servus tuus custodit ea : in custodiendis illis retributio multa.

Delicta quis intelligit? ab occultis meis munda me : et ab alienis parce servo tuo.

Si mei non fuerint dominati, tunc immaculatus ero : et emundabor a delicto maximo.

Et erunt ut complaceant eloquia oris mei : et meditatio cordis mei in conspectu tuo semper.

Domine adjutor meus : et redemptor meus.

Gloria Patri.   Sicut erat.

PSALMUS XXIV.

De illorum innocentiâ, qui cœlum petituri sunt : et de Christi resurrectione.

DOMINI est terra, et plenitudo ejus : orbis terrarum, et universi qui habitant in eo.

Quia ipse super maria fundavit eum : et super flumina præparavit eum.

Quis ascendet in montem Domini? aut quis stabit in loco sancto ejus?

Innocens manibus et mundo corde ; qui non accepit in vano animam suam : nec juravit in dolo proximo suo.

Hic accipiet benedictionem a Domino : et misericordiam a Deo salutari suo.

Hæc est generatio quærentium eum : quærentium faciem Dei Jacob.

Attollite portas principes vestras, et elevamini portæ æternales : et introibit rex gloriæ.

Quis est iste rex gloriæ ? Dominus fortis et potens, Dominus potens in prœlio.

Attollite portas principes vestras, et elevamini portæ æternales : et introibit rex gloriæ.

Quis est iste rex gloriæ ? Dominus virtutum, ipse est rex gloriæ.

Gloria Patri. Sicut erat.

Antiphona. Salvare in perpetuum potest Christus accedentes per semetipsum ad Deum : semper vivens ad interpellandum pro nobis. Heb. vii. 25.

℣. In ipsum cœlum introivit Jesus.

℟. Ut appareat nunc vultui Dei pro nobis.

Deinde a Lectore solo.

PATER noster, qui es in cœlis : Sanctificetur nomen tuum. Adveniat regnum tuum. Fiat·voluntas tua, sicut in cœlo, et in terrâ. Panem nostrum quotidianum da nobis hodie. Et dimitte nobis debita nostra, sicut et nos dimittimus debitoribus nostris.

Et ne nos inducas in tentationem.

Sed libera nos a malo.

Benedictio. Benedictione perpetuâ benedicat nos Pater æternus.

℟. Amen.

LECTIO PRIMA. Isa. xi. 1.

EGREDIETUR virga de radice Jesse, et flos de radice ejus ascendet. Et requiescet super eum Spiritus Domini; spiritus sapientiæ, et intellectûs, spiritus consilii et fortitudinis, spiritus scientiæ, et pietatis; et replebit eum spiritus timoris Domini. Non secundum visionem oculorum judicebit, neque secundum auditum aurium arguet, sed judicabit in justitiâ pauperes, et arguet in æquitate pro mansuetis terræ. Et percutiet terram virgâ oris sui, et spiritu labiorum suorum interficiet impium : et erit justitia cingulum lumborum ejus, et fides cinctorium renum ejus. Hæc dicit Dominus Deus, Convertimini ad me, et salvi eritis.

Benedictio. Unigenitus Dei Filius nos benedicere et adjuvare dignetur.
R⁄. Amen.

LECTIO SECUNDA. Luc. i. 26.

MISSUS est Angelus Gabriel a Deo in civitatem Galilææ, cui nomen Nazareth, ad virginem desponsatam viro, cui nomen erat Joseph, de domo David, et nomen virginis Maria. Et ingressus Angelus ad eam, dixit : Ave gratiâ plena; Dominus tecum, benedicta tu in mulieribus. Quæ quum audîsset, turbata est in sermone ejus, et cogitabat qualis esset ista salutatio. Et ait Angelus ei, Ne timeas Maria, invenisti enim gratiam apud Deum : ecce concipies in utero, et paries filium, et vocabis nomen ejus Jesum. Hic erit magnus, et Filius Altissimi vocabitur, et dabit illi Dominus Deus sedem David, patris ejus, et regnabit in domo Jacob in æternum, et regni ejus non erit finis. Hæc dicit Dominus Deus, Convertimini ad me, et salvi eritis.

AD MATUTINUM.

Benedictio. Spiritûs Sancti gratia illuminet sensus et corda nostra.

℟. Amen.

LECTIO TERTIA.

DIXIT autem Maria ad Angelum, Quomodo fiet istud, quoniam virum non cognosco? Et respondens Angelus dixit ei: Spiritus Sanctus superveniet in te, et virtus Altissimi obumbrabit tibi. Ideoque et quod nascetur ex te Sanctum, vocabitur Filius Dei. Et ecce Elisabeth cognata tua, et ipsa concepit filium in senectute suâ: et hic mensis sextus est illi, quæ vocatur sterilis: quia non erit impossibile apud Deum omne verbum. Dixit autem Maria: Ecce ancilla Domini, fiat mihi secundum verbum tuum. HÆC DICIT DOMINUS DEUS, CONVERTIMINI AD ME, ET SALVI ERITIS.

HYMNUS SS. AMBROSII ET AUGUSTINI.

Laus Dei Patris et Filii et Spiritûs Sancti.

TE Deum laudamus : te Dominum confitemur.
  Te æternum Patrem : omnis terra veneratur.
  Tibi omnes Angeli : tibi cœli et universæ potestates.
  Tibi Cherubin et Seraphin, incessabili voce proclamant:
  Sanctus, Sanctus, Sanctus : Dominus, Deus Sabaoth.
  Pleni sunt cœli et terra : majestatis gloriæ tuæ.
  Te gloriosus Apostolorum chorus,
  Te Prophetarum laudabilis numerus,
  Te Martyrum candidatus : laudat exercitus.

Te per orbem terrarum : sancta confitetur Ecclesia.

Patrem immensæ majestatis.

Venerandum tuum, verum et unicum Filium.

Sanctum quoque Paraclitum Spiritum.

Tu Rex gloriæ, Christe.

Tu Patris sempiternus es Filius.

Tu ad liberandum suscepturus hominem : non horruisti Virginis uterum.

Tu devicto mortis aculeo : aperuisti credentibus regna cœlorum.

Tu ad dexteram Dei sedes : in gloriâ Patris.

Judex crederis esse venturus.

Te ergo quæsumus, famulis tuis subveni : quos pretioso sanguine redemisti.

Æternâ fac cum Sanctis tuis : in gloriâ numerari.

Salvum fac populum tuum, Domine : et benedic hæreditati tuæ.

Et rege eos et extolle illos usque in æternum.

Per singulos dies, benedicimus te.

Et laudamus nomen tuum in sæculum : et in sæculum sæculi.

Dignare, Domine, die isto : sine peccato nos custodire.

Miserere nostri, Domine : miserere nostri.

Fiat misericordia tua, Domine, super nos : quemadmodum speravimus in te.

In te, Domine, speravi : non confundar in æternum.

℣. Misericordiâ tuâ, Domine, plena est terra.

℞. Justificationes tuas doce me.

Ad Laudes.

℣. Deus, in adjutorium meum intende.

℟. Domine, ad adjuvandum me festina.

Gloria Patri, et Filio : et Spiritui Sancto.

Sicut erat in principio, et nunc, et semper : et in sæcula sæculorum. Amen.

ALLELUIA.

Antiphona. Ecce oculi Domini.

PSALMUS LXVII.

Oratio ad impetrandam gratiam et scientiam Dei, ut laus ejus per totum orbem divulgetur.

DEUS misereatur nostri, et benedicat nobis : illuminet vultum suum super nos, et misereatur nostri.

Ut cognoscamus in terrâ viam tuam : in omnibus gentibus salutare tuum.

Confiteantur tibi populi, Deus : confiteantur tibi populi omnes.

Lætentur et exsultent gentes, quoniam judicas populos in æquitate : et gentes in terrâ dirigis.

Confiteantur tibi populi, Deus, confiteantur tibi populi omnes : terra dedit fructum suum.

Benedicat nos Deus, Deus noster; benedicat nos Deus : et metuant eum omnes fines terræ.

Gloria Patri. Sicut erat.

CANTICUM TRIUM PUERORUM

Qui in fornace perambulantes Deum magnificabant.

Dan. iii. 57.

BENEDICITE, omnia opera Domini, Domino : laudate et superexaltate eum in sæcula.

Benedicite, angeli Domini, Domino : benedicite cœli Domino.

Benedicite, aquæ omnes, quæ super cœlos sunt, Domino : benedicite, omnes virtutes Domini, Domino.

Benedicite, sol et luna, Domino : benedicite, stellæ cœli, Domino.

Benedicite, omnis imber et ros, Domino : benedicite, omnes spiritus Dei, Domino.

Benedicite, ignis et æstus, Domino : benedicite, frigus et æstas, Domino.

Benedicite, rores et pruina, Domino : benedicite, gelu et frigus, Domino.

Benedicite, glacies et nives, Domino : benedicite, noctes et dies, Domino.

Benedicite, lux et ténebræ, Domino : benedicite, fulgura et nubes, Domino.

Benedicat terra Dominum : laudet et superexaltet eum in sæcula.

Benedicite, montes et colles, Domino : benedicite, universa germinantia in terrâ Domino.

Benedicite, fontes, Domino : benedicite, maria et flumina, Domino.

Benedicite, cete et omnia quæ moventur in aquis, Domino : benedicite, omnes volucres cœli, Domino.

Benedicite omnes bestiæ et pecora, Domino : benedicite, filii hominum, Domino.

Benedicat Israel Dominum : laudet et superexaltet eum in sæcula.

Benedicite, sacerdotes Domini, Domino : benedicite, servi Domini, Domino.

Benedicite, spiritus et animæ justorum, Domino : benedicite, sancti et humiles corde, Domino.

Benedicite, Anania, Azaria, Misael, Domino : laudate et superexaltate eum in sæcula.

Benedicamus Patrem et Filium cum Sancto Spiritu : laudemus et superexaltemus eum in sæcula.

Benedictus es, Domine, in firmamento cœli : et laudabilis, et gloriosus, et superexaltatus in sæcula.

PSALMUS CXLVIII.

Omnes creaturæ ad Dei laudem excitantur.

LAUDATE Dominum de cœlis : laudate eum in excelsis.

Laudate eum, omnes angeli ejus : laudate eum, omnes virtutes ejus.

Laudate eum, sol et luna : laudate eum, omnes stellæ et lumen.

Laudate eum, cœli cœlorum : et aquæ omnes, quæ super cœlos sunt, laudent nomen Domini.

Quia ipse dixit, et facta sunt : ipse mandavit, et creata sunt.

Statuit ea in æternum, et in sæculum sæculi : præceptum posuit, et non præteribit.

Laudate Dominum de terra : dracones, et omnes abyssi.

Ignis, grando, nix, glacies, spiritus procellarum : quæ faciunt verbum ejus.

Montes, et omnes colles : ligna fructifera, et omnes cedri.

Bestiæ, et universa pecora : serpentes, et volucres pennatæ :

AD LAUDES.

Reges terræ, et omnes populi : principes et omnes judices terræ.

Juvenes et virgines, senes cum junioribus laudent nomen Domini : quia exaltatum est nomen ejus solius.

Confessio ejus super cœlum et terram : et exaltavit cornu populi sui.

Hymnus omnibus sanctis ejus : filiis Israël, populo appropinquanti sibi. **Alleluia.**

Gloria Patri. Sicut erat.

Antiphona. Ecce oculi Domini super metuentes eum; et in eis, qui sperant super misericordia ejus, ut eruat a morte animas eorum, et alat eos in fame. Ps. xxxiii. 17.

CAPITULUM. Jer. ix. 23.

HÆC dicit Dominus; Non glorietur sapiens in sapientiâ suâ, et non glorietur fortis in fortitudine suâ, et non glorietur dives in divitiis suis : sed in hoc glorietur, qui gloriatur, scire et nosse me, quia ego sum Dominus, qui facio misericordiam, et judicium, et justitiam in terrâ.

℞. Deo gratias.

HYMNUS.

ALES dieï nuncius
Lucem propinquam præcinit :
Nos excitator mentium
Jam Christus ad vitam vocat.

Jesum ciamus vocibus
Flentes, precantes, sobrii :
Intenta supplicatio
Dormire cor mundum vetat.

Tu, Christe, somnum discute ;
Tu rumpe noctis vincula ;
Tu solve peccatum vetus,
Novumque lumen ingere. Amen.

℣. Sit nomen Domini benedictum.

℟. Ex hoc nunc et usque in sæculum.

𝔄ntiphona. Benignitas et humanitas.

CANTICUM ZACHARIÆ.
Gratiarum actio ob præstitum Dei promissum.

BENEDICTUS Dominus Deus Israel : quia visitavit, et fecit redemptionem plebis suæ ;

Et erexit cornu salutis nobis : in domo David pueri sui ;

Sicut locutus est per os sanctorum : qui a sæculo sunt, Prophetarum ejus ;

Salutem ex inimicis nostris : et de manu omnium qui oderunt nos ;

Ad faciendam misericordiam cum patribus nostris : et memorari Testamenti sui sancti ;

Jusjurandum quod juravit ad Abraham patrem nostrum : daturum se nobis ;

Ut sine timore, de manu inimicorum nostrorum liberati : serviamus illi ;

In sanctitate et justitia coram ipso : omnibus diebus nostris.

Et tu, puer, Propheta Altissimi vocaberis : præibis enim ante faciem Domini parare vias ejus ;

Ad dandam scientiam salutis plebi ejus : in remissionem peccatorum eorum.

Per viscera misericordiæ Dei nostri : in quibus visitavit nos oriens ex alto ;

Illuminare his qui in tenebris et in umbrâ mortis sedent : ad dirigendos pedes nostros in viam pacis.

Gloria Patri, et Filio : et Spiritui Sancto ;

Sicut erat in principio, et nunc, et semper : et in sæcula sæculorum. Amen.

Antiphona. Benignitas et humanitas apparuit Salvatoris nostri Dei; non ex operibus justitiæ quæ fecimus nos, sed secundum suam misericordiam salvos nos fecit, per lavacrum regenerationis et renovationis Spiritûs Sancti, quem effudit in nos abunde per Jesum Christum Salvatorem nostrum, ut justificati gratiâ ipsius, hæredes simus secundum spem vitæ æternæ.

Tit. iii. 4.

℣. Ostende nobis, Domine, misericordiam tuam.

℟. Et salutare tuum da nobis.

Oremus.

¶ *Hic dicatur* ORATIO DE DIE, *genibus flexis, deinde sequentia.*

CONCEDE nos famulos tuos, quæsumus, Domine Deus, perpetuâ mentis et corporis salute gaudere, et a præsenti liberari tristitiâ, et æternâ perfrui lætitiâ; per Christum Dominum nostrum. Amen.

℣. Benedicamus Domino.

℟. Deo gratias.

¶ *Deinde fiant hæ sequentes Commemorationes, una vel plures, secundum occasionem; cum Benedictione et Oratione Dominicâ in fine, p. xxi.*

Commemorationes.

I.

DE SANCTO SPIRITU.

Ant. Veni, Sancte Spiritus, reple tuorum corda fidelium, et tui amoris in eis ignem accende.

℣. Emittes Spiritum tuum, et creabuntur.

℟. Et renovabis faciem terræ.

Oremus.

DEUS, qui corda fidelium, Sancti Spiritûs illustratione, docuisti; da nobis in eodem Spiritu recta sapere, et de ejus semper sanctâ consolatione gaudere; per Christum Dominum nostrum. Amen.

II.

DE SANCTISSIMA TRINITATE.

Ant. Libera nos, salva nos, justifica nos, O Beata Trinitas.

℣. Benedicamus Patrem, et Filium, et Spiritum Sanctum.

℟. Laudemus et superexaltemus eum in sæcula.

AD LAUDES.

Oremus.

OMNIPOTENS, sempiterne Deus, qui dedisti nobis famulis tuis, in confessione veræ fidei, æternæ Trinitatis gloriam agnoscere, et in potentiâ divinæ majestatis adorare Unitatem; Quæsumus ut, ejusdem fidei firmitate, ab omnibus semper muniamur adversis, qui vivis et regnas Deus, per omnia sæcula sæculorum. Amen.

II.

PRO SANCTITATE.

Ant. In hoc scimus quoniam cognovimus Deum, si mandata ejus observemus. Qui dicit se nosse eum, et mandata ejus non custodit, mendax est, et in hoc veritas non est. Qui autem servat verbum ejus verè in hoc caritas Dei perfecta est. *1 Joan. iii. 2.*

℣. Doce me facere voluntatem tuam, Domine.

℟. Quia Deus meus es tu.

Oremus.

LARGIRE nobis, quæsumus, Domine, semper spiritum cogitandi quæ recta sunt, propitius, et agendi: ut qui sine te nihil boni agere possumus secundum te vivere te adjuvante valeamus: per Jesum Christum Dominum nostrum. Amen.

IV.

PRO GRATIA.

Ant. Misereator et misericors Dominus: longanimis et multum misericors. Quoniam secundum altitudinem cœli a terrâ : corroboravit misericordiam suam super timentes se. Quantum distat ortus ab occidente, longè fecit a nobis iniquitates nostras. Quomodo miseretur pater filiorum, misertus est Dominus timentibus se.

Ps. ciii. 11.

℣. Exultabit cor meum in salutari tuo, Domine.

℞. Cantabo Domino, qui bona tribuit mihi : et psallam nomini Domini altissimi.

Oremus.

TUA nos, Domine, quæsumus, gratia semper et præveniat et sequatur, ac bonis operibus jugitèr præstet esse intentos ; per Jesum Christum Dominum nostrum.

V.
PRO REGINA.

Ant. Quia fuisti adjutor meus, in velamento alarum tuarum exultabo ; adhæsit anima mea post te : me suscepit dextera tua. Ipsi vero in vanum quæsiverunt animam meam ; introibunt in inferiora terræ : rex vero lætabitur in Deo.

℣. Domine, salvam fac reginam.

℞. Et exaudi nos in die quâ invocaverimus te.

Oremus.

DOMINE, Pater cœlestis, Rex regum et Dominator dominantium, omnium principum gubernator et rector, intimis votis te supplices quæsumus, reginam nostram Victoriam benigno vultu respicias, eique, singulari gratiâ et Spiritu

Sancto, ita semper assistere digneris, et voluntatem tuam ubique exsequatur, et secundum saluberrimam normam mandatorum tuorum omnem vitam transigat. Accumula in illam cœlestia tua dona, ut diu feliciter nobis imperet, hostes fortiter devincat, tandemque tecum in cœlesti gloriâ vivat in æternum: Qui vivis et regnas Deus, per omnia sæcula sæculorum. Amen.

VI.
PRO PACE.

Ant. Da pacem Domine, in diebus nostris, quia non est alius qui pugnet pro nobis, nisi tu solus, Domine.

℣. Fiat pax in virtute tuâ.

℟. Et abundantia in turribus tuis.

Oremus.

DEUS a quo sancta desideria, recta consilia, et justa sunt opera, da servis tuis illam, quam mundus dare non potest, pacem: ut et corda nostra mandatis tuis dedita, et hostium ablatâ formidine, tempora sint tuâ protectione tranquilla: per Christum Dominum nostrum. Amen.

VII.
DE PASSIONE.

Ant. Christus passus est pro nobis, nobis relinquens exemplum, ut sequamur vestigia ipsius: qui peccatum non fecit, neque dolus inventus est in ore ejus. _{1 Pet. ii. 21.}

℣. Adoramus te, Christe, et benedicimus tibi.

℟. Quia ab afflictione mundum redemisti.

Oremus.

DOMINE Jesu Christe, Fili Dei vivi, pone passionem, crucem, et mortem tuam inter Judicium tuum et animas nostras, nunc et in horâ mortis nostræ; et largiri digneris vivis misericordiam et gratiam, defunctis veniam et requiem, Ecclesiæ tuæ Sanctæ pacem et concordiam, et nobis peccatoribus vitam et lætitiam sempiternam: Qui vivis et regnas, cum Deo Patre, in unitate Spiritûs Sancti Deus, per omnia sæcula sæculorum. Amen.

℣. Benedicamus Domino.

℟. Deo gratias.

GLORIOSA et salutaris mors et passio Domini nostri Jesu Christi eruat nos a dolore tristi, et perducat ad gaudia Paradisi.

℟. Amen.

¶ *Deinde dicatur* PATER NOSTER *secreto.*

Ad Primam.

℣. Deus, in adjutorium meum intende.

℟. Domine, ad adjuvandum me festina.

Gloria Patri, et Filio : et Spiritui Sancto.

Sicut erat in principio, et nunc, et semper : et in sæcula sæculorum.   Amen.

ALLELUIA.

Hymnus.

CONSORS paterni luminis,
Lux ipse lucis et Dies,
Christe, qui noctem discutis,
Assiste postulantibus.

Aufer tenebras mentium,
Fuga catervas dæmonum :
Expelle somnolentiam,
Ne pigritantes obruat.

Sic, Christe, nobis omnibus
Indulgeas credentibus ;
Ut prosit exorantibus
Quod præcinentes psallimus.   Amen.

Antiphona.   Beati pauperes spiritu.

PSALMUS CXVIII.

Pii provocantur ad laudem Dei.

CONFITEMINI Domino quoniam bonus : quoniam in sæculum misericordia ejus.

Dicat nunc Israel quoniam bonus : quoniam in sæculum misericordia ejus.

Dicat nunc domus Aaron : quoniam in sæculum misericordia ejus.

Dicant nunc omnes qui timent Dominum : quoniam in sæculum misericordia ejus.

De tribulatione invocavi Dominum : et exaudivit me in latitudine Dominus.

Dominus mihi adjutor : non timebo quid faciat mihi homo.

Dominus mihi adjutor : et ego despiciam inimicos meos.

Bonum est confidere in Domino : quàm confidere in homine :

Bonum est sperare in Domino : quàm sperare in principibus.

Omnes gentes circuierunt me : et in nomine Domini quia ultus sum in eos.

Circumdantes circumdederunt me : et in nomine Domini quia ultus sum in eos.

Circumdederunt me sicut apes, et exarserunt sicut ignis in spinis : et in nomine Domini quia ultus sum in eos.

Impulsus eversus sum ut caderem : et Dominus suscepit me.

Fortitudo mea, et canticum meum Dominus : et factus est mihi in salutem.

Vox exultationis, et salutis : in tabernaculis justorum.

Dextera Domini fecit virtutem : dextera Domini exaltavit me, dextera Domini fecit virtutem.

Non moriar, sed vivam : et narrabo opera Domini.

Castigans castigavit me Dominus : et morti non tradidit me.

Aperite mihi portas justitiæ : et ingressus in eas confitebor Domino.

Hæc porta Domini : justi intrabunt in eam.

Confitebor tibi Domine, quoniam exaudisti me : et factus es mihi in salutem.

Lapidem, quem reprobaverunt ædificantes : hic factus est in caput anguli.

A Domino factum est istud : et est mirabile in oculis nostris.

Hæc est dies, quam fecit Dominus : exultemus, et lætemur in eâ.

O Domine salvum me fac : ô Domine da nunc prosperitatem.

Benedictus qui venit in nomine Domini : benediximus vobis de domo Domini.

Deus Dominus, et illuxit nobis : constituite diem sollennem cum frondibus usque ad cornu altaris.

Deus meus es tu, et confitebor tibi : Deus meus es tu, et exaltabo te.

Confitebor tibi, Domine, quoniam exaudisti me : et factus es mihi in salutem.

Confitemini Domino quoniam bonus : quoniam in sæculum misericordia ejus.

Gloria Patri.   Sicut erat.

Antiphona. Beati pauperes spiritu, quoniam ipsorum est regnum cœlorum : beati qui lugent, quoniam ipsi consolabuntur.   <small>Matth. v. 3.</small>

¶ *Deinde cantetur vel dicatur Symbolum Apostolorum ab omnibus stantibus et in Orientem reverenter conversis.*

CREDO in Deum, Patrem Omnipotentem, Creatorem cœli et terræ.

Et in Jesum Christum Filium ejus unicum, Dominum nostrum : Qui conceptus est de Spiritu Sancto; Natus ex Mariâ Virgine; Passus sub Pontio Pilato; Crucifixus, mortuus et sepultus; Descendit ad inferos; Tertiâ die resurrexit a mortuis; Ascendit ad cœlos; Sedet ad dexteram

AD PRIMAM.

Dei Patris omnipotentis; Inde venturus est judicare vivos et mortuos.

Credo in Spiritum Sanctum; Sanctam Ecclesiam Catholicam; Sanctorum communionem; Remissionem peccatorum; Carnis resurrectionem; Vitam æternam. Amen.

⁋ *Et postea hæ sequentes Preces omnibus religiose genuflexis.*

℣. Domine, exaudi orationem meam.

℟. Et clamor meus ad te veniat.

Oremus.

⁋ *Hic dicatur* ORATIO DE DIE, *genibus flexis, deinde sequentia.*

DOMINE Jesu Christe, spiritu longe pauperrime, qui ob peccata et infidelitatem nostram luxisti: Concede nobis ut similes, hoc est spiritu simus pauperes; atque ut sic peccata nostra lugeamus ut cœlestis regni tui participes esse possimus, Qui vivis et regnas cum Patre et Spiritu Sancto Deus, per omnia sæcula sæculorum. Amen.

℣. Benedicamus Domino.

℟. Deo gratias.

⁋ *Deinde dicatur* PATER NOSTER *secreto.*

Ad Tertiam.

℣. Deus, in adjutorium meum intende.

℟. Domine, ad adjuvandum me festina.

Gloria Patri, et Filio : et Spiritui Sancto,

Sicut erat in principio, et nunc, et semper : et in sæcula sæculorum.   Amen.

ALLELUIA.

HYMNUS.

RECTOR potens, verax Deus,
   Qui temperas rerum vices ;
Splendore mane instruis,
Et ignibus meridiem :

Extingue flammas litium,
Aufer calorem noxium :
Confer salutem corporum,
Veramque pacem cordium.

Os, lingua, mens, sensus, vigor,
Confessionem personet :
Tua nos accendat caritas,
Ad te colendum sedulò.   Amen.

Antiphona.   Beati mites.

PSALMUS CXX.

Oratio ut liberemur a mundi vanitate.

AD Dominum cum tribularer clamavi : et exaudivit me.

AD TERTIAM.

Domine, libera animam meam a labiis iniquis : et a linguâ dolosâ.

Quid detur tibi, aut quid apponatur tibi : ad linguam dolosam?

Sagittæ potentis acutæ : cum carbonibus desolatoriis.

Heu mihi, quia incolatus meus prolongatus est; habitavi cum habitantibus Cedar : multum incola fuit anima mea.

Cum his qui oderunt pacem eram pacificus : cum loquebar illis, impugnabant me gratis.

Gloria Patri. Sicut erat.

𝔄ntíphona. Beati mites : quoniam ipsi possidebunt terram. Beati, qui lugent : quoniam ipsi consolabuntur. Matth. v. 4.

℣. Domine, exaudi orationem meam.

℟. Et clamor meus ad te veniat.

Oremus.

¶ *Hic dicatur* ORATIO DE DIE, *genibus flexis, deinde sequentia.*

DOMINE Jesu Christe, cujus tota vita nihil nisi mansuetudo, quique solus es nostra justitia : Da nobis ut mansueto et humili corde te colamus, et per totam vitam nostram in operibus justitiæ conversemur : Qui vivis et regnas Deus, per omnia sæcula sæculorum. Amen.

℣. Benedicamus Domino.

℟. Deo gratias.

¶ *Deinde dicatur* PATER NOSTER *secreto.*

Ad Sextam.

℣. Deus, in adjutorium meum intende.

℟. Domine, ad adjuvandum me festina.

Gloria Patri, et Filio : et Spiritui Sancto.

Sicut erat in principio, et nunc, et semper : et in sæcula sæculorum.   Amen.

Alleluia.

Hymnus.

RERUM creator omnium,
    Rectorque semper aspice :
Nos, a quiete noxiâ,
Mersos sopore, libera.

Te, Christe sancte, poscimus,
Ignosce tu criminibus ;
Ad confitendum surgimus,
Morasque noctis rumpimus.

Quicquid malorum gessimus,
Occulta nostra pandimus,
Preces gementes fundimus,
Dimitte quod peccavimus.   Amen.

Antiphona.   Beati misericordes.

PSALMUS CXXIII.

Oratio ut liberemur ab impiorum ludibriis.

AD te levavi oculos meos : qui habitas in cœlis.

AD SEXTAM.

Ecce sicut oculi servorum : in manibus dominorum suorum :

Sicut oculi ancillæ in manibus dominæ suæ : ita oculi nostri ad Dominum Deum nostrum, donec misereatur nostri.

Miserere nostri, Domine, miserere nostri : quia multum repleti sumus despectione :

Quia multum repleta est anima nostra, opprobrium abundantibus : et despectio superbis.

Gloria Patri. Sicut erat.

Antiphona. Beati misericordes, quoniam ipsi misericordiam consequentur; beati mundo corde, quoniam ipsi Deum videbunt. _{Matth. v. 7.}

℣. Domine, exaudi orationem meam.

℞. Et clamor meus ad te veniat.

Oremus.

¶ *Hic dicatur* ORATIO DE DIE, *genibus flexis, deinde sequentia.*

DOMINE Jesu Christe, cui proprium est misereri, quique purus ac mundus es absque ullâ peccati maculâ : gratiâ tuâ nos imbue, ut te sequamur, misericordiam proximis nostris prestando, et nunquam non puro ac mundo corde simus erga te, ut, post hanc vitam, te intueamur in æternâ gloriâ : Qui vivis et regnas Deus, per omnia sæcula sæculorum. Amen.

℣. Benedicamus Domino.

℞. Deo gratias.

¶ *Deinde dicatur* PATER NOSTER *secreto.*

Ad Nonam.

℣. Deus, in adjutorium meum intende.

℟. Domine, ad adjuvandum me festina.

Gloria Patri, et Filio : et Spiritui Sancto.

Sicut erat in principio, et nunc, et semper : et in sæcula sæculorum.   Amen.

ALLELUIA.

HYMNUS.

ÆTERNA cœli gloria,
    Beata spes mortalium,
Celsi tonantis unice,
Castæque proles Virginis.

Da dexteram surgentibus,
Exsurgat ut mens sobria,
Flagransque in laudem Dei,
Grates rependat debitas.

Te, Christe, Deum poscimus
Fidem inde nostris sensibus;
Ut, spe futuræ gloriæ,
Amore cor sit fervidum.   Amen.

Antiphona. Beati pacifici.

PSALMUS XV.

Pie viventes ingredientur vitam æternam.

DOMINE, quis habitabit in tabernaculo tuo : aut quis requiescet in monte sancto tuo?

AD NONAM.

Qui ingreditur sine maculâ : et operatur justitiam.

Qui loquitur veritatem in corde suo : qui non egit dolum in linguâ suâ.

Nec fecit proximo suo malum : et opprobrium non accepit adversus proximos suos.

Ad nihilum deductus est in conspectu ejus malignus : timentes autem Dominum glorificat :

Qui jurat proximo suo, et non decipit : qui pecuniam suam non dedit ad usuram, et munera super innocentem non accepit.

Qui facit hæc : non movebitur in æternum.

Gloria Patri. Sicut erat.

Antiphona. Beati pacifici, quoniam hi filii Dei vocabuntur : beati qui persecutionem patientur propter justitiam, quoniam ipsorum est regnum cœlorum. _{Matth. v. 9.}

℣. Domine exaudi orationem meam.

℟. Et clamor meus ad te veniat.

Oremus.

¶ *Hic dicatur* ORATIO DE DIE, *genibus flexis, deinde sequentia.*

DOMINE Jesu Christe, qui pacem conciliasti inter Deum Patrem et nos miseros peccatores, nihilo seciùs tamen injurias et afflictiones pertulisti : Concede nobis gratiam tuam, ut pacem per te factam custodiamus, patienterque injurias omnes et persecutiones patiamur, ut filii tui vocemur, et cœlestis regni tui hæredes simus; Qui vivis et regnas Deus, per omnia sæcula sæculorum. Amen.

℣. Benedicamus Domino.

℟. Deo gratias.

¶ *Deinde dicatur* PATER NOSTER *secreto.*

Ad Vesperas.

℣. Deus, in adjutorium meum intende.

℟. Domine, ad adjuvandum me festina.

Gloria Patri, et Filio : et Spiritui Sancto.

Sicut erat in principio, et nunc, et semper : et in sæcula sæculorum. Amen.

ALLELUIA.

Antiphona. Mandatum novum.

PSALMUS CXIII.

Hic instigamur ad laudandum et glorificandum Deum.

LAUDATE pueri Dominum : laudate nomen Domini.

Sit nomen Domini benedictum : ex hoc nunc et usque in sæculum.

A solis ortu usque ad occasum : laudabile nomen Domini.

Excelsus super omnes gentes Dominus : et super cœlos gloria ejus.

Quis sicut Dominus Deus noster, qui in altis habitat : et humilia respicit in cœlo et in terrâ?

Suscitans a terrâ inopem : et de stercore erigens pauperem :

Ut collocet eum cum principibus : cum principibus populi sui.

Qui habitare facit sterilem in domo : matrem filiorum lætantem.

Gloria Patri. Sicut erat.

PSALMUS CXXXV.
Laudandus Deus ob admiranda opera et beneficia.

LAUDATE nomen Domini : laudate servi Dominum,

Qui statis in domo Domini : in atriis domûs Dei nostri.

Laudate Dominum, quia bonus Dominus : psallite nomini ejus, quoniam suave.

Quoniam Jacob elegit sibi Dominus : Israël in possessionem sibi.

Quia ego cognovi quod magnus est Dominus : et Deus noster præ omnibus diis.

Omnia quæcumque voluit, Dominus fecit in cœlo, in terrâ : in mari, et in omnibus abyssis.

Educens nubes ab extremo terræ : fulgura in pluviam fecit.

Qui producit ventos de thesauris suis : qui percussit primogenita Ægypti, ab homine usque ad pecus.

Et misit signa et prodigia in medio tui, Ægypte : in Pharaonem et in omnes servos ejus.

Qui percussit gentes multas : et occidit reges fortes.

Sehon regem Amorrhæorum, et Og regem Basan : et omnia regna Chanaan.

Et dedit terram eorum hæreditatem : hæreditatem Israël populo suo.

Domine, nomen tuum in æternum : Domine, memoriale tuum in generationem et generationem.

Quia judicabit Dominus populum suum : et in servis suis deprecabitur.

Simulacra gentium argentum et aurum : opera manuum hominum.

Os habent, et non loquentur : oculos habent, et non videbunt.

Aures habent, et non audient : neque enim est spiritus in ore ipsorum.

Similes illis fiant qui faciunt ea : et omnes qui confidunt in eis.

Domus Israël, benedicite Domino : domus Aaron, benedicite Domino.

Domus Levi, benedicite Domino : qui timetis Dominum, benedicite Domino.

Benedictus Dominus ex Sion : qui habitat in Hierusalem.

Gloria Patri. Sicut erat.

PSALMUS CXXXVIII.

Laus Dei simul et gratiarum actio.

CONFITEBOR tibi, Domine, in toto corde meo : quoniam audisti verba oris mei.

In conspectu angelorum psallam tibi : adorabo ad templum sanctum tuum, et confitebor nomini tuo.

Super misericordiâ tuâ et veritate tuâ : quoniam magnificasti super omne nomen sanctum tuum.

In quâcumque die invocavero te, exaudi me : multiplicabis in animâ meâ virtutem.

Confiteantur tibi, Domine, omnes reges terræ : quia audierunt omnia verba oris tui.

Et cantent in viis Domini : quoniam magna est gloria Domini.

Quoniam excelsus Dominus, et humilia respicit : et alta a longe cognoscit.

Si ambulavero in medio tribulationis, vivificabis me : et super iram inimicorum meorum extendisti manum tuam, et salvum me facit dextera tua.

Dominus retribuet pro me; Domine, misericordia tua in sæculum : opera manuum tuarum ne despicias.

Gloria Patri. Sicut erat.

𝔄ntiphona. Mandatum novum do vobis, ut diligatis invicem, sicut ego dilexi vos : in hoc cognoscent omnes, quia discipuli mei estis, si dilectionem habueritis ad invicem. Joan. xiii. 34.

CAPITULUM. Isa. lxvi. lv.

LÆTAMINI cum Jerusalem et exultate in eâ, omnes qui diligitis eam, gaudete cum eâ gaudio universi qui eugetis super eam, ut repleamini ab ubere consolationis ejus. Omnes sitientes venite ad aquas, et qui non habetis argentum, properate, emite et comedite : venite, emite, absque argento et absque ullâ commutatione, vinum et lac.

℞. Deo gratias.

HYMNUS.

SALVATOR mundi, Domine,
Qui nos salvasti hodie,
In hac nocte nos protege,
Et salva omni tempore.

Adesto nunc propitius,
Et parce supplicantibus;
Tu dele nostra crimina,
Tu tenebras illumina.

Ne mentem somnus opprimat,
Nec hostis nos surripiat;
Nec ullis caro, petimus,
Commaculetur sordibus.

Te, reformator sensuum,
Votis precamur cordium,
Ut puri, castis mentibus,
Surgamus a cubilibus. Amen.

℣. Cor mundum crea in me, Deus.

℟. Et spiritum rectum innova in visceribus meis.

Antiphona. Si Deus pro nobis.

CANTICUM MARIÆ. Luc. i. 46.
Exultantis et laudantis bonitatem Dei.

MAGNIFICAT : anima mea Dominum.

Et exultavit spiritus meus : in Deo salutari meo.

Quia respexit humilitatem ancillæ suæ : ecce enim ex hoc beatam me dicent omnes generationes.

Quia fecit mihi magna qui potens est : et sanctum nomen ejus.

Et misericordia ejus a progenie in progenies : timentibus eum.

Fecit potentiam in brachio suo : dispersit superbos mente cordis sui.

Deposuit potentes de sede : et exaltavit humiles.

Esurientes implevit bonis : et divites dimisit inanes.

Suscepit Israel puerum suum : recordatus misericordiæ suæ.

Sicut locutus est ad patres nostros : Abraham et semini ejus in sæcula.

Gloria Patri, et Filio : et Spiritui Sancto;

Sicut erat in principio, et nunc, et semper : et in sæcula sæculorum. Amen.

Antiphona. Si Deus pro nobis, quis contra nos? Qui enim proprio Filio suo non pepercit, sed pro nobis omnibus tradidit illum : quomodo non etiam cum illo omnia nobis donabit?

Rom. viii. 31, 32.

AD VESPERAS.

℣. Domine, exaudi orationem meam.

℞. Et clamor meus ad te veniat.

Oremus.

¶ *Hic dicatur* ORATIO DE DIE, *genibus flexis, deinde sequentia.*

OMNIPOTENS Domine Deus, ex cujus ordine et voluntate jam nox et tenebræ appetunt, tuam clementiam deprecamur, ut nos misericorditer in tutelam tuam accipias, ne in nos principes tenebrarum aliquid potestatis habeant; et quum dormiendum pro corporis necessitate sit, nihilominùs cor et animus noster ad te semper vigilent; et effice ne in conspectu tuo filii noctis et tenebrarum, sed diei et lucis inveniamur; qui vivis et regnas Deus, per omnia sæcula sæculorum. Amen.

℣. Benedicamus Domino.

℞. Deo gratias.

¶ *Fiant hic, si tempus requirat, nonnullæ ex Commemorationibus, ut supra in* LAUDIBUS, *p. xvii.; modo in fine officii fiat hæc Commemoratio de Passione, ut ibi habetur.*

COMMEMORATIO DE PASSIONE.

𝔄ntiphona. Christus passus est pro nobis, nobis relinquens exemplum, ut sequamur vestigia ipsius: qui peccatum non fecit, neque dolus inventus est in ore ejus. 1 Pet. ii. 21.

℣. Adoramus te, Christe, et benedicimus tibi.

℞. Quia ab afflictione mundum redemisti.

AD VESPERAS.

Oremus.

DOMINE Jesu Christe, Fili Dei vivi, pone passionem, crucem, et mortem tuam inter Judicium tuum et animas nostras, nunc et in horâ mortis nostræ; et largiri digneris vivis misericordiam et gratiam, defunctis veniam et requiem, Ecclesiæ tuæ Sanctæ pacem et concordiam, et nobis peccatoribus vitam et lætitiam sempiternam: Qui vivis et regnas, cum Deo Patre, in unitate Spiritûs Sancti Deus, per omnia sæcula sæculorum. Amen.

℣. Benedicamus Domino.

℟. Deo gratias.

GLORIOSA et salutaris mors et passio Domini nostri Jesu Christi eruat nos a dolore tristi, et perducat ad gaudia Paradisi.

℟. Amen.

⁋ *Deinde dicatur* PATER NOSTER *secreto.*

Ad Completorium.

℣. Converte nos, Deus salutaris noster.

℟. Et averte iram tuam a nobis.

℣. Deus, in adjutorium meum intende.

℟. Domine, ad adjuvandum me festina.

Gloria Patri, et Filio : et Spiritui Sancto.

Sicut erat in principio, et nunc, et semper : et in sæcula sæculorum. Amen.

ALLELUIA.

Antiphona. Salva nos.

PSALMUS XIII.

Oratio contra tentationem.

USQUEQUO Domine obliviscéris me in finem : Usquequo avertis faciem tuam a me?

Quamdiu ponam consilia in animâ meâ : dolorem in corde meo per diem.

Usquequo exaltabitur inimicus meus super me : respice, et exaudi me Domine Deus meus.

Illumina oculos meos, ne unquam obdormiam in morte : nequando dicat inimicus meus, Prævalui adversus eum.

Qui tribulant me, exultabunt si motus fuero : ego autem in misericordiâ tuâ speravi.

Exultabit cor meum in salutari tuo ; cantabo

Domino, qui bona tribuit mihi : et psallam nomini Domini altissimi.

Gloria Patri. Sicut erat.

PSALMUS XLIII.

Oratio ut liberemur ab hostibus ad cantandum laudem Dei.

JUDICA me, Deus, et discerne causam meam de gente non sanctâ : ab homine iniquo et doloso erue me.

Quia tu es Deus fortitudo mea, quare me repulisti : et quare tristis incedo, dum affligit me inimicus?

Emitte lucem tuam et veritatem tuam : ipsa me deduxerunt, et adduxerunt in montem sanctum tuum, et in tabernacula tua.

Et introibo ad altare Dei : ad Deum, qui lætificat juventutem meam.

Confitebor tibi in citharâ, Deus, Deus meus : quare tristis es, anima mea : et quare conturbas me?

Spera in Deo, quoniam adhuc confitebor illi : salutare vultûs mei, et Deus meus.

Gloria Patri. Sicut erat.

Antiphona. Salva nos, Domine, vigilantes, custodi nos dormientes; ut vigilemus in Christo, et requiescamus in pace.

CAPITULUM. Jer. xiv. 9.

TU in nobis es, Domine, et nomen sanctum tuum invocatum est super nos : ne derelinquas nos, Domine, Deus noster.

℞. Deo gratias.

HYMNUS.

RERUM Creator omnium,
Te poscimus hoc vesperi,

Defende nos per gratiam
Ab hostis nostri fraudibus.

Nullo ludamur, Domine,
Vel somnio vel phasmate:
In te cor nostrum vigilet,
Nec dormiat in crimine.

Summe Pater, per Filium
Largire quod te poscimus:
Cui per Sanctum Spiritum
Æterna detur Gloria. Amen.

℣. Qui habitat in adjutorio altissimi.

℞. In protectione Dei cœli commorabitur.

Antiphona. Lucem tuam.

CANTICUM SIMEONIS JUSTI.

NUNC dimittis servum tuum, Domine: secundum verbum tuum in pace.

Quia viderunt oculi mei: salutare tuum.

Quod parâsti: ante faciem omnium populorum.

Lumen ad revelationem gentium: et gloriam plebis tuæ Israel.

Gloria Patri, et Filio: et Spiritui Sancto.

Sicut erat in principio, et nunc, et semper: et in sæcula sæculorum. Amen.

Antiphona. Lucem tuam, Domine, nobis concede; ut, depulsis cordium tenebris, pervenire possimus ad lumen quod est Christus.

¶ *Deinde cantetur vel dicatur Symbolum Apostolorum ab omnibus stantibus et in Orientem reverenter conversis.*

CREDO in Deum, Patrem Omnipotentem, Creatorem cœli et terræ:

Et in Jesum Christum, Filium ejus unicum, Dominum nostrum: Qui conceptus est de Spiritu Sancto; Natus ex Mariâ Virgine; Passus sub Pontio Pilato; Crucifixus, mortuus, et sepultus; Descendit ad inferos: Tertiâ die resurrexit a mortuis; Ascendit ad cœlos; Sedet ad dexteram Dei Patris Omnipotentis: Inde venturus est judicare vivos et mortuos.

Credo in Spiritum Sanctum; Sanctam Ecclesiam Catholicam; Sanctorum Communionem; Remissionem peccatorum; Carnis Resurrectionem; Vitam æternam. Amen.

¶ *Et postea, hæ sequentes Preces, omnibus religiose genuflexis.*

℣. Domine, exaudi orationem meam.

℞. Et clamor meus ad te veniat.

Oremus.

¶ *Hic dicatur* ORATIO DE DIE, *deinde sequentia.*

ILLUMINA quæsumus, Domine Deus, tenebras nostras, et totius noctis insidias tu a nobis repelle propitius; propter caritatem Filii tui unigeniti, Jesu Christi, Servatoris nostri. Amen.

Aut hoc.

DOMINE Jesu Christe, Redemptor mundi, æternum Patris verbum, per quem omnia creata sunt et conservantur, oramus te ut sub umbrâ misericordiæ tuæ nos per hanc noctem accipias, nec sinas nos cadere, neque Satanæ terroribus consternari. Effice ut lumen in tenebris videamus, qui es lux æterna, et cum cœlesti Patre et Sancto Spiritu vivis et regnas Deus per omnia sæcula sæculorum. Amen.

℣. Benedicamus Domino.

℟. Deo gratias.

GRATIA Domini nostri Jesu Christi, caritas Dei, communicatio Sancti Spiritûs sit semper cum omnibus.

℟. Amen.

¶ *Deinde dicatur* Pater Noster *secreto.*

SEPTEM PSALMI PŒNITENTIALES.

Una cum succinctis orationibus, Psalmi uniuscujusque summam breviter complectentibus.

Antiphona. Ne reminiscaris.

I. DOMINICÂ.

PSALMUS VI.

Peccator morbum curari, ac hostes prosterni optat.

DOMINE, ne in furore tuo arguas me : neque in irâ tuâ corripias me.

Miserere mei, Domine, quoniam infirmus sum : sana me, Domine, quoniam conturbata sunt ossa mea.

Et anima mea turbata est valde : sed tu, Domine, usquequo?

Convertere, Domine, et eripe animam meam : salvum me fac propter misericordiam tuam.

Quoniam non est in morte qui memor sit tui : in inferno autem quis confitebitur tibi?

Laboravi in gemitu meo, lavabo per singulas noctes lectum meum : lacrymis meis stratum meum rigabo.

Turbatus est a furore oculus meus : inveteravi inter omnes inimicos meos.

Discedite a me omnes qui operamini iniquitatem : quoniam exaudivit Dominus vocem fletûs mei.

Exaudivit Dominus deprecationem meam : Dominus orationem meam suscepit.

Erubescant et conturbentur vehementer omnes inimici mei : convertantur et erubescant valde velociter.

Gloria Patri. Sicut erat.

ORATIO.

DOMINE, qui in terribili et tremendâ majestate tuâ genus humanum judicaturus advenies, miserere nobis miserrimis peccatoribus in hac vitâ, ne in die iræ, furoris, et vindictæ, ad æterna supplicia condemnemur. Dignare etiam te de rigore justitiæ ad dulcorem misericordiæ convertere, ut et de potestate tenebrarum animas nostras eripias, atque in omnibus infirmitatibus et gemitibus nostris tuâ semper gratiâ muniamur; Per Christum Dominum nostrum. *Amen.*

II. FERIÂ SECUNDÂ.

PSALMUS XXXII.

Quomodo lugenda peccata, orandus Deus, et in ipso exultandum.

BEATI quorum remissæ sunt iniquitates : et quorum tecta sunt peccata.

Beatus vir cui non imputavit Dominus peccatum : nec est in spiritu ejus dolus.

Quoniam tacui, inveteraverunt ossa mea : dum clamarem totâ die.

Quoniam die ac nocte gravata est super me manus tua : conversus sum in ærumnâ meâ, dum configitur spina.

Delictum meum cognitum tibi feci : et injustitiam meam non abscondi.

Dixi, Confitebor adversum me injustitiam meam Domino : et tu remisisti impietatem peccati mei.

Pro hac orabit ad te omnis sanctus : in tempore opportuno.

Verumtamen in diluvio aquarum multarum : ad eum non approximabunt.

Tu es refugium meum a tribulatione quæ circumdedit me : exultatio mea, erue me a circumdantibus me.

Intellectum tibi dabo, et instruam te in viâ hac quâ gradieris : firmabo super te oculos meos.

Nolite fieri sicut equus et mulus : quibus non est intellectus.

In camo et freno maxillas eorum constringe : qui non approximant ad te.

Multa flagella peccatoris : sperantem autem in Domino misericordia circumdabit.

Lætamini in Domino, et exultate, justi : et gloriamini omnes recti corde.

Gloria Patri.   Sicut erat.

ORATIO.

QUÆSUMUS, Domine, intellectum sapientiæ tuæ divinæ nobis tribuere digneris : nosque in viâ hac peregrinationis nostræ, armis justitiæ tam benignè instrue, figendo in nos oculos gratiæ et misericordiæ tuæ qui confitemur injustitias nostras : ut, obtectis per veniam et clementiam tuam peccatis, nec imputatis ultrà delictis, sic justificati unà cum sanctis et electis tuis in omnem æternitatem exultemus : Per Christum Dominum nostrum.   *Amen.*

III. FERIÂ TERTIÂ.

PSALMUS XXXVIII.

Peccator, peccatorum pondere pressus, implorat opem Dei; cujus misericordiæ sese committit.

Domine, ne in furore tuo arguas me : neque in irâ tuâ corripias me.

Quoniam sagittæ tuæ infixæ sunt mihi : et confirmasti super me manum tuam.

Non est sanitas in carne meâ a facie iræ tuæ : non est pax ossibus meis a facie peccatorum meorum.

Quoniam iniquitates meæ supergressæ sunt caput meum : et sicut onus grave gravatæ sunt super me.

Putruerunt et corruptæ sunt cicatrices meæ : a facie insipientiæ meæ.

Miser factus sum et curvatus sum usque in finem : totâ die contristatus ingrediebar.

Quoniam lumbi mei impleti sunt illusionibus : et non est sanitas in carne meâ.

Afflictus sum et humiliatus sum nimis : rugiebam a gemitu cordis mei.

Domine, ante te omne desiderium meum : et gemitus meus a te non est absconditus.

Cor meum conturbatum est, dereliquit me virtus mea : et lumen oculorum meorum, et ipsum non est mecum.

Amici mei et proximi mei : adversum me appropinquaverunt, et steterunt.

Et qui juxta me erant, de longe steterunt : et vim faciebant qui quærebant animam meam.

Et qui inquirebant mala mihi locuti sunt vanitates : et dolos totâ die meditabantur.

Ego autem tanquam surdus non audiebam : et sicut mutus non aperiens os suum.

Et factus sum sicut homo non audiens : et non habens in ore suo redargutiones.

Quoniam in te, Domine, speravi : tu exaudies me, Domine Deus meus.

Quia dixi, Nequando supergaudeant mihi inimici mei : et dum commoventur pedes mei, super me magna locuti sunt.

Quoniam ego in flagella paratus sum : et dolor meus in conspectu meo semper.

Quoniam iniquitatem meam annuntiabo : et cogitabo pro peccato meo.

Inimici autem mei vivunt et confirmati sunt super me : et multiplicati sunt qui oderunt me inique.

Qui retribuunt mala pro bonis detrahebant mihi : quoniam sequebar bonitatem.

Ne derelinquas me, Domine Deus meus : ne discesseris a me.

Intende in adjutorium meum : Domine, Deus salutis meæ.

Gloria Patri. Sicut erat.

ORATIO.

DOMINE, ne in furore tuo excandescenti arguas nos ; neque cum reprobis in æternum damnes. Agnoscimus culpam, et precamur veniam. Reminiscentia peccatorum nos affligit ; cor conturbatum est ; non est sanitas in carne nostra. Ne derelinquas nos, Domine Deus noster, neque subtrahas gratiam tuam a nobis : sed intende in adjutorium nostrum, auctor salutis nostræ, Jesu Christe, qui es benedictus in sæcula. *Amen.*

IV. FERIÂ QUARTA.

PSALMUS LI.

Peccator agnoscit ac dolet sceleratam vitam, quærit purgari, implorat Spiritum Dei, ut renovetur ac confirmetur.

MISERERE mei, Deus : secundum magnam misericordiam tuam.

Et secundum multitudinem miserationum tuarum : dele iniquitatem meam.

Amplius lava me ab iniquitate meâ : et a peccato meo munda me.

Quoniam iniquitatem meam ego cognosco : et peccatum meum contra me est semper.

Tibi soli peccavi, et malum coram te feci : ut justificeris in sermonibus tuis, et vincas cum judicaris.

Ecce enim in iniquitatibus conceptus sum : et in peccatis concepit me mater mea.

Ecce enim veritatem dilexisti : incerta et occulta sapientiæ tuæ manifestasti mihi.

Asperges me hyssopo, et mundabor : lavabis me, et super nivem dealbabor.

Auditui meo dabis gaudium et lætitiam : et exultabunt ossa humiliata.

Averte faciem tuam a peccatis meis : et omnes iniquitates meas dele.

Cor mundum crea in me, Deus : et spiritum rectum innova in visceribus meis.

Ne projicias me a facie tuâ : et Spiritum Sanctum tuum ne auferas a me.

Redde mihi lætitiam salutaris tui : et Spiritu principali confirma me.

Docebo iniquos vias tuas : et impii ad te convertentur.

Libera me de sanguinibus, Deus, Deus salutis meæ : et exultabit lingua mea justitiam tuam.

SEPTEM PSALMI PŒNITENTIALES.

Domine, labia mea aperies : et os meum annuntiabit laudem tuam.

Quoniam si voluisses sacrificium, dedissem utique : holocaustis non delectaberis.

Sacrificium Deo spiritus contribulatus : cor contritum et humiliatum, Deus, non despicies.

Benigne fac, Domine, in bonâ voluntate tuâ Sion : ut ædificentur muri Hierusalem.

Tunc acceptabis sacrificium justitiæ, oblationes, et holocausta : tunc imponent super altare tuum vitulos.

Gloria Patri. Sicut erat.

ORATIO.

DELE, quæso, iniquitates nostras Domine, secundum magnam misericordiam tuam. Munda et lava nos super candorem nivis, a peccatis nostris, quibus malum coram te fecimus. Cor nostrum contritum et humiliatum non despicias, Domine; sed innova in cordibus nostris Spiritum Sanctum tuum; quo laudem tuam annunciare possimus, et recto principalique Spiritu tuo confirmati in cœlestem Hierusalem tandem perveniamus; Per Christum Dominum nostrum. *Amen.*

V. FERIÂ QUINTÂ.

PSALMUS CII.

Querela pii ad Deum, ab impiis graviter vexati.

DOMINE, exaudi orationem meam : et clamor meus ad te veniat.

Non avertas faciem tuam a me : in quâcumque die tribulor, inclina ad me aurem tuam.

In quâcumque die invocavero te : velociter exaudi me.

Quia defecerunt sicut fumus dies mei : et ossa mea sicut cremium aruerunt.

Percussus sum ut fœnum, et aruit cor meum : quia oblitus sum comedere panem meum.

A voce gemitus mei : adhæsit os meum carni meæ.

Similis factus sum pellicano solitudinis : factus sum sicut nycticorax in domicilio.

Vigilavi : et factus sum sicut passer solitarius in tecto.

Totâ die exprobrabant mihi inimici mei : et qui laudabant me adversum me jurabant.

Quia cinerem tanquam panem manducabam : et potum meum cum fletu miscebam.

A facie iræ et indignationis tuæ : quia elevans allisisti me.

Dies mei sicut umbra declinaverunt : et ego sicut fœnum arui.

Tu autem, Domine, in æternum permanes : et memoriale tuum in generationem et generationem.

Tu exsurgens misereberis Sion : quia tempus miserendi ejus, quia venit tempus.

Quoniam placuerunt servis tuis lapides ejus : et terræ ejus miserebuntur.

Et timebunt gentes nomen tuum, Domine : et omnes reges terræ gloriam tuam.

Quia ædificavit Dominus Sion : et videbitur in gloriâ suâ.

Respexit in orationem humilium : et non sprevit precem eorum.

Scribantur hæc in generatione alterâ : et populus, qui creabitur, laudabit Dominum :

Quia prospexit de excelso sancto suo : Dominus de cœlo in terram aspexit ;

Ut audiret gemitus compeditorum : ut solveret filios interemtorum :

Ut annuntient in Sion nomen Domini : et laudem ejus in Hierusalem.

In conveniendo populos in unum : et reges ut serviant Domino.

Respondit ei in viâ virtutis suæ : paucitatem dierum meorum nuntia mihi.

Ne revoces me in dimidio dierum meorum : in generationem et generationem anni tui.

Initio tu, Domine, terram fundasti : et opera manuum tuarum sunt cœli.

Ipsi peribunt, tu autem permanes : et omnes sicut vestimentum veterascent.

Et sicut opertorium mutabis eos, et mutabuntur : tu autem idem ipse es, et anni tui non deficient.

Filii servorum tuorum habitabunt : et semen eorum in sæculum dirigetur.

Gloria Patri. Sicut erat.

ORATIO.

BENIGNE Salvator, sinum tuæ pietatis nobis aperi, ut hæreditatem cœlestem, quam amisimus per culpam, recuperemus per pœnitentiam. Subinde præsta ut dignis resipiscentiæ fructibus peccata quæ fecimus salubriter abstergamus, utque nomen tuum tam piè revereamur, ut et tu clementer respicias orationes nostras, et nos semenque nostrum tandem ad æternam vitam aspiremus, gratiâ et misericordiâ Domini nostri Jesu Christi. *Amen.*

VI. FERIÂ SEXTÂ.

PSALMUS CXXX.

Peccator ob peccata mulctatus, petit solvi a peccato et a peccati pœnâ.

DE profundis clamavi ad te Domine : Domine exaudi vocem meam.

Fiant aures tuæ intendentes : in vocem deprecationis meæ.

Si iniquitates observaveris Domine : Domine quis sustinebit?

Quia apud te propitiatio est : et propter legem tuam sustinui te, Domine.

Sustinuit anima mea in verbo ejus : speravit anima mea in Domino.

A custodiâ matutinâ usque ad noctem : speret Israel in Domino.

Quia apud Dominum misericordia : et copiosa apud eum redemptio.

Et ipse redimet Israel : ex omnibus iniquitatibus ejus.

Gloria Patri. Sicut erat.

ORATIO.

DE profundis cordis clamamus ad te, Domine, ut de profundis peccatorum liberes nos. Quia apud te solum verum Deum est propitiatio et reconciliatio nostra. Ne observes itaque iniquitates nostras, qui speramus in misericordiâ tuâ, quique redempti sumus pretioso sanguine tuo, Domine Deus noster. *Amen.*

VII. SABBATO.

PSALMUS CXLIII.

Justus, malis affectus, orat ut eripiatur a malis.

DOMINE, exaudi orationem meam; auribus percipe observationem meam : in veritate tuâ exaudi me, in tuâ justitiâ.

Et non intres in judicium cum servo tuo : quia non justificabitur in conspectu tuo omnis vivens.

Quia persecutus est inimicus animam meam : humiliavit in terrâ vitam meam.

Collocavit me in obscuris sicut mortuos sæculi : et anxiatus est super me spiritus meus; in me turbatum est cor meum.

Memor fui dierum antiquorum; meditatus sum in omnibus operibus tuis : in factis manuum tuarum meditabar.

Expandi manus meas ad te : anima mea sicut terra sine aquâ tibi.

Velociter exaudi me, Domine : deficit spiritus meus.

Non avertas faciem tuam a me : et similis ero descendentibus in lacum.

Auditam fac mihi manè misericordiam tuam : quia in te speravi.

Notam fac mihi viam, in quâ ambulem : quia ad te levavi animam meam.

Eripe me de inimicis meis, Domine; ad te confugi : doce me facere voluntatem tuam, quia Deus meus es tu.

Spiritus tuus bonus deducet me in terram rectam : propter nomen tuum, Domine, vivificabis me, in æquitate tuâ.

Educes de tribulatione animam meam : et in misericordiâ tuâ disperdes omnes inimicos meos.

Et perdes omnes, qui tribulant animam meam : quoniam ego servus tuus sum.

Gloria Patri. Sicut erat.

ORATIO.

NON avertas, Domine, tanquam offensus, faciem misericordiæ tuæ a nobis pœnitentibus, neque intres in judicium nobiscum in cujus conspectu nullus mortalium justicabitur : sed velociter exaudi et adjuva nos qui in te solo speramus, et ad te fontem gratiæ levamus animas nostras. Erue, quæso, de tribulatione animam nostram. Auditam fac nobis manè misericordiam tuam. Notam etiam fac nobis viam tuam, ut in eâ, itinere recto, ambulantes ad patriam cœlestem tandem feliciter perveniamus, propter nomen tuum quod Jesus est. *Amen.*

Antiphona. Ne reminiscaris, Domine, iniquitatum nostrarum antiquarum, sed misericordia tua præveniat nos: sumus enim miserrimi. Adjuva nos, Deus, Servator noster, et propter gloriam nominis tui libera nos. Esto nobis propitius, et propter nomen tuum condona nobis peccata nostra. Ne dicant impii, Ubi est Deus eorum? Nos autem populus tuus et oves pascuæ tuæ semper gratias agemus tibi: a generatione in generationem promulgabimus laudem tuam. Tibi honor et gloria in æternum. *Amen.*

LITANIA.

Kyrie, eleïson.
   Christe, eleïson.
Kyrie, eleïson.
Christe, audi nos.
   Christe, exaudi nos.

Pater de cœlis Deus, *miserere nobis.*
Fili Redemptor mundi Deus, *miserere nobis.*
Spiritus Sancte Deus, *miserere nobis.*
Sancta Trinitas, unus Deus, *miserere nobis.*
Propitius esto, *Parce nobis, Domine.*

Ab omni malo,
Ab insidiis diaboli,
A damnatione perpetuâ,
Ab imminentibus peccatorum nostrorum periculis,
Ab infestationibus demonum,
A spiritu fornicationis,
Ab appetitu inanis gloriæ,
Ab omnibus immunditiis mentis et corporis,
Ab irâ et odio, et omni malâ voluntate,
Ab immundis cogitationibus,
A cæcitate cordis,
A fulgure et tempestate,
A subitaneâ et improvisâ morte,
Per mysterium sanctæ Incarnationis tuæ,
} *Libera nos, Domine.*

Per Nativitatem tuam,
Per sanctam Circumcisionem tuam,
Per Baptismum tuum,
Per Jejunium tuum,
Per Passionem et Crucem tuam,
Per pretiosam Mortem tuam,
Per gloriosam Resurrectionem tuam,
Per admirabilem Ascensionem tuam,
Per gratiam Sancti Spiritûs Paracliti,

} *Libera nos, Domine.*

In horâ mortis, *Succurre nobis, Domine.*
In die Judicii, *Libera nos, Domine.*

Peccatores,
Ut pacem nobis dones,
Ut misericordia et pietas tua nos semper custodiat,
Ut Ecclesiam tuam regere et defensare digneris,
Ut domnum Apostolicum et omnes gradus Ecclesiæ in sanctâ religione conservare digneris,
Ut reginæ nostræ et principibus nostris pacem et concordiam atque victoriam donare digneris,
Ut episcopos nostros et omnes congregationes illis commissas in sanctâ religione conservare digneris,
Ut congregationes omnium sanctorum in tuo sancto servitio conservare digneris,
Ut cunctum populum Christianum pretioso sanguine tuo redemptum conservare digneris,
Ut omnibus benefactoribus nostris sempiterna bona retribuas,
Ut animas nostras et parentum nostrorum ab æternâ damnatione eripias,
Ut fructus terræ dare et conservare digneris,

} *Te rogamus, audi nos.*

Ut oculos misericordiæ tuæ super nos reducere digneris,
Ut obsequium servitutis nostræ rationabile facias,
Ut mentes nostras ad cœlestia desideria erigas,
Ut miserias pauperum et captivorum intueri et relevare digneris,
Ut omnibus fidelibus vivis ac defunctis requiem æternam dones,
Ut nos exaudire digneris,

} *Te rogamus, audi nos.*

Fili Dei, *Te rogamus, audi nos.*
Fili Dei, *Te rogamus, audi nos.*
Fili Dei, *Te rogamus, audi nos.*

Agnus Dei, qui tollis peccata mundi, *Exaudi nos, Domine.*
Agnus Dei, qui tollis peccata mundi, *Parce nobis, Domine.*
Agnus Dei, qui tollis peccata mundi, *Miserere nobis.*

Kyrie eleïson.
 Christe eleïson.
Kyrie eleïson.

Pater noster, &c.
Et ne nos inducas in tentationem.
 Sed libera nos a malo.
Ostende nobis, Domine, misericordiam tuam.
 Et salutare tuum da nobis.
Et veniat super nos misericordia tua, Domine.
 Salutare tuum, secundum eloquium tuum.
Peccavimus cum patribus nostris;

LITANIA.

Injustè egimus, iniquitatem fecimus.

Domine, non secundum peccata nostra facias nobis.

Neque secundum iniquitates nostras retribuas nobis.

Oremus pro omni gradu Ecclesiæ:

Sacerdotes tui induantur justitiam; et sancti tui exultent.

Pro fratribus et sororibus nostris:

Salvos fac servos tuos et ancillas tuas, Deus meus, sperantes in te.

Oremus pro cuncto populo Christiano:

Salvum fac populum tuum, Domine, et benedic hereditatem tuam, et rege illos et extolle illos usque in æternum.

Domine, fiat pax in virtute tuâ,

Et abundantia in turribus tuis.

Animæ famulorum famularumque tuarum

Requiescant in pace. Amen.

Domine exaudi orationem meam.

Et clamor meus ad te veniat.

ORATIONES *dicendæ, una vel plures.*

DEUS cui proprium est misereri semper et parcere, suscipe deprecationes nostras; ut quos delictorum catena constringit, miseratio tuæ pietatis absolvat; Per Christum Dominum nostrum. *Amen.*

OMNIPOTENS sempiterne Deus, qui facis mirabilia magna solus, pretende super famulos pontifices et super cunctas congregationes illis commissas Spiritum gratiæ salutaris; et ut in veritate tibi complaceant, perpetuum eis rorem tuæ benedictionis infunde; Per Christum Dominum nostrum. *Amen.*

DEUS qui caritatis dona, per gratiam Sancti Spiritûs, tuorum cordibus fidelium infundis, da famulis et famulabus tuis, pro quibus tuam deprecamur clementiam, salutem mentis et corporis; ut te totâ virtute diligant, et quæ tibi placita sunt totâ dilectione perficiant; Per Christum Dominum nostrum. *Amen.*

DEUS, a quo sancta desideria, recta consilia, et justa sunt opera, da servis tuis illam quam mundus dare non potest pacem, ut et corda nostra mandatis tuis dedita, et, hostium sublatâ formidine, tempora sint tuâ protectione tranquilla; Per Christum Dominum nostrum. *Amen.*

GRATIA Domini nostri Jesu Christi, caritas Dei, communicatio Sancti Spiritûs sit semper cum omnibus. *Amen.*

INDEX.

	PAGE
Ante omnes horas dicendæ orationes	ii
Aquinas, S. Thomas, Prayer of	260
Asa, King, Prayer of	240
Ascension, Metrical Litany of	275
Benedicite	19, xii
Benedictus	23, 107
Bernardine, S., Prayer of	261
Commemorationes	xvii
Commendatory Litany, Metrical	271
Communion, Prayer of Erasmus before	227
Communion, Prayer of Dying S. Jerome before	228
Communion, Prayer of the Passion before	220
Communion, Thanksgiving after	230
Completorium, ad	xxxix
Compline	55
Contemplation of the Cross	206
Creed	1, 34, 58
Decalogue	2
Departed, Prayers for the	29, 90, 110
De Profundis, Psalm and Collect	72
Dirge Hours	84
Erasmus, Prayer of, for the Peace of the Church	247
Erasmus, Prayer of, before Communion	227
Evensong	46
Evensong for Penitential Seasons	84
Fifteen Psalms of Prayer	113
Friday, Penitential Psalm and Collect for	72

INDEX.

	PAGE
Graces before and after meals	3
Hezekiah, Song of	103
History of the Primer	(Introduction) v
Holy Ghost, Invocation to	235
Horarium	iii
Hymns—	
Æterna cœli gloria	43, xxx
Ales diei nuncius	22, xiv
Consors paterni luminis	31, xxii
Jam lucis orto sidere	8, iv
Rector potens, verax Deus	37, xxvi
Rerum Creator omnium	40, xxix
Rerum Creator omnium	57, xl
Salvator mundi Domine	50, xxxv
Jeremiah, Prayer of	242
Jerome, S., Prayer of, before Communion	228
Jesus son of Sirac, Prayer of	244
Job, Prayer of	242
Laudes, ad	xi
Lauds	18
Lauds for Penitential Seasons	102
Litania	lvi
Litany	76
Litanies, Metrical	269
Lord's Prayer	1
Magnificat	51, 88
Manasses, Prayer of	240
Matins	7
Matins for Penitential Seasons	92
Matutinum, ad	iii
Memorials in Lauds	25
Memorials in Evensong	53
Metrical Litanies	269
Miserere Psalm	67, 100
Monday, Penitential Psalm and Collect for	63
Morning Prayers (three)	223

	PAGE
Night Litany, Metrical	269
Night Prayers (three)	225
Ninth Hour	43
Nonam, ad	xxx
Nunc Dimittis	58, xli
Passion of our Lord from S. John's Gospel	197
Passion, Prayers of the	218
Passion, Psalms of the	186
Penitential Offices	84
Penitential Psalms and Collects for each day of the week	61
Plain directions for using the Hours (Introduc.)	xxii
Prayer, Seven Hours of	7
Prayer against anger	257
Prayer against enemies of Christ's truth	234
Prayer against envy	257
Prayer against pride	256
Prayer against sin	240
Prayer against unchasteness	256
Prayer against worldliness	255
Prayer for competent living	243
Prayer for concord	233
Prayer for desire of the life to come	268
Prayer for Holy Communion	227
Prayer for patience in trouble	232
Prayer for peace of the Church	247
Prayer for Sunday Morning	231
Prayer for trust in God	231
Prayer in adversity	258
Prayer in prosperity	259
Prayer in the hour of death	263
Prayer in trouble of conscience	238
Prayer of S. Thomas Aquinas	260
Prayer of Asa, King	240
Prayer of S. Bernardine	261
Prayer of David	237
Prayer of Erasmus for Holy Communion	227
Prayer of Erasmus for peace of the Church	247
Prayer of Jeremiah	242

INDEX.

	PAGE
Prayer of Jesus, son of Sirac, for wisdom	244
Prayer of Job, in distress	242
Prayer of Manasses, King	240
Prayer of Solomon, King, for competent living	243
Prayers to be said before any of the Hours	6
Prayers of the Passion	218
Preface	i
Primam, ad	xxii
Prime	31
Primer, History of (Introduction)	v
Primer, Hours of the, how to use them and when (Introduction)	xxix
Psalms of the Passion	186
Psalms of Prayer	113
Saturday, Penitential Psalm and Collect for	73
Septem Psalmi Pœnitentiales cum orationibus	xliv
Seven Penitential Psalms and Collects	61
Sextam, ad	xxviii
Sixth Hour	40
Solomon, Prayer of	243
Sunday, Penitential Psalm and Collect for	61
Sunday Morning, Prayer for	231
Te Deum	15
Ten Commandments	2
Tertiam, ad	xxvi
Third Hour	37
Thursday, Penitential Psalm and Collect for	69
Tuesday, Penitential Psalm and Collect for	64
Venite	7, iii
Vesperas, ad	xxxii
Wednesday, Penitential Psalm and Collect for	67

JOSEPH MASTERS AND SON, PRINTERS, ALBION BUILDINGS,
BARTHOLOMEW CLOSE, E.C.

Fcap. 8vo., price 6s.

HYMNS AND LYRICS

For the Seasons and Saints' Days of the Church.

BY THE

REV. GERARD MOULTRIE, M.A.,
Of Exeter College, Oxford,
Vicar of South Leigh, Oxfordshire.

"In Mr. Moultrie's volume we have lighted upon an oasis in the desert. It is poetry, it is original poetry, and it is of very varied character."—*Literary Churchman.*

"Full of refined thought and pure religious feeling."—*Ecclesiastic.*

"One of the best, if not, indeed, the very best volume of sacred poetry we have seen for some years."—*Standard.*

"Bespeaks high cultivation of the poetic faculty, and no small aptitude for graceful composition."—*Churchman.*

"We note with especial pleasure that there are several pieces in Mr. Moultrie's volume which can be thrown into our still scantily furnished treasury of Church song."—*Church Times.*

"A work which will give great pleasure to all who are at once devotionally-minded and capable of appreciating poetry of a very high tone."—*Churchman's Companion.*

"Mr. Moultrie is already well known as a sacred poet of no common ability and power. We can cordially recommend this book as a valuable addition to our stock of hymns and sacred lyrics."—*Churchman's Shilling Magazine.*

"We are bound to record our deliberate conviction that it is a volume of high poetical merit; that it contains lofty thoughts and Catholic truths, well expressed, and most poetically rendered; and finally, that it deserves to be circulated far and wide, as well for its admirable principles as for its poetical merits."—*Church News.*

"Our readers will see that there are some unusual elements in the writer of the following hymn for S. Mark's Day . . . We have here a number of images grouped together almost grotesquely, but linked to each other by a true imaginative affinity, such as cannot be recognized, much less invented, by a mind which moves only on a low prosaic level."—*Guardian.*

"Of a very high order of merit, and contains many hymns of singular power and beauty, which are certain to become deservedly popular."—*Union Review.*

BY THE SAME AUTHOR.

Fcap. 8vo., cloth, 2s. 6d.

THE ESPOUSALS OF S. DOROTHEA,

And other Poems.

In 8vo., 1s.

THE MARTYRDOM OF POLYCARP.

A Poem.

"Graceful in composition. Full of true depth of thought and real poetical ability."—*Union Review.*

18mo., price 3s.

OFFICES FOR HOLY WEEK AND EASTER,

AFTER THE PRIMER USE,

TOGETHER WITH

Meditations and Prayers on the Passion.

"Comes nearest to our idea of what a devotional manual should be of any which we have seen for a long time. We can recommend no more fitting manual than this."—*Churchman.*

London: JOSEPH MASTERS, 78, New Bond Street.

www.ingramcontent.com/pod-product-compliance
Lightning Source LLC
Chambersburg PA
CBHW031417230426
43668CB00007B/333